ARCHAEOLOGY OF THE BURREN

Prehistoric Forts and Dolmens
in North Clare

To Imelda,
With Best Wishes

Also published by CLASP PRESS

County Clare: A History and Topography
by Samuel Lewis.

Poverty Before the Famine: County Clare 1835;
first report from His Majesty's commissioners
for inquiring into the condition
of the poorer classes in Ireland

Two Months at Kilkee
by Mary John Knott.
(originally published 1836)

The Antiquities of County Clare;
letters containing information relative to the
Antiquities of the County of Clare
collected during the progress of
the Ordnance Survey in 1839
& letters and extracts relative to
Ancient Territories in Thomond, 1841
by John O'Donovan and Eugene O'Curry

Kilrush Union Minute Books, 1849.

A Handbook to Lisdoonvarna and its vicinity
giving a detailed account of its
curative waters, and tours to
the principal places of interest
in the County Clare
by Philip Dwyer (originally published 1876)

Sable Wings Over the Land;
Ennis, County Clare, and its wider community
during the Great Famine
by Ciarán Ó Murchadha

The Strangers Gaze;
Travels in County Clare
1534-1950
edited by Brian Ó Dálaigh

Archaeology of the Burren

Prehistoric Forts and Dolmens in North Clare

THOMAS J. WESTROPP

CLASP PRESS

Published by

CLASP PRESS, 1999.

ISBN 1 900545 10 1

Edited by
Maureen Comber

Text prepared by
Andrea Lynch, Michelle Moloney, Tara Considine, Suzanne Quinn, Carole Keane,
Zelda Ryan, Karen McInerney, Ailin McAllister, Tina Robinson, Siobhán Kelleher,
Imelda Greene, Margaret Clancy, Emer Kinsella, Joanne Considine, Yamile Berry,
Áine Clune, Catriona Malone, Siobhán Murphy, Joyce Cronin, Lorna Downes, Maria
Meaney, Siobhán Kenny, Tracey Hayes, Sharon Considine-Meaney, Jackie Dermody
& especially Linda Burke and Martina Crowley-Hayes .

Designed by
Anthony Edwards

Layout by
M. Comber & J. Dermody

Cover design: A. Edwards
Cover layout: S. McCooey & A. Edwards

Printed by Colour Books, Dublin

CLASP PRESS,
Clare County Library Headquarters,
Mill Road, Ennis, Co. Clare.

CHAIRMAN OF CLASP

Clare Local Studies Project, set up as an independent organisation by members of the Clare Library staff, continues to grow in both structure and confidence. It is a perfect marriage between the training objectives of FÁS, the dedication of the Board of CLASP and the mission of said board "to develop awareness of, and increase access to sources for local studies in county Clare".

The support of FÁS continues to be the most important ingredient in the success of the Clare Local Studies Project (CLASP). We are deeply indebted to the training authority for their continued support over the last four years. With their assistance we confidently look forward to the challenges of the new millennium and already have a number of new titles in preparation.

We also have worked closely with Clare County Council and, indeed, have had links with Ennis Urban Council, Kilrush Urban Council and Kilkee Town Commissioners, all of whom have contributed in varying degrees.

The great strength of the organisation is the expertise that each individual brings to each task – Ted Finn, Administration; Anthony Edwards, Projects & Design; and Maureen Comber, Editorial. Collectively, along with Gerry Collison, External Director, they make my task as Chairman very easy. Of course, many people continue to play an active role in ensuring our continued success. The day to day training, supervision and in-house co-ordination of trainees and projects is expertly led by Project Supervisor, Martina Crowley-Hayes and Senior Trainee, Linda Burke. Without the dedication of this team, our work could never achieve its high standards, not alone in publications but in job and educational opportunities for our young people.

I would also like to thank Carol Gleeson for her excellent introduction, Siobhán McCooey for her cover artwork, Trish Murphy for her jacket photographs and plate reproductions of T.J. Westropp's original photographs, and the ever reliable Jackie Dermody.

The Burren area of County Clare holds a great fascination for people all over the world, yet few will know of the incredible work done by Thomas J. Westropp in surveying, describing and illustrating the area and its archaeological monuments. *Archaeology of the Burren : Prehistoric Forts and Dolmens in North Clare* is now, for the first time, made available in a single volume and is the perfect companion for the explorer of the Burren. Indeed, if one has room for a second book on your travels then, I would recommend that you also pack the *Antiquities of County Clare*, published by CLASP PRESS in 1997.

The research done by Thomas J. Westropp, not alone in archaeology, but in topography, history and folklore will provide us with the opportunity to, hopefully, bring his work to a greater audience over the next few years. It is appropriate that we honour T.J. Westropp this year on the 150th anniversary of the foundation of the Royal Society of Antiquaries of Ireland – a society in which he held membership for thirty six years, and of which he eventually became President.

Noel Crowley

Photographs

*All plates from Thomas J. Westropp's photographic album courtesy Clare County Library and reproduced for this publication by Trish Murphy, L.R.P.S.

ILLUSTRATIONS

Editorial Note

The volumes of the *Journal of the Royal Society of Antiquaries of Ireland* in which the articles republished here originally appeared are given below with the corresponding page numbers of this edition.

When these volumes are referred to within the text, the corresponding page numbers of this edition are given in square brackets, after the original citation.

Contents

THOMAS JOHNSON WESTROPP

The person who begins any attempt at researching the history, archaeology or folklore of County Clare, and the Burren in particular, will invariably be led to the work of Thomas J. Westropp. He has been referred to as the Father of Burren Archaeology. This compilation of articles on the Burren (which originally appeared in the *Journal of the Royal Society of Antiquaries of Ireland* between 1895 and 1915) illustrates why. His recordings and analysis of the topography, archaeology, history and folklore of the Burren is as highly regarded today as when first published and is an indicator of the incalculable debt owed to such people who laid the ground work for subsequent generations of researchers and archaeologists.

Thomas Johnson Westropp was born in 1860 at Attyflyn, County Limerick, of an important family with many branches in the counties of Clare and Limerick. He spent his boyhood in these counties, where he developed an interest in their topography and folklore and immersed himself in the traditions which still survived in the rural areas. Educated at Trinity College, Dublin, his subsequent career as an engineer and surveyor allowed him to travel all over the country. In the course of this work he began to research and record in great detail the archaeological remains all around him.

He became a member of the Royal Society of Antiquaries in 1886, and eventually was honoured with the role of President of the Society in 1916. He held this office during a period of immense political and social upheaval in Ireland:

'The duties of the office were, in consequence, for him more than usually exacting, but he carried them through with dignity and with unremitting ardour, forgetting his uncertain health with that perfect unselfishness which was one of the leading features of his character.'

The details of his life are not well known, the only glimpse of the man behind the copious amount of invaluable work being in the personal allusions in his obituary notice, published in the Proceedings of the Royal Society of Antiquaries of Ireland in 1923, and through the personality of his own work, art and writing.

'As a field worker he had no rival; not even the advancing ill health which for several of his last years caused his friends anxiety, or the restrictions which military and other exigencies placed upon transport and photography during the past troubled decade, could check his enthusiasm.'

Westropp had a prodigious memory and kept detailed notes. By the time of his death on the 9th April, 1922, he had contributed an astonishing amount of work on the recording of antiquities and traditions. He wrote and published extensively on a wide variety of subjects from megalithic tombs to folklore. The Royal Irish Academy holds his notebooks, meticulous recordings of sites and customs, which are richly illustrated with maps and sketches.

'His interests were all embracing: folklore, ancient and modern; comparative religion; topography; prehistoric forts and sanctuaries; mediaeval castles; Gothic churches; historical records - all were studied with a catholic zeal.'

On County Clare alone he published 'The Antiquities of Co. Clare'; 'Churches and Monasteries of Co. Clare'; 'Co. Clare Folk Tales and Myths'; 'A Folklore Survey of Co. Clare'; 'Killaloe, its ancient places and Cathedral'; 'King Brian, hero of Clontarf'; 'Wars of Turlough O'Brien and Thomas de Clare, 1275-85' (in Irish); 'Prehistoric remains of Co. Clare'; 'Prehistoric stone forts of central Clare'; and a paper on Bunratty.

He had a scholarly and speculative mind, a sense of humour and a fresh approach to the recording of monuments. His notebooks contain beautiful illustrations and colourful maps of the areas he worked in. His artistic eye combined with the disciplined training of the engineer and the surveyor's sense of scale to create a versatile and well rounded talent for recording. These recordings, and the many photographs he took, allow the contemporary archaeologist to assess the changes to sites and the landscape since his day. His talent for recording was not limited to the visual. He had an ear for old tales and traditions, his publications and recording of the folklore of rural Clare and Limerick illustrating his obvious appreciation of and sensitivity towards such traditions, which he held in equal esteem to archaeological remains as legitimate evidence of our cultural past.

Westropp's presidential address charts the development of antiquarian interest and speculation through the eighteenth and nineteenth centuries and is worth reading for its content and the humour of its style. This address, which takes no prisoners, is a testimony to his quick wit, innate good sense, intelligence and open mind. He gave credit where credit was due, ridiculed the ridiculous and reiterated the need for a balanced and scientific approach to archaeology. A section worth quoting refers to the theories purported by the Vallancey School, prominent in the latter part of the 18th century, which 'attributed to the early Irish a high culture, comparable with that of the Mediterranean civilizations'.

He continues,

'First of these discoveries elucidated by the new learning was that of the Ogham stone of Mount Callan in Co. Clare. I myself regard it as an innocent scholastic freak of the Mac Brodies, a bardic family living close to its site, between 1650 and 1720. It was found by John Lloyd of Theophilus O Flanagan about 1778, and the latter, though confessedly ignorant of old Irish epigraphy, settled the whole question to the satisfaction of himself and his hearers. He read it forward and backward, right side up and wrong side up, he changed the value of two letters and tortured it till it said anything he wanted. He thus got five readings out of a single line:
i.   Beneath this stone lies Conaf (Conan) the fierce and swift footed;
ii. Obscure not the remains of Conaf the fierce and swift footed;
iii. Long may he lie at his ease on the brink of the lake beneath this hieroglyphic, darling of the sacred;

iv. Long may he lie at his ease on the brink of this lake who never saw his faithful clan depressed;

v. Hail with reverential sorrow the drooping heath around his lamentable tomb.

Such was archaeology then.'

His clear and balanced thinking contributed to the development of a more scientific approach to archaeology. He was an able successor to 'the sober truth-seeking school of Petrie and O'Donovan' and fought a continuous battle against the 'hardy perennials of error... we shall never be in a satisfactory position 'til in archaeology, as in natural science, the man who attempts to revive an exploded error only slays his reputation and deceives no one but himself.'

His fundamental belief in the future of Irish archaeology is encapsulated in the summary of his Presidential Address:

'Most hopeful is it to recall that in Ireland our work always advanced, not by State aid and popular applause, but by self-sacrifice; and having no ambition save the objects of our research. These endowments cannot fail if we continue true.'

Irish archaeologists are indebted to the zeal and dedication of antiquarians such as Westropp. He and his colleagues, working under conditions of limited transport, rudimentary equipment and no financial support, laid the foundations for modern Irish archaeology, field working, historical research and the collection of folklore.

It is a pity that not more is known about the man Thomas Johnson Westropp. However, his legacy of ground breaking work lives on. The summation of his obituary notice is eloquent in its assessment of this inspiring man:

'His genial presence, his kindly humour, his inexhaustible fund of reminiscences of times and conditions that have disappeared, and his immense knowledge will no longer brighten the meetings and excursions of the Society. But his memory will live as an inspiration of those who knew him: and his name will remain, written high on the Roll of Honour of Ireland, long after many men, who make a much greater noise in these times of ours, have dropped into the oblivion that awaits them.'

Carol Gleeson,
May 1999.

1

FOREIGN AND IRISH FORTS
KILNABOY
NOUGHAVAL - KILFENORA

Prehistoric[1] events in Ireland have too often been treated in an extreme spirit of acceptance or negation. Some speak of our pre-Christian kings with a certainty scarcely suitable to the reigns of Brian or Roderic; others write of Laoghaire's predecessors as if all were as mythic as the heroes of the Nibelungs Lay. In all probability the centuries preceding St. Patrick handed down not a little real history[2] to his scribes, whose successors passed it on, but possibly with added errors, to the compilers of the earlier encyclopædias of Irish literature. In the earliest of these we meet a legend versified by Mac Liag, Brian's bard, who died 1016, and ascribed to Amergin mac Amalgaidh, *circa* 550, on which an unreasonable stress has been laid to make it support a popular theory. On its supposed authority most of our antiquaries, begging the question, attribute the great forts of Aran and Clare to the Huamorian Firbolgs in the first century. Now the *Lay of Carn Chonoill* certainly connects Oengus with Dun Oengus, but names no other western fort, nor does it even state[3] that the fugitives entrenched themselves. Even if it did so, a writer, as far removed from the period of his legend as we are from the time of Alfred the Great, cannot be taken as an unimpeachable authority, and, where the old poem, *The taking of Dun Oengusa*, is lost, we have practically no earlier legend than that in Roderic O'Flaherty's *HIar Connaught*, 1686, which attributes the building of two only of the Aran forts to the Firbolgs, no fort in Clare being mentioned.

---

[1] This Paper forms a continuation of 'Prehistoric Stone Forts in Central Clare' in our *Journal [of the Royal Society of Antiquaries of Ireland]*, 1893, pp. 281 and 432. By the terms 'prehistoric' and 'fort,' I only imply that the origin of the cahers is un-recorded, and their use more or less defensive, few being forts in the modern sense.

[2] The commencement of St. Patrick's mission was probably nearer to the death of Cormac mac Airt than the present year is to the accession of George II. This leaves abundant room, however, for a plentiful growth of myths, had we even fifth-century manuscripts to aid us, without the added errors of seven more centuries, a period as long as that which separates us from the reign of Richard I.

[3] Another manuscript, however, says, 'They dwelt thus in fortresses.' - *Revue Celtique*, 1894, p. 481.

The original story so often alluded to, and so little known, is thus translated by Dr. Whitley Stokes[1]:-

'Conall, the slender, son of Oengus, son of Umor, fell there (at Carn Conoill). Once upon a time, when the sons of Umor made a flitting over sea out of the province of the Picts (of Scotland), they come to the plain of Meath to Cairbre Nia-fer, the Lord of Tara, and of him they sought land, the best in Meath, to wit, Rath Cennaig, Rath Commair, Cnogba, Brug Mna Elcmair, Taltiu, Cermna, Tlachtga, Ath Sige, Bri-dam Dile. Cairpre required them (to perform the) base service of Tara, like everyone whom he permitted to dwell in Banba (Ireland) and (especially) Bregia. So for this (performance) the children of Umor gave four sureties, namely, Cet mac Magach, Ross, son of Deda, Conall Cernach, and Cuchulainn. Afterwards Cairpre imposed on the children of Umor a rent which could not be endured: so they decamped from him, with their possessions, westward to Ailill and Medb, and set up beside the sea. Oengus in Dun Oengusa in Ara; Cutra to Lough Cutra; Cimbe Fourheads[2] at Lough Cimbi; Adar at Mag Adair; Mil at Muirbech Mil; Daelach on Dail and Ennach, from whom is Ennach's house (Tech nEnnaich); Bir at Rind Bera Sirraim; Mod at Insi Mod (the Clew Bay Islands); Irgus at Rind Boirne[3]; Cingid at Cruach Aigli; Bairnech Barannbel at Laiglinni; Conchiurn at Inis Medon (Middle Island Aran); Lathrach at Lathrach's Hill (Tulaich Lathraich); Taman at Taman's Point (Rind Tamain); Conall the slender at Aidne; Mesc on Lough Mask. So then the four sureties and guarantors are summoned by (the creditor) Cairpre, Conall comes with his (comrade) Cuchulainn from the Ulaid; Ross, son of Deda, from the Ernai; and Cet went out of Connaught to Cairpre's house. Cairpre demanded their honour or their soul (life). So then, under Cet's safeguard, the sureties repaired to Cruachan, and there, on the green of the fortress, they commenced their fasting. Cet's wife entreated the respite of a single night (that the children of Umor might consider what was to be done). On the morrow Oengus comes, and said that his son, with his three brothers, would fight on his behalf with the sureties. Cing against Ross, Cimbe Fourheaded against Conall Cernach, Irgus against Cet mac Magach, and Conall, son of Oengus, against Cuchulainn. So the sons of Umor were

---

[1] 'Dindseanchas,' in *Revue Celtique*, 1894, pp. 478, 480. Professor Rhys goes so far as to consider the legend a solar myth, the Firbolgs seeking refuge from the heroes of Tara in the isles of the Western Ocean, as darkness flies before the rising sun (Hibbert Lectures, 1886). For the lost poem, *Togail Duine Oengusa* (Taking of Dun Oengus), see M. Darbois de Jubainville's *Catalogue of Epic Literature of Ireland*, p. 244.
[2] As he and his three relatives only afforded four heads as trophies, the epithet is not so ogre-like as some imagine. Lough Cime is Lough Hackett, near Headford, Galway, round which, within a few square miles, are ninety-one forts, of which over a dozen cahers have names. (Sheet 42, 6 inch Survey of Galway.) Magh Adhair, the district north of Quin, Clare; the name survives in Moy Eir, near Corbally, and the mound in the adjoining Toonagh (Tuanamoyre, 1584). Muirbech Mil, probably Kilmurvey, Aran, Aidne, is Hy Fiacra Aidne, barony of Kiltartan. In it and the adjoining parishes in Dunkellin, we have no less than fifty-eight caher names. Dail, the river Daelach, near Ennistymon, Clare, Taman, Tawin Island, south of Galway.
[3] Perhaps Black Head, 'Ceann Boirne,' still crowned with the fort of Fergus, query Irgus?

killed, and the sureties brought their four heads to Cairbre to boast of them. Then Oengus was buried, with his son Conall, under this cairn.'

Elsewhere, in the Dindseanchas,[1] we learn that Maistiu, sister of Conall the slender, and Maer, who was twin with him, died of sorrow at his death.

Every passage of the story is excessively improbable, from the Firbolgs getting the royal forts of Taltiu and Tlactga, and the royal cemeteries of Knowth (Cnogba) and Newgrange (Bru), down to the death of Oengus and his daughters; and a tribe that could find space among the Milesians in nine raths in Meath must have been very small, so we can give this story little weight in any question relating to the forts. We are left equally in the dark by the early records and legends of possible historic value. Ptolemy places the Ganganoi near the Shannon estuary, there the Firbolgs Gann, Genann, and Sengan[2] appear. Cormac mac Airt wages war on the inhabitants of the Burren, defeating them on Slieve Elva in the third century, while in the fifth the Dalcassian kings have their palaces in Co. Limerick, and do not yet hold Aughty or Elva, and the king of Aran seeks refuge with the pagans of Corcomroe. If the smith legend of Glasgeivnagh is ancient,[3] the Celtic warriors of the third century found the hills behind the Fergus at Corofin garrisoned by Tuatha De Danann. This may represent, in outline, an early fact of the Dalcassian conquest,[4] and that proud tribe boasted to the king of Cashel, about 840, that they had won the land by their own swords; yet many of the fort-names and legends are of Celts alone.[5]

It cannot be sufficiently emphasised that our forts are not a unique and isolated class of structures, as several seem to have considered them. Ours may be some of the finest and best preserved, but they are only the latest and most remote of a series extending across all Europe, wherever the Celtic race held sway. This people attained the summit of their power between 450 B.C. and 220 B.C. The Phoenicians were over-lords of Spain, under Hiram of Tyre, 537 B.C.; but by the time of Herodotus, 450 B.C., the Gauls had gained

---

[1] *Reveue Celtique*, 1894, p. 334. The curious legend states that Maistiu embroidered a cross on the tunic of her father Oengus, in Mullaghmast, which place derives its name from her. Asal (Tory Hill), near Croom, Co. Limerick, was named from another son of Umor. Mend, son of Umor, a poet, is also given. - *Ibid.*, p. 481.

[2] For these tribes, see our *Journal*, 1879-1882, pp. 469, 475. It may be a mere coincidence, but we find the Ganganoi round the Shannon mouth in Clare, and the Ganganon Akron in Carnarvonshire, both districts having these stone forts. Gan and Sengann's cupbearer wooed Echtge 'the awful,' from whom Slieve Aughty is named (*Revue Celtique*, 1894, p. 458). This connects their legend with Clare.

[3] See our *Journal*, 1895, p. 227.

[4] The Dalcassians under Lughad Menn engaged in the conquest of Thomond from the King of Connaught soon after King Crimthann's death, *circa* 378, well within the limit of reliable tradition: see *inter alia Silva Gadelica*, p. 377, from Book of Ballymote.

[5] It is just possible that the legend of Crochan and Dolv, son of Dal, two of the Tuatha De Danann of Slieve Echtge, found its counterpart at Cahercrochain and Lisdundalheen, at Loop Head (see O'Donovan, Ordnance Survey Letters, Galway II., p. 36, on Ceanncrochain and Drumcrochain). Petrie, in 'Military Architecture of Ireland', p. 122, points out that dry stone forts in parts of Western Scotland are called 'Dun na Firbolg.'

the upper hand. About 390, the Celts overran Etruria, and destroyed Rome. In 280, they invaded Thrace and Macedonia, defeated Ptolemy Keraunos, raided up the very glen of Delphi, and formed a colony in Galatia, giving that country its name. Internecine feuds and lack of writers crippled their power and obscured their fame. Their 'empire' was 2000 miles from east to west, from the mouth of the Danube to the Tagus and Shannon, from Etruria to Northern Scotland; all across the district the names and remains of 'duns' occur, from Singidunum (Belgrade), on the Danube, to the uttermost verge of the old world, as a well-known antiquary writes[1]: 'The names of Gaulish villages handed down the ages the living remembrance of the dominion exercised by a people which preceded the Romans in empire, the Germans in civilization.' The fall of this many-headed 'empire' was speedy. It began historically in Spain, Hamilcar Barca 238 B.C., Hasdrubal, 230, and Hannibal, 219, drove back the Celts and Iberians from the Mediterranean; the resistless hordes of the Germans pressed the Eastern Gael over the Rhine. The arms of Cæsar broke their power in Gaul, and it may well have been that many a dislodged tribe, whose traditions may have descended from those who saw the hill-forts of Greece and Asia Minor,[2] fled into this island during the two centuries before our era, bringing knowledge of fort-building. We find forts of dry stone or earth, very similar in plan, construction, and features to ours, scattered across Europe, almost from the borders of Thrace, the traditional starting-point of the Firbolgs. In Bosnia Herzegovina[3] they are oval, or with several concentric walls, and sometimes have stone huts near them. A triple concentric fort near Cserevics and a 'hring' of three semicircles, on the edge of a steep hill at Bény, occur in Hungary[4]: they are called 'Poganvyar' (or pagan forts), Földvar (or earth forts), and 'Devils' ditches' in that country. Still northward, in Bohemia, we find many forts, notably the Haditsch, near Strakonitz, Ginetz, and the Knezihora, near Katovic.[5]

In Baden we find examples (possibly Celtic, though attributed to the Ubii), probably earlier than 100 B.C. Their great stone 'Wallburgs' and 'Ringwalls'

---

[1] M. de Jubainville in *Revue Archéologique*, xxix., 1875, p. 53; also see same on Celts, Galatians, and Gauls, xxx., 1875, p. 4.

[2] 'Les Gaulois eurent pour maîtres les Phocèens ou Marseillais.' - *Soc. Ant. Normandy*, 1835, p. 228. For Celtic Conquest of Spain, see *Early Man in Britain*, p. 320.

[3] *Rambles and Studies in Bosnia Herzegovina*, by Dr. Robert Munro. Debelobrdo is an oval fort about 330 feet x 110 feet, with stone huts near it. Ograc (see p. [5], fig. 21) is an oval 'caher,' surrounded by a long irregular enclosure; Kicin and Pleschiwetz; also *L'Anthropologie*, 1894, v., pp. 563-568 – 'Notice of Ringwalls, Tumuli, and Circles of Bronze Age at Glasinac and Rusanovic.' See p. [5], figs. 9, 21 and 25.

[4] *Congrés Internationale d'Anthropologie et d'Archéologie Prehistoriques* at Buda Pesth, 1876, vol. viii., pp. 62, 79. 'Hring de Bény' measures about 1500 feet x 1300 feet, slightly larger than Moghane. Sixty-six of these forts are given, some are still named 'duna.' See also *Revue Archéologique*, 1879, p. 158; *La Dominion Celtique en Hongrie*. For plans, see p. [5], figs. 3 and 10.

[5] *Proc. Soc. Ant., Scotland*, 1868-1870, pp. 158-161. The Bohemian forts are of dry stones, vitrified in some cases. See p. [5], figs. 19 and 22.

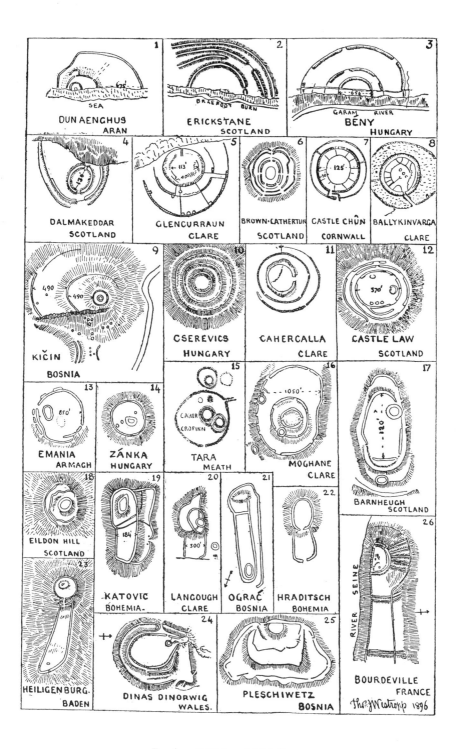

Foreign, British and Irish Forts.

gird the Altkönig in the Taunus and the wooded crests of the beautiful Heiligenburg[1] overhanging Heidelberg. Dry stone ramparts sometimes semicircular, called 'Heydenmauer' (or heathen walls) exists in the Vosges Mountains[2]; others are found in Oldenburgh and in Switzerland on the Jura,[3] and in Zurich; several occur in Alsace Lorraine[4] as the 'Altschloss' (old fort) of Haspelscheidt, an elliptical ring 980 feet across, of rude stones with a side enclosure to the north as at Dun Conor. In France along the bank of the Seine[5] in Normandy and between that river and the Loire[6] there are many forts like our Irish ones, and the series runs out to the sea in Brittany, especially in Côtes du Nord and Finistere,[7] scattered examples occurring as far south as the Pyrenees, and in Great Britain, in Cornwall, and Wales, with numerous examples in Scotland.[8] They are of every period from the Flint Age to the Roman Conquest, while in Scotland they undoubtedly date

---

[1] Mons Pirus. I have examined this fort since writing the present Paper. It is of small sandstone blocks, and much dilapidated and overgrown with oak and beech. It consists of a round fort, about 650 feet in diameter on the higher peak, with a crescent-shaped annexe to the south, whence a long loop of wall surrounds the southern peak. It measures over all about 2640 feet x 440 feet, a lesser area than Moghane. See plan, p. [5], fig. 23.

[2] The Vosges forts: see *Mémoires de la Soc. Royale des Ant. de France*, vol. v., p. 106. Masonry like Langough, county Clare. Also *Ibid.*, vol. xii., p. 8.

[3] *Dictionnaire Archéologique de Gaule époque Celtique*, 1875. Deveher (Jura), p. 339. Cheteley, p. 284. Chateau Chalon, p. 271. Siesberg, p. 93. Also in Zurich, Birchweil, p. 162. Bassersdorf, p. 122. The Swiss forts are usually curved entrenchments across the necks of spurs.

[4] *Mémoires de la Soc. Arch. et Hist. de la Moselle*, 1859, p. 58; 1862, p. 275. *Dictionnaire Archéologique de la Gaule*, Haspelscheidt, p. 5; Hommert, 'ring' on isolated rock, p. 26. Laguille's *History of Alsace*, vol. vii., and *Soc. Ant.*, Normandy, 1835, p. 247, describe the great dry stone fort of Mont St. Odille.

[5] *Dictionnaire Archéologique de la Gaule*. La Cheppe (Marne), p. 283. Bar Sur Aube, p. 121. Baillu sur Thérain (Oise), p. 114. Arces (Yonne), p. 73. Champ Cevrais (same), p. 259.

[6] *Société des Antiquaires de la Normandie*, 1835, pp. 188, &c. 'Entrenched enclosures on the banks of the Seine' (plate vi. and vii.). The fort of Bourdeville, 150 acres in extent, a great semicircle on the edge of a cliff, with radiating enclosures and great curved trenches, forming a second ring. A 'Druidic' stone stands in the inner enclosure (plan, p. [5], fig. 26). Of somewhat similar plan is the great fort above Caudebec. On the opposite hill a large circular 'rath' enclosed a Roman villa. M. Fallue, the author, does not consider the remains to be early Gaulish work, but as he does not take into account similar, though smaller forts, in places never held by Romans, or threatened by Saxons, we may hesitate to accept all his conclusions.

[7] Henansal (Côte du Nord), p. 18 (*Dict. Arch.*, as quoted). Langast (same), p. 66. Laz (Finisterè), p. 78. Cléden (same), p. 291. Cléguérec (Morbihan), p. 292.

[8] For the British forts - Borlase's *Antiquities of Cornwall*, pp. 346, 347. Mac Arthur's *Arran: Its Antiquities*, &c., pp. 80-83. Roy's *Military Antiquities*, plate xlviii. Martin's *Western Isles*, 1703, pp. 34, 152. *Proc. Soc. Ant., Scotland*, 1886 to 1895; and our *Journal*, 1894, pp. 408, 416. George Chalmers' *Caledonia*, vol. i., pp. 88, 92, 131. *Archæologia Cambrensis. Archæological Journal.* Pennant's *Tour in Wales*, vol. ii. For Celtic invasion of the British Isles, see *Early Man in Britain* (Mr. W. B. Dawkins), p. 342.

to the legendary period of the sons of Huamore. Flint weapons have been found in Dun Aenghus,[1] but iron objects were found in the walls of Cahercalla, Clare, and iron axes in Caherspeenaun on Lough Corrib. There are forts in France, Scotland, and in this island, as at Moytura-Cong, Deerpark, Co. Sligo, Ballykinvarga, and Tullycommane, Clare, and elsewhere associated with stone circles, cromlechs, and primitive burials,[2] while the furrowed and weatherworn tops of the pillars of the *chevaux-de-frise* of Dun Aenghus and Ballykinvarga testify to the long period which has passed since their erection

On the other hand the Clare cahers[3] are manifestly of very different periods, many are residential rather than defensive, resembling our enclosed yards rather than castles; others are not the hurried entrenchments of a small and hunted tribe, but the deliberately built citadels of a settled and powerful nation, fearing assault rather than siege. Antiquities found in their enclosures may have lain there long before the fort was built. If a great caher were erected in our day from the crag blocks, it would look venerable and antique even in the lifetime of its builders, for its materials would be already fretted with more ages of storms than have lashed the ramparts of Aenghus and Conor, while some of the churches of the eighth and ninth centuries[4] are of more massive masonry and even more weatherbeaten than some of our forts. There is no hint that the buildings were regarded as unusual or non-Milesian; some bear Celtic proper names, even later than the eleventh century, and were used for ordinary residence through the Middle Ages to recent years.

In 1317 Donchad O'Brien, before the fatal battle of Corcomroe, did not leave 'a man dwelling in an 'ooan''[5] (caher's souterrain) unsummoned to his army. Dromore Caher was inhabited 1569; Cahermacnaughten in 1675, and Caherballiny to 1839. As a result one is driven first to merely negative conclusions: (1), it is more than questionable whether any of these cahers are the work of Firbolgs who built none in their undisturbed settlements[6] and had hardly leisure or resources to build the huge fortresses of Aran and Clare; (2), nor can they be the work of sea-rovers for the same reason, and the occurrence of many important cahers on mountains difficult of access from the sea;[7] (3), nor by the Dalcassian kings who never settled in the districts where they most abound, and built none in the neighbourhood of

---

[1] 'Age of Dun Aenghus,' by Dr. Colley March. *Proc. Soc. Ant., London*, vol. xv., 1894, p. 222; and our *Journal*, 1895, p. 257. *Early Man in Britain*, p. 336.

[2] See Petrie's 'Military Architecture,' MSS. R.I.A.; Dr. Fergusson's *Rude Stone Monuments*, chap. v.; and Mr. Milligan on Sligo Forts, in our *Journal*, 1890-1891.

[3] The total number is about 2300. Of these over 300 are in Burren, and about 200 each in Corcomroe and Inchiquin.

[4] One Scotch dry stone fort is attributed to a certain Tuathal, who died 865.

[5] Mr. Standish Hayes O'Grady first called my attention to the true meaning of this passage in the 'Triumphs of Torlough.' Cahers are still 'Uamhs,' 'Ooans,' and 'Nooans' in Burren and Inchiquin.

[6] In eastern Galway and Roscommon and around Emly. They rather figure as builders of earthern forts, *e.g.* Talti and Rath Croaghan.

[7] In Mayo fifteen out of twenty-two are inland. We shall see how inaccessible were many forts in Clare.

their own residences;[1] (4), nor by the Danes[2] for similar reasons; (5), nor by the monks, who in this district seldom attempted even a slight mound and ditch and left their chief monasteries unfenced in the open fields; (6), nor as cattlepens, to which such ramparts, terraces, and steps are unsuitable; (7), nor *primarily* as fortresses, for overhanging hills and want of water seem to have been matters of indifference to their builders.[3] Where unquarried stone was so easily procured and in suitable blocks[4] it is probable that a series of cahers, necessarily in one nearly invariable style, were built, rebuilt, and repaired from early pagan times down perhaps to the fourteenth century, when they were superseded by square towers; the straight-sided cahers and mortar-built gateways in circular forts being transitional. The more elaborate forts are not necessarily the latest; they only imply better organisation and greater population. Moghane required the collection and laying of some 1,177,000 cubic feet of blocks, the average fort of at least 40,000 cubic feet. A group of six or more cahers (we shall examine several such groups) implies a much denser population than in the thirteenth century or even now; but it may equally imply that the country being overgrown and wild, men congregated into the cleared districts. O'Donovan[5] noticed this in 1839, though he was a firm believer in the pagan origin of the Aran cahers and attributed Dubh Caher to 1000 B.C. 'The Firbolgs were never more than a handful of men in Ireland, and it must have required a dense population and several centuries to erect all these cahirs.'

The stone forts of Clare lie mainly in Burren and the adjoining parishes: most of the others in eastern Clare lie on two lines running more or less from the N.W.[6] from the hills of Glasgeivnagh and Inchiquin to Cratloe Hill, all three being noted in pre-Christian tradition.[7] The only noteworthy

---

[1] The Grianan Lachtna is of earth, though convenient slate blocks lay loose to hand, and indeed were used for the base of the inner building. Balboruma is entirely of earth (see our *Journal*, 1893, p. 191). In face of this fact, it is more probable that the great cahers in Tradree were dismantled and useless before the Danish wars, in which they played no recorded part, than that Brian, or his successors, undertook such vast works to the neglect of their own residences.

[2] See, first, Giraldus Cambrensis, 'Topog. Hib.', III. 37, who states that the Danes made 'entrenchments both deep and circular, for the most part triple'; also Martin's *Western Islands*, 1703, p. 34; Lady Chatterton's *Rambles in South of Ireland*, vol. i., p. 280; Borlase, *Cornwall*, &c.

[3] I must allude to the strange theory that they were places for games or combats. We find it in White's *Tour in Scotland*, 1769, p. 273; Vallancey's *Tract on Staig Fort*; Scott's *Marmion*; the 'Legend of Moghane' in our *Journal*, 1893, p. 281, and in Bohemia, in *Proc. Soc. Ant. Scot.*, 1868-70, p. 158.

[4] Too much stress is often laid on style of masonry or questions of material; both depended on the facilities of getting stone and the natural cleavage of the blocks.

[5] Ordnance Survey Letters, Clare, p. 187.

[6] This also occurs in Scotland (see *Forts and Camps of Dumfries*, by Dr. D. Christison). 'Two broad lines of forts appear to cross Annandale from east to west, and nearly half of the Eskdale forts occur in a band running N.E. and S.W.' - *Proc. Soc. Ant. Scotland*, 1890-1891, p. 203.

[7] On the more northern line are Cahereen, Caherlough, Cahernavillare, Caher-macrea, Cahershaughnessy, and Cahercalla; also the mounds of Inauguration of Magh Adhair: see for these our *Journal*, 1890-1891, p. 463; 1893, pp. 287, 432. On

group in the S.W. is that of Loop Head. Though excelled by the Duns in Aran (which, however, belonged to Clare till the later part of the sixteenth century, and were evidently built by the same race as those in the Burren) their number enables us to form a more accurate notion as to what is exceptional and what commonplace in the former and in others of our cahers. The traces of structures in their enclosures, if we except the oval cloghans and the souterrains, are probably fences round wooden houses.

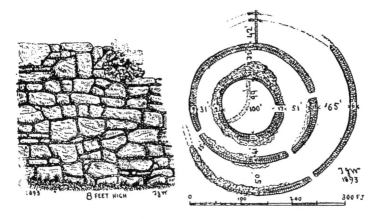

Cahercalla, near Quin.

Cahermacnaughten and, perhaps, Ballyallavan have foundations of late mediæval buildings. The older residences must have been groups of huts with cup-shaped roofs of wicker and thatch, such as we see in the Gaulish huts on the Antonine column. The walls were of wood and clay, decorated at times with carved yew posts, bronze studs, and designs in colours and lime; the outer rampart was often whitewashed,[1] lime being used for the purpose before being used for mortar. We find round pits, perhaps the bases of wooden huts (the Germans made wooden souterrains, possibly the Irish occasionally did the same), for timber was more plentiful even on the heights of Burren when such names as Ardross, Behagh, Feenagh, and Killoghil were first adopted than in 1652 when Ludlow made his grim joke, 'There is not wood enough to hang a man.'

This Paper is intended to collect facts rather than to advance theories. Baffled in our search into the records, lost in the mazes of tradition, and

---

the second line lie Caheragaleagh, Cahergurraun, Moghane, and Langough (see our *Journal*, 1893, pp. 281, 284); for the other forts see *infra*. As I did not then illustrate the interesting triple fort of Cahercalla, I give here its plan and masonry; it needs little other explanation, its steps and terraces, if it ever had any, being defaced. If triple walls mark a royal fort, its nearness to the place of inauguration implies its importance, and the comparative preservation of its rudely-built and small masonry suggests a rebuilding in later times. It may be safely asserted that it was never a permanent royal residence since A.D. 840. The finding of iron objects in its walls has been already noticed. In the adjoining townland of Creevaghbeg is a very perfect but featureless caher, 84 feet internal diameter; walls, 7 and 8 feet thick; door, E.N.E.

[1] Introduction to O'Curry's *Manners and Customs*, pp. 298, 303, and vol. iii., p. 11.

getting no certain answer from the forts, we must lay up careful descriptions for that future scholar who can answer the riddle of the ruins. For the rabbit-catcher and road-contractor are overthrowing the walls, and even where conserved they have too often been rashly modernized; 'palaces and castles,' it has been said, 'are more attractive objects in ruins than in complete repair.' I cannot pretend to describe even the most interesting of some 400 forts, nor to give popular accounts of bardic glories, 'duns, snow white, with roofs striped crimson and blue, chariots . . . bearing the warrior and his charioteer,' for such fall as little as landscape-drawing within the scope of this Paper; but I hope to help better antiquaries than myself in their libraries, and to save them on their journeys from the disappointment of taking a long and weary drive to find some fort attractive and conspicuous on the map reduced to mere heaps of featureless moss-grown stones.

INCHIQUIN BARONY - KILNABOY PARISH

TULLYCOMMANE[1] (O.S. 10). - Turning off from the main road to Kilfenora, on the rising ground north of Kilnaboy Church, we enter a very wild district, and ascending, in zigzags, a steep hill, a bastion of the great Glasgeivnagh rampart, the true edge of Burren, we reach a plateau, with a glorious view over Inchiquin Lake to Moghane fort and Cratloe. The road turns northward, at one time through low bushes and mossy rocks, at another, unenclosed, through sheets of shining grey crags, like the waves of some vast lake of stone; past the cromlechs and cairns of Leanna, till we drop sharply from the table-land into the deep rugged gorge of Glencurraun. We may conjecture this to be the 'blind valley of Burren,' Caechan Boirne - 'constant the road of the king' - named in the Book of Rights. Perhaps 'the road of the king' is Boher na mic righ (of the king's sons), running to the foot of these hills. No other valley suits the term Caechan, and possesses a triple (or royal) fort to meet the requirement of the venerable record. It is a curious coincidence that Dermot O'Brien's army, in 1317, took this very route, up the Boher, over the white crags of Mullachgall, through 'Leanna's dairy land,' and 'along the fastness-begirt tracks,' on their way to the battle of Corcomroe Abbey. The probability is increased when we find in the same poem with 'Caechan Boirne,' the fort of Kilfenora and Inchiquin hill (Ceann Nathrach).

CASHLAUN GAR. - At the entrance of Glencurraun rise two great natural domes of limestone, and on the nearer,[2] towering over the road, we see the broken walls of Cashlaun Gar like the acropolis of some lost city. Climbing, with some difficulty, up the steep slope, over heaps of stone that are slipping down the hill, we stand in the interior in deep grass and moss covering

---

[1] The map form 'Tullycommon' is deceptive, 'Chuman' appearing both in the local form and the 'Tulach Chumann' of the 'Four Masters.' Lord Dunraven vaguely locates the two great forts 'between Clifden and Termon' ('Notes,' vol. i., p. 17). The 6 inch Map only gives 'Glencrawne cave.'

[2] The *Proceedings, Soc. Ant., Scotland*, 1888-1889, p. 400, gives several forts in Lorne in similar positions.

rough crags and treacherous fissures. To the N.W. side are the remains ofthree cloghauns, so ruined that we cannot trace the entire face of their walls; a fourth stands in the very centre of the enclosure opposite the eastern gate.

Cashlaun Gar, from S.E.

They were probably thatched and not vaulted, as the walls are slight, and no great quantity of stones appear. The ramparts are well built of long blocks, with upright joints at intervals, attaining their greatest height of 13 feet 6 inches to the north, and from 9 feet to 10 feet thick, increasing at the gateway to 11 feet 8 inches, with two faces and large blocks for filling.

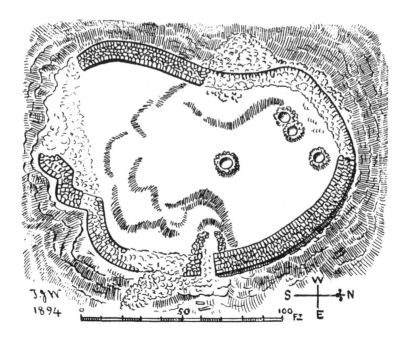

Plan of Cashlaun Gar.

A long reach to the N.E. is 8 feet high. It ends in the well-built north pier
of the gate, the south pier being much injured. The gate faces E.N.E., and
opens on the edge of a precipitous slope and a rock 10 feet high, sheltering a
badger's den. The inhabitants must have entered the fort by ladders, which
suggests the theory that some cahers with no gates were entered by similar
means; and if the ancient builders[1] used wooden scaffolds, the construction
of a ladder would have been easy. At the foot of the slope lie long fragments
of stone, probably the broken lintels of the gate. The fort is very irregular,
being 133 feet 6 inches north and south, and 76 feet east and west internally.
The south wall has two re-entrant angles, dipping in 5 feet, in 19 feet, and 6
feet 9 inches, in 29 feet. They are beautifully constructed to cling, with
unnecessary accuracy, to the edge of the perpendicular cliff. There is a
similar but more shallow dip, in the west rampart, much of which has fallen.[2]

Gateway, Cashlaun Gar.

---

[1] Book of Lecan: 'Active Garvan proceeded to work with art (on Grianan Aileach)
and to chip. Imcheall placed a scaffold.' - Ordnance Survey, Templemore.

[2] I have since found the foundations of an outer enclosure of massive blocks, often 5
to 7 feet long, overgrown with hazel bushes, on the northern flank of the knoll.

LOWER FORT. - On the opposite edge of the table-land, and across the valley, about 300 feet from Cashlaun Gar, is a straight-sided enclosure, irregular, and somewhat diamond-shaped, 153 feet north and south, and 135 feet east and west internally. It is much defaced, the walls only 3 feet 6 inches thick, and about 5 feet at the highest part, being built of long 'stretchers,' several 8 feet 6 inches long, and in parts cyclopean in character. The S.W. corner is rounded, and constructed with a facing of large stones set on end. It may have been a cattle enclosure.

Masonry in Lower Fort

CAHERCOMMANE TRIPLE FORT. - Following the windings of the glen for about half a mile, we find on the edge of a lofty and steep cliff, opposite which another huge dome rises, a large and very interesting fort, remarkably like Dun Aenghus, though its cliff overhangs a narrow gorge instead of the vast swirling abyss of foam-flecked sea beneath the Aran fortress.[1]

The outer wall is entirely destroyed for 24 feet from the cliff, both on the east and west sides, much of it is 7 feet or 8 feet high, and 8 feet thick. It has two faces, well bonded, with several upright joints. Near one of these, to the south, the inner face has been rebuilt, the stones being laid slope-wise,

Masonry, Cahercommane

with flat blocks here and there to prevent their slipping. The wedge-shape of many of the stones helps this arrangement. Similarly we see a course like a flat arch in the inner caher, and in some of the other Clare forts.[2] Against the wall were built several small huts of uncertain date; and the foundations

---

[1] We find forts of similar plan at Dunriachy (*Archæol. Scot.*, iv., p. 199); Dalmakeddar and Erickstane, Dumfries, and Twyholm, Kircudbright (*Proc. Soc. Ant., Scotland*, 1890-1891, p. 234; 1892-1893, p. 136), in Scotland; Bourdeville and Caudebec though vastly larger (*Soc. Ant. Normandy*), in France; and at Bény (*Congrès Internat.*, Buda-Pesth, 1876, pp. 62, 63), in Hungary. See plans, p. [5], figs. 1 to 5 and 26.

[2] See illustration of Caherscrebeen, *infra* [p. 21]. As a clue to the origin of upright joints we find provision made in the 'Seanchas Mór', IV., p. 123, for the employment of joint labour on the enclosure round a dwelling. Evidently each section of the wall was entrusted to a different gang.

of an oval cloghaun,[1] 27 feet x 18 feet, lie 54 feet outside, and S.E. of the fort. The enclosure between the outer and second wall varies, being 54 feet west, 50 feet south, and 60 feet east.[2] It is crossed by several radiating walls much overthrown. The southern runs from the central caher to the outer wall, where is a very small hut or kennel. It enclosed a round hut in the second enclosure. A parallel wall forms a passage with it across the latter space only, and a second hut is built to the left of the opening against the outer face of the second rampart. The second radiating wall runs across both enclosures; the third and fourth are parallel, forming a passage 6 ft. wide from the second to the outer rampart, the more northern crossing the second enclosure to the caher, and in every case the walls are sufficiently perfect to show that no gate existed at either passage.

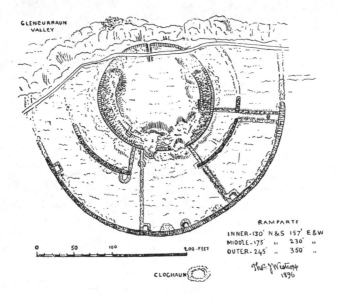

Cahercommane

Lord Dunraven suggests that the northern one was covered; but it only ran along the surface, and there are no traces of flags or corbelling, so it remains a problem. Perhaps these huts and cross-walls may represent the work of herdsmen long after the caher was deserted. The district for five hundred years[3] has been much used for grazing. The outer rampart runs for

---

[1] Mr. Seaton Milligan, in our *Journal*, 1890-1891, p. 579, describes a small 'fort,' 29 feet in diameter, lying 25 feet outside the second cashel of Deerpark.

[2] In the Leabhar Breac there is a curious description of the Heavenly City, evidently founded on the recollection of a triple caher. It is surrounded by three ramparts, each 1/3rd larger than the next inner enclosure. Within is the square city, with four gates, and a flowering lawn in front of each. - Todd Lecture Series, R.I.A., vol. iii., No. 830.

[3] 'Leanna's dairy lands.' 'Burren's hilly, grey expanse of jagged points and slippery steeps, flowing with milk, and yielding luscious grass.' - (Magrath's 'Triumphs of Torlough,' 1317, and the cattle tributes in the Book of Rights). The Book of

60 feet north of the passage, about 18 feet from which the ground sinks into a regular area from the inner caher for at least 100 feet outside of the fort.

The second rampart is 5 feet thick, and 3 feet or 4 feet high; it lies 30 feet from the caher, is better built, and seems to have been disused and partly demolished when the outer rampart was constructed. The central caher is massive and imposing, whether seen from the road or from the depth of the glen, rising like a great knoll of rock against the sky. It is 12 feet high at the east, and 14 feet to the south, being there fairly perfect, but leaning out. It is of rude masonry, from 20 feet to 22 feet thick, and had at least one terrace, which has a recess, probably for a ladder, whence shallow steps built of flags led to a second platform, or to the summit. The north side has fallen down the cliff, but a rock-cut passage, 3 feet wide, crosses its base, and probably formed the only gate of the caher. The enclosures measure respectively - the inner, 85 feet north and south; 113 feet 4 inches east and west internally; 130 feet[1] and 157 feet externally. The second 175 feet x 230 feet externally, the outer about 350 feet along the cliff x 245 feet deep.

On the opposite ridge lie two circular enclosures, one coarsely built and nearly overthrown, the second, of very regular masonry, called Cahereen-moyle, its wall only a few feet high. It is scarcely possible to conceive surroundings more desolate and melancholy than those of Glencurraun. The pale flat ridges shutting out the more distant view; the dark glen and ghastly sheets of grey rock, rendering more dismal the storm-worn ruins - homes of tribes, forgotten with the kings and rulers of the earth – 'Qui ædificant sibi solitudines.'

Cahercommane Triple Fort.

Distribution (1655), p. 520, mentions Tullycommon, 'whose meares cannot be shown.' Gleacrane (Glencurraun), Leahesse (Lisheen), Slewbegg, Lisheenageeragh, Dullisheen, Cahercomaine, alias Lysidlyane, stony pasture. Creevagh is described as covered with dwarf wood (p. 442).

[1] By later examination, I find that it probably extended to a ridge 8 feet in advance of the present remains, *i.e.* up to 138 feet north and south.

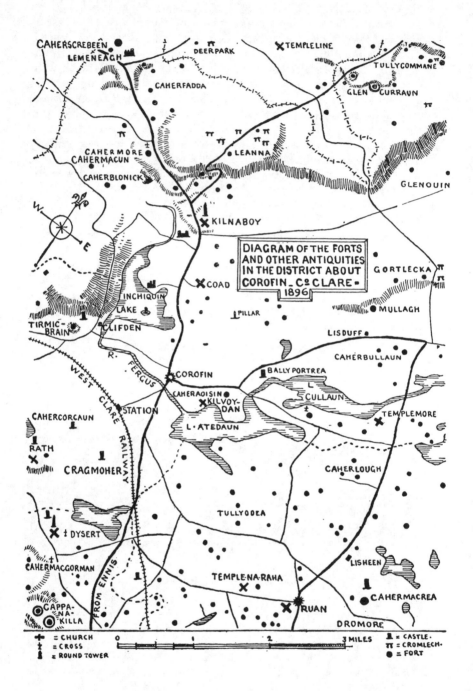

Plan of Forts in the Barony of Inchiquin.

GLASGEIVNAGH HILL.[1] - This range of hills rises gradually from the west to a steep eastern cliff; the top is a plateau of fissured crags, with here and there a shallow valley, and in the spring is very attractive, abounding in gentians, anemones, and numerous ferns and flowers. The remains on this plateau call for some notice. I carefully examined them in company with Dr. George U. Macnamara, our Local Secretary, to whose wide traditional and topographical knowledge, and constant practical help, I am much indebted for the completion of this Paper; moreover, the crags are difficult, wearisome, and, even to some extent, dangerous to traverse, and not likely to be much visited.

KNOCKAUN FORT (not to be confounded with Knockans townlands) stands on the ridge of Tullycommane, north of Cahercommane. It is not oval, as shown on the 6-inch Ordnance Survey map, but consists of a poorly built, slight wall, forming an angular enclosure on the crags. Inside is a souterrain of the usual type, two nearly parallel walls 3 feet apart, roofed by a slab about 7 feet square, and leading into an enclosure of slabs set on edge, 21 feet x 17 feet, with a door to the south flanked by two regular blocks like seats; smaller but somewhat similar structures exist at Ballyganner.

Several interesting remains lie westward along the ridge in line with each other and Knockaun fort: a large long cromlech, which the scope of this Paper does not permit me to describe; a circular caher of well-laid slabs, levelled to a couple of feet in height, its gate facing east-south-east; a circular cairn, its middle dug out, and reputed to have more fairies than all the other forts of the hill; near it a smaller cairn or giant's grave: these crown a rounded green hill, possibly the 'Tulach chumann,' which gives the townland its name; a rath of earth and stones, south of it a thick-walled enclosure like a small house; finally, crossing the road, we find a small fort nearly levelled, and a larger caher, part of its western segment well preserved, with traces of a second ring nearly 300 feet in diameter. A short distance N.E. from this is the hamlet of Castletown, with a lofty fragment of one of the O'Loughlin's castles; passing round the hill we find north of the road:-

CAHERSAVAUN,[2] a well built fort of large blocks, which in winter forms a sort of crannoge in the temporary lough of Castletown, it surrounds a knoll on the very edge of Tullycommane, and indeed of the baronies of Inchiquin and Burren. Its gateway faces S.E., and is destroyed.

Again ascending the ridge, we pass a late-looking enclosure, near which, in the rock, are three basins, so regular as to suggest their being artificial.

In Cappaghkennedy, east of Knockaun, is a large cairn, at the highest point of the ridge, 780 feet above the sea, with a noble view across Galway and Clare, from Loughrea and Kilmacduagh ruins to Cratloe and Inchiquin. Near it is a fine cromlech quite perfect, and long inhabited by poor families,

---

[1] Ordnance Survey (six-inch scale), Co. Clare, Sheet No. 10.
[2] A similar 'crannoge caher,' 'quayed round with a stone wall,' in a lake in county Antrim, is described in *Ulster Journal of Archæology*, vol. viii., p. 238. There is a Cahersavane in county Kerry, Sheet 89, Ordnance Survey. (See Wilkinson's *Ancient Architecture of Ireland*, p. 58).

though now unoccupied; at which is a block with three very small cup-markings, and two more just marked out, bearing distinct trace of having been picked, and not ground.[1]

Cahersavaun in Winter.

CAHERMORE, or MOHER NA CARTAN, a fine caher on the borders of Cappaghkennedy and Knockans. It measures 138 feet north and south, with walls 10 feet thick and high, formed of large headers, often 2 feet 6 inches square, and 4 feet to 7 feet long.[2] It has a souterrain 3 feet 6 inches x 16 feet, roofed with blocks 6 feet long, level with the ground. The wall conforms to the edge of the projecting crag, jutting above the grassy depression of Mohernacartan, called, like the fort, after the Tuatha De Danann smith, Lon, who traditionally resided there, and whose legend I gave at some length in our *Journal*, 1895, p. 227. Near the south-west end of the depression, a long cromlech, much injured by fire, stands on the ridge; it was partially destroyed by a crazy lad named MacMahon, employed on the farm about fifteen years ago.

In the next field is a well-built, but nearly demolished, circular caher; and, nearer the waterfall, where the 'Seven Streams' of Teeskagh fall into their verdant, shrubby glen, is a fort like Knockaun, called Moher na glasha, after the legendary cow 'Glas Geivnagh'; it has some cloghauns, which probably, like the enclosure, are of no great age, the only noteworthy feature being a series of slabs set on end all round the interior with their edges to the wall. The entrance faces westward, and commands a fine view of Cahercommane and Glencurraun down the slope, with the tower of Lemeneagh far away. There is a large cairn in the deep gorge near the waterfall.

---

[1] Bullaun stones also occur with prehistoric remains at the cromlechs of Newgrove, Kiltanon, and the Mound of Magh Adhair, all near Tulla, county Clare.
[2] In the 'Dindseanchus' (*Revue Celtique*, xv., p. 449), Curoi is advised to direct the clans of Deda to gather 'pillar-stones' to build his caher.

Cahermore, Glenquin, from South.

GLENQUIN[1] (110 ft. x 112 ft. and 166 ft. x 170 ft.,[2] O.S. 10). – Under the cliffs of Glasgeivnagh, on the hill behind Mr. W. Russell's house, is the double fort of Cahermore,[3] looking over Glenquin valley, to its strangely terraced hills, and across all central Clare. As I saw it, with its fields and crags, blue with gentians and violets, it was one of the most picturesque forts in the county. It is fairly perfect, its wall 10 feet thick at base, and up to 11 feet 6 inches high, having a terrace 4 feet above the ground-level inside, varying from 1 foot 10 inches to 4 feet wide. The outer face is of good large masonry, diminishing up-wards, and having filling as small as road metal, which has probably bulged it into its curious convex outline.[4] The defaced gate faces S.E.; its lintel was 6 feet long. A souterrain lies N.W. and S.E. at 12 feet from the wall at the N.W. segment. The outer ring has fallen, save to the N.E. where it is 4 feet thick and 5 feet high; it is not circular, but 20 feet at N., W. and S. to 29 feet at E. and S.W. out from the inner rampart. A wall ran across this enclosure from the gate, and a house adjoined it to the south. On the grassy knoll S.W. is a small cairn 'Lishaun' overlooking the narrow and cliff-girt Lough Avalla, locally called Aphoilla, and, at the foot of the slope, are the foundations of the oratory and friar's house of Templepatrick and Correen, a stream and bank enclosing the so-called 'battlefield,' whose history I fail to discover.

MULLAGH (129 ft. to 138 ft., O.S. 17), a caher of regular masonry on the hill-side in Dabrien. The walls are most perfect to N.E., being 9 feet thick and high, with a terrace inside, 5 feet high and 2 feet 6 inches wide, and a

---

[1] 'Caherwoughtereen or Caherougherlinny' (einny?) in Book of Distribution, p. 512.
[2] Unless the contrary is stated my measurements are external diameters. Where two are given the first is N. and S., the second E. and W.; where four numbers are given the fort is double.
[3] Rev. T. Warren, (*Member*), first called my attention to Glenquin fort.
[4] This also occurs, *inter alia*, in Grianan Aileach, Staig, Duns Oghil, Conor, and Ballycarbery fort, in this country, and certain forts in Caithness and Sutherland.

batter of 1 in 4. Two defaced sets of steps[1] lead up the terrace and wall at the N.; the defaced gate looks S.-E. Inside is a rock-cut tank or souterrain 33 feet from S.W. A large earth fort, 'Lisvetty,' lies to the N.

CAHERAHOAGH (95 ft. x 103 ft., O.S. 17), half a mile east from the last, in Caherbullaun, 3 miles N. from Corofin. - It is nearly oval in plan, slightly flattened to the E. and W. Its walls are roughly built in two sections, with small filling; the outer, 5 feet x 9 feet high; the inner, a terrace, 3 feet 6 in. x 5 feet high, with an interesting 'stone ladder' in a recess 3 feet wide to the N.; five steps show above the rubbish, the top one having fallen, and four steps lead thence up the wall, to the left. The gate faces S.E., and has been rebuilt about the fifteenth century, with dressed stone and mortar, retaining the old batter 1 in 12 (the outer face reset for 12 feet west and 5 feet east). The passage

Stone Ladder, Caherahoagh Fort.

splays inward, from 5 feet 2 inches to 6 feet 5 inches, being 4 feet 4 inches wide, at two projecting jambs, 19 inches thick. Three inches behind these are bolt holes, showing how thin a door was used. A flight of four steps leads from the terrace up the south pier. Caherbullaun (82 feet), lies 58 feet to W., and Lisduff, a similar fort of earth and stones, in equal decay, lies beyond the road in a labyrinthine grove.

ROUGHAN (130 ft. x 127 ft., O.S. 16). - On a steep slope[2] near Kilnaboy cross and Lemeneagh gate, stands Cahermore.[3] Its wall is of finely fitted masonry, many of the blocks 5 feet x 3 feet; it is 10 feet thick, 7 feet high to S., and 2 or 3 feet high to N. and E. The outer face, though perfect, shows no gate[4]; the inner face, with much of the filling, has been removed; an

---

[1] More likely recesses for ladders.
[2] Such a site is common among Scotch forts. (See several striking examples in *Proc. Soc. Ant., Scot.*, 1895, pp. 113, 131, 137, 151).
[3] The only fort fully described in the 'Ord. Survey Letters on Clare,' R.I.A., vol. i., p. 47, copied in *Diocese of Killaloe*, p. 494.
[4] Some remains, apparently of a gateway, facing the east, and 3 feet wide, exist in a brake of bramble. Mr. George FitzGerald, some years ago, found a cist of four stones and a top slab to the S.E. in the adjoining field. The remains of two skeletons, laid with the legs to the east, were found, and replaced under the belief

inaccessible souterrain lies 17 feet from the wall to S.E. In the next field, westward, lies the long cromlech of Ballycasheen.

CAHERSCREBEEN[1] (129 x 135 feet, O.S. 16) is on the ridge behind Lemeneagh Castle, a shallow valley leads to its western face. The present wall seems built outside an older one, to enlarge the area,[2] and is 12 feet to

17 feet thick, and 7 feet high, with patches of good masonry, but much is built of small field stones, and much has fallen; no gate is visible; the interior is level with the top of the wall, and crossed by four foundations (N. and S.); a small hut stood in the centre, and an inaccessible souterrain 9 feet from the west. A shepherd told Dr. G. Macnamara, 'it is one of the richest forts in Ireland: it has a room full of gold, another of deer's tallow, and a third of 'beor lochlanagh,' or 'Dane's beer.'[3] Pits dug by treasure-seekers appear everywhere.

Masonry - Cahermore, Roughan.

Masonry - Caherscrebeen, near Lemeneagh Castle.

---

that the cist was a Christian burial-place. The top slab is visible, and being only 5 feet 4 inches by 3 feet 3 inches, suggests that the bodies were not in an extended position.

[1] Compare 'Dun Scribin,' north of Loch Ness, in Scotland.

[2] This is also noticeable at Caherbullog, near Slieve Elva, in the Burren.

[3] Similarly in Bohemia the peasants tell of 'giants' cellars' under the Wlader fort, 'filled with treasure and wine,' the fort being 'pitted with the diggings of treasure-seekers.' - *Proc. Soc. Ant., Scot.*, 1868-70, p. 161.

OTHER FORTS IN INCHIQUIN. - Cappanakilla, a long ridge in Dysert, has two double[1] forts, Caheragaleagh (the western, 100 feet x 60 feet, and 200 feet x 150 feet), and Cahergurraun (the eastern, 130 feet x 150 feet and 300 feet x 300 feet); both are overthrown and of rather small stones. The plateau has a fine outlook, extending from the spires of Ennis to Inchiquin Lake, and ends in steep crags covered with hazels. Cahermacgorman, levelled. Caherclancy, a high fort cut by the road. Cahermacrea (300 feet x 250 feet), quite overthrown, in a dense wood. To the S.W., is a smaller fort (130 feet), a ring of filling 6 feet high x 9 feet thick, the outer face rebuilt to protect a plantation. Ballyharaghan, overgrown and featureless.[2] Cahereen, Caherlough, and Cahervillare, defaced. Caheraoisin, (220 feet x 250 feet), of earth and stones, had gates to E and W., an old road leads to latter. Cahermacatier, of coarse blocks, much broken. Caherblonick, Cahermacon and Caherfadda, defaced. Cahermore, in Killeen, S.E. from Coad, perfect but featureless, the walls 6 feet high. Tirvicbrain, two enclosures of doubtful age on an abrupt crag. Roughan, a fort at opposite end to Cahermore (p. [20] *supra*), feature-less and overgrown.[3]

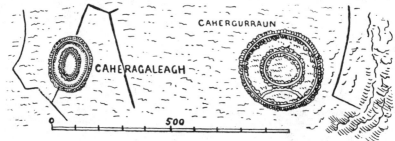

Plan of Forts on Cappanakilla. Scale, 400 feet to an inch.

---

[1] For a foreign example, see *Congrès International*, Buda Pesth, vol. viii., p. 94.

[2] This is one of the best examples of a stone fort in the parish of Ruan, but there are many interesting earth forts with souterrains, justifying Macgrath's epithet (in 1317): 'Ruan of the grass-topped 'ooans," *ooan* being used both for cahers and caves in this barony.

[3] The following names are now forgotten:- In 1652, Cahermoyle or Cahermeenrow; Cahershillagh or Cahernahaille (perhaps Parc-na-hilly, in Caherblonick), in Kilnaboy; Cahergar (perhaps near Lough Gar and Cahermacrea); Cahernamart, and Cahervicknea, in Ruan.

Other interesting names in Inchiquin and its borders are: - Caherbannagh, in Kilnamona; Cahervickaun, in Dysert; Cahergal, Cahernamona, and Cahercorcaun, in Rath. (The last, called Cragcorcaun in 'Annals of Four Masters,' but Cahercorcaun in other documents of the period.) Caherdermotygriffa, in Templemally, on border of Dysert.

THE BORDER OF BURREN. NOUGHAVAL (O.S. 9).

Along the desolate ridges between Noughaval and Ballyganner lie a group of forts so numerous and implying so much labour that we may conclude that an actual city and considerable population occupied this lonely site.[1]

> 'Their raths are not dwelt in –
> Their ancient cathairs –
> Whereon great duration was wrought –
> They are waste . . . like Lugaid's House.'[2]

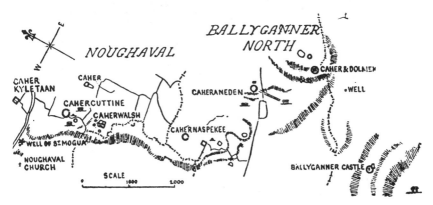

Plan of Noughaval and Ballyganner.

Six 'forts' and two cromlechs run in line nearly N. and S. towards the summit of Ballyganner hill. From Cahernaspekee, and the last of these, five more lie eastward with four cromlechs. Small 'caves,' cairns, circles, and hut-sites abound; and near the N. end are the venerable church of Noughaval[3] with two crosses, the 'O'Davoren's chapel' and the well of St. Mogua with its uncouth and ancient ash tree.

At the south end are the huge cromlech, castle, and three cahers of Ballyganner. The ridge has a wide view over Kilfenora, while Liscannor Bay is visible through a gap in the hills, from the gate of Cahercuttine. The whole site abounds in beautiful crag flowers.

CAHERKYLETAAN (105 feet x 120 feet). - A straight-sided fort, walls 4 feet or 5 feet high and 10 feet thick, of large slabs; it has a cross wall and some prostrate pillar stones, but no trace of a gateway.

---

[1] Ten fine forts stand near St. Abb's Head, Scotland, where only three farmhouses are now inhabited. - *Proc. Soc. Ant., Scot.*, 1895, p. 171. 'The battle of Magh Leana,' p. 79, also mentions a group of 'three strong duns . . . three lofty murs of assembly, and three strong cathairs.'

[2] 'Calendar of Oengus,' p. 18.

[3] *Nua-congabhaile*, the latter word one of our oldest terms for a monastery, *Tripartite Life*, p. clv. A 'Mughain, virgin, of Cluain Boirenn,' is given under Dec. 15th, in 'Calendar of Oengus.' A description of Noughaval Church appears in the *Report of the Society for the Preservation of Memorials of the Dead (Ireland)*, 1896.

Cahercuttine – Fort and Cromlech, from south.

CAHERCUTTINE[1] (137 ft. x 130 ft.). - A well preserved fort on the summit of the ridge, commanding a view of most of the other cahers of the group and those of Doon and Ballykinvarga. Its wall is 11 feet 4 inches to 12 feet 6 inches thick, and up to 10 feet high, very well built, of large stones, with two faces, the inner having a plinth 9 inches wide.[2] The gateway had corner posts and large lintels, removed to admit cattle, the main lintel was 8 ft. 6 in. x 2 ft. x 1 foot; the passage, 5 ft. 8 in. within, widens outward: it faces S. S. E.[3]; near it to the west is a fine flight of six steps, 3 feet 9 inches x 10 inches x 4 inches to 6 inches tread and two feet deep.

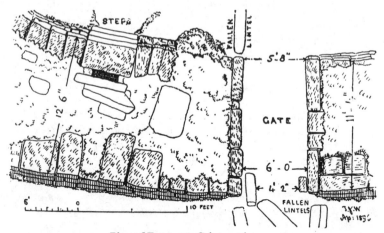

Plan of Entrance, Cahercuttine.

This fort is a veritable garden of ferns, harebells, and cranesbills. In the field to the west are a small cromlech 8 ft. x 6 ft., a ring wall of large slabs

---

[1] The fort name appears as Cahirgotten or Cahirnegotten in the Patent of Donough, Earl of Thomond, 1612.
[2] A similar feature occurs at Morbihan, Brittany, *Revue Archéologique*, 1895, p. 64, and at Cahergrillaun, in the parish of Carran, county Clare.
[3] Canon Philip Dwyer describes this caher of 'Knickknocktheen' (Knockcottine), in 1876, as having an entrance with a 'flat single stone lintel' in excellent preservation. - *Handbook to Lisdoonvarna*, p. 57.

24 feet diameter, with walls 3 feet 6 inches thick, and a miniature souterrain. Two flights of five and four steps remain nearly hidden by grass and weeds to the E.S.E. and N.W. by N. They are similar to the third southern flight, and lead upwards from the plinth or narrow platform.

Steps and Gate, Cahercuttine

A cairn,[1] semicircle, and pile of large blocks occur in the same field, while south of the fort are another cairn and an overthrown cromlech 7 feet x 12 feet. A small oval fort stands about 200 yards to the east. It is featureless and defaced, with coarse walls 9 feet thick, and an enclosure about 85 feet long, tapering to the south.[2]

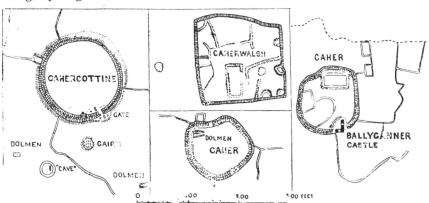

Plans of Forts near Noughaval.

---

[1] Small cairns abound near the stone fort of Cair Conan, Cornwall (Royal Inst. of Cornwall, 1862, p. 56), also at Chûn Castle in same shire.
[2] Compare plans, *Journal*, 1896, p. 147 [5], fig. 19 to 23.

CAHERWALSH (162 feet x 156 feet), an irregular enclosure of large stretchers, 9 feet thick. It is late, and much levelled, and several house-sites remain in the garth. A slab enclosure, nearly 16 feet square, stands outside the fort to the west. There seems to be part of a small caher farther south, but it is evidently rebuilt.

CAHERNASPEKEE (105 feet), a circular caher, its walls 8 feet thick, with a terrace 'veneered' with flat slabs, and much dug up by rabbit and treasure seekers. The gate faced the south, in which direction lie an oblong garth, coarsely built, a small cairn, and a ring of stones, the latter perhaps was set to mark out the ground for an intended fort.

We now turn eastward, and meet two rude enclosures, with a grassy valley between; the western surrounds a much defaced oblong slab-hut, and is 'veneered' with most fantastic water-fretted blocks. Beyond these is a very fine cromlech, 25 feet x 6 feet, of three chambers, the central marked by four pillars, the eastern pair being 5 feet high; they supported a lintel now fallen.

CAHERANEDEN (100 feet), a fort fairly built of large blocks, often 5 feet long, stands eastward on a low ridge, whence it is named. The wall is 8 feet thick, with very small filling; the face towards the south is removed, and only three courses remain along the ridge. An oblong slab-hut stands to the east; it is 12 feet × 6 feet, with a little annexe 3 feet square. A green road,[1] formed by the removal of the top strata of the crag, leads from the caher southward to a fallen cromlech; two of its slabs are 9 feet 6 inches ×6 feet.

Caheraneden - Fort and Slab Hut.[2]

We then ascend a slightly rising ground to the east; on the summit, near a large strangely-shaped boulder, are a late and badly built oval enclosure (140 feet north and south) a small ring wall surrounding a sort of cairn, and lower down the slope a caher (111 feet). A large cromlech stands inside,

---

[1] Cormac's Glossary gives Ramhat 'an open space or street which is in front of the fort of Kings'; every neighbour was bound to clean it.
[2] The forts in the background are - 1. The oblong garth; 2. Cahernaspekee;
3. Cahercuttine; and 4. (extreme right), Caher, with side enclosure.

partly embedded in its wall. Probably the followers of some chief laid him (like Joab) 'in his own house in the wilderness.'[1]

Eastward in the valley a perfect cromlech stands in a levelled cairn. Turning from it, towards Ballyganner hill and castle, we pass a curious rock basin, forming a well, and reach the small and broken castle embedded in the ring of a caher (115 feet); the wall of the latter is 12 feet thick, and in it stands a late-looking house-site, 41 feet × 24 feet, and two other enclosures. Two cahers on the hill top, near the seventh cromlech (one slab of which is 18 feet 6 inches × 6 feet), and a large caher on the southern slope, are greatly broken and nearly levelled; nor are three or four others between it and Lemeneagh, nor Cahermore and Caheraclarig, in Sheshy, near Caherscrebeen, in much better condition. The unusual number of early remains in this district, and the pains taken by the present staff of the Ordnance Survey to mark the same accurately on the large scale maps, lead me to give a fuller account and list than I should otherwise have thought of doing.

CAHERMACNAUGHTEN (O.S. 9), 127 feet × 130 feet. Two miles north from Noughaval stands this fine caher, noteworthy as being the place where our great scholar, Duald Mac Firbis, studied the Brehon law under Donald O'Davoren, who was himself (in the earlier years of Elizabeth's reign) author of a glossary of Irish terms.[2] We have also the rare but welcome aid of a full description of the place when it formed the centre of the O'Davoren's 'town' in 1675. The sons of Gillananeave O'Davoren in that year made a deed of family arrangement which their father confirmed as his will.

'The following is the partition of the 'keannait,' or village of Cahermac-naughten, viz., the site of the large house of the caher within, and the site of the kitchen-house, which belongs to the house within the caher, and the site of the house of the churchyard on the west side of the caher and all the gardens, extending westward from the road of the garden of Teig roe mac Gillapheen (not including Teig roe's garden), and the house site between the front of the large house and the door of the caher, at the north-west (*sic*) side and the large house which is outside the door of the caher.' The 'green of the booley,' water supply, and several townlands are also distributed. We find a very similar arrangement recorded in the *Tripartite Life of St. Patrick*. A 'caher' or fortified monastery being surrounded by a vallum, and having a 'tech mor' or 'great house,' a church, an 'aregal,' a kitchen, a 'pranntech' or refectory, a guest-house, and a graveyard.

The caher consists of a nearly circular wall 10 feet high and thick, nearly perfect, and of massive blocks, many 4 feet 6 inches × 1 foot 6 inches, the

---

[1] 'A fort, in this again a colossal sepulchre.' - *Silva Gadelica*, ii, p. 131. Hely Dutton, in 1808, when describing Ballyganner, mentions 'the remains of a stone rath in which part of a covered passage is still visible.' - *Statistical Survey of Clare*, p. 137.

[2] O'Curry, *Manners and Customs*, iii., p. 322. O'Donovan sensibly asks (in the Ordnance Survey Letters, R.I.A., p. 187) 'who built Caher mac Naughten? Did the Firbolgs erect *all* the Cahers in the Burren? Never.' (See Ordnance Survey Letters, vol. i., for ensuing deed. - MSS., R.I.A.).

longest being laid as headers, bonding into the filling for 3 feet. The gate faces E.S.E., and is a late mediæval porch, two side walls with roof corbels; it has a batter of 1 in 8; this is not apparent in the dry stone wall. The foundations of the houses rise but little above the dark earth and rich grass of the interior. A large house (48 feet N.E. and S.W. ×15 feet 6 inches internally, the walls 3 feet thick) occupies the southern segment; another building with three rooms lies in the northern. There are traces of two other small huts inside and of some others outside the caher, but no 'churchyard' is visible. A well lies a few hundred feet to the S.W.

CAHERYHOOLAGH (Cathair Ui Dhualachta, O'Douloughty's fort, probably the 'caherwooly' of 1641) lies in a state of great dilapidation on the western edge of the townland of Cahermacnaughten.

KILFENORA (O.S. 9).

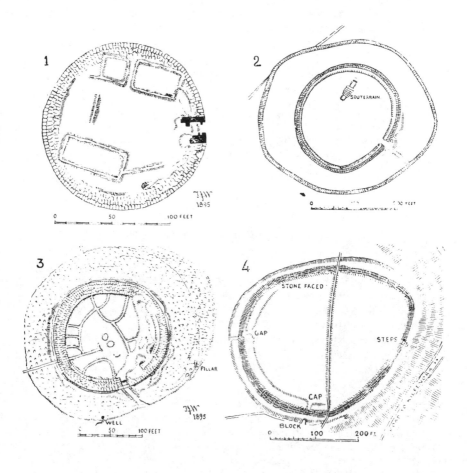

1. Cahermacnaughten. 2. Glenquin. 3. Ballykinvarga. 4. Doon Fort.

BALLYKINVARGA[1] ('of the head of the market'), 135 feet × 155 feet. This very fine fort, possibly the 'Cathair Fhionnabhrach,' reserved to the King of Cashel in the Book of Rights, appears in O'Brien's Rental,[2] about 1380, as '*baile cin mhargadh.*' It is first described by Eugene O'Curry, 1839, as 'a very large caher. . . around which were formerly a great number of stones forming a circle about it.' S.F. (? Ferguson) notices it thus:- 'Close to Kilfenora is one of those stone plashed cyclopean fortresses. . . Caherflaherty.

View of Ballykinvarga Caher, near Kilfenora.

Its dimensions are not comparable to those of the great Arran citadel, but the arrangement of the ramparts and the distribution of the stone caltrops in the space between the body of the fortress and the outer circumvallation are the same.'[3] Lord Dunraven's description is equally misleading, as he omits any account of its *chevaux de frise*, monoliths, and hut sites, and says its wall is double and its passage curved, which is not the case; he only calls it 'one (fort) near Kilfenora.' Mr. T. Foote also alludes to it in a letter to Du Noyer, 1862, 'a fort that has pointed stones planted upright all around it.'[4]

When perfect it must have been a beautiful specimen; now the vandal country lads, rabbit-hunting and tearing blocks out of its wall, must soon bring it to complete ruin. It is well built of large blocks, 3 feet to 5 feet long, and where most perfect to the east, is 15 feet high. The wall consists of three sections; the central 4 feet thick, the others 5 feet; it probably had another terrace, 4 feet 6 inches thick, as it is 19 feet 6 inches thick in other parts. The walls have several upright joints. The gate faces S.S.E., its lintel, 7 feet 9 inches × 1 foot 4 inches × 3 feet, resting on side walls and corner

---

[1] The old name seems to have been 'Caher Loglin' in east Ballykenuarga, Book of Distribution, p. 189. Another fort in the western division (now apparently incorporated with Caherminane) was Caheryline, perhaps that described [*infra* p. 32].

[2] *Trans. R.I.A.*, xv. (1828), p. 37.

[3] *Dublin University Magazine*, Jan. 1853, vol. xli., p. 505, 'Caherflaherty' is, I suppose, the name 'Caherlahertagh'; besides this mistake we have 'the outer circumvallation' which never existed. The writer seems not to have seen the 6-inch Survey.

[4] Ord. Survey Letters, Clare, vol. i., p. 287. Dunraven's 'Notes,' vol. i., p. 18. Du Noyer's 'Sketches,' R.S.A.I., vol. vii.

posts;[1] its outer face was blocked; and, as I saw it, the space was occupied by
a colony of hedgehogs. A walled and sunken passage led eastward through
the *chevaux de frise*, probably, as in the Greek and Esthonian forts,[2] to
compel assailants to advance with their shield arm away from the wall. The
inner enclosures extend in a fairly regular band round the western edge,
where the wall is 7 feet high.

Gateway, Ballykinvarga Caher.

They recall the still more even compartments in Castle Chûn.[3] The
chevaux de frise[4] is in two sections: the inner, about 46 feet wide, thickly set
with pillars about 3 feet high, with smaller spikes between, and still nearly

[1] The (alleged) poem by Flan Mainistrech given in the Book of Fenagh, p. 121,
mentions 'the pillar stone in the principal door of the cathair,' *circa* 1050. Caher
gates were sufficiently familiar to furnish illustrations, even in legendary literature,
e.g., 'The Hunt of Sliab Truim,' p. 115, for a '*piast* (monster) with ears as large as the
gate of a *caher.*'

[2] At Tiryns, but not at Mycenæ. Also at Möhne in the Baltic.

[3] Compare plans, p. 147 [5], Nos. 7, 8, *Journal*, 1896, and 1893, p. 288. Possibly
these were both enclosures for wooden huts and to pen cattle. Iuchna the Firbolg
kept herds of cows in his *liss* (*Silva Gadelica*, ii., p. 131), and each of the stone forts,
stormed and burned near Ventry, harboured 150 men, besides women, children,
horses, and dogs. (*Cath Fintraga*, edited by Dr. Kuno Meyer, p. 5.)

[4] *Chevaux de frise* also occur at Dun Aenghus and Dubh Caher, Aran (Dunraven's
'Notes,' I. pp. 6, 10. Our *Journal*, 1895, pp. 257, 258, and 266); Dunamoe, Mayo
(*Journal*, 1889, p. 182); Pen Caer Helen, Caernarvon (*Archæologia Cambrensis*, series
iv., vol. 12, p. 345, and vol. 14, p. 192, with fine views), 'large stones, with sharp
slate splinters, set between' (*Archæolog. Journal*, xxv., p. 228. The writer considers
this fort earlier than an adjoining Roman camp). Cademuir and Dreva, Peebleshire
(*Proc. Soc. Ant., Scot.*, 1866, pp. 21, 24). The 'monumental theory,' in *Pagan Ireland*,
p. 186, is very improbable. *Archæologia Cambrensis*, 1870, p. 286, describes one at
Castel coz, Finistère, France, a pre-Roman fort on a headland.

impassible, save to the south. A second band extends for 50 feet more, but is less thickly set with stones; it has a border mound set with large blocks,[1]

Pillar-stone and *chevaux-de-frise*, Ballykinvarga.

one nearly 7 feet x 2 feet 7 inches x 1 foot.[2] A large hoard of silver coins 'of Edward II.' were found at the foot of a pillar and, much more precious to the occupants, a streamlet wells out on the southern side.[3] Several groups of blocks remain in the adjoining field. I am not satisfied that any one was a cromlech. A small rude fort, overthrown for 95 feet, crowns the ridge 235 feet to the N.E. Two curved walls cross its garth, and a two-doored cloghaun stood in the northern loop. From its roughness and choice site it may be the older fort of the two. There must have been some danger apprehended from this direction as an addition seems to have been made to the *chevaux de frise* at the same side.

Five more cahers stand within 2000 feet east of the great fort. Kilcameen is quite levelled, and is now a burial place for children. It stands on a knoll, and has a few rude pillars and cairns, and two ancient graves marked out by a kerb of great slabs, like the sides of a cromlech; the western is 6 feet long, the eastern 9 feet, and traces of a third adjoin. Tobercameen well lies in the depression southward, and is dry in summer. Beyond, on a grassy knoll, a few scattered stones mark another small fort. It had a sharp angle to the

---

[1] This feature occurs in a prehistoric fort, or 'bauerberge,' in the Island of Möhne, in the Gulf of Riga, where also a passage runs slantwise to the gate.

[2] In old Irish works note 'a pillar-stone on the green before a rath' (Táin Bo Cuailgne). Fergus fights a battle in this very district of Burren from 'cloch comuir to the stone of meeting by the three mounds of walled fortresses' (Poem of Seanchan, *circa* A.D 647, in Book of Lecan). Pillar-stones were erected to celebrate victories, and cairns heaped to commemorate slaughters (Leabhar na h-Uidhri, p. 86), &c.

[3] This is not unusual, *e.g.* Inismurray (our *Journal*, 1885, p. 98), Hillsborough, Devon (*Gentleman's Magazine*, 1865, Part II., pp. 715, 716), and several Cornish forts (Royal Inst. Cornwall, 1863, p. 60). We also find it in old writers as Adamnan, where Columba prophesies the well *near* a fort will be defiled with blood; and 'Colloquy of the Ancients' for a *hidden* well on the *south* side of a fort (*Silva Gadelica*, p. 195. also pp. 103, 131). Capt. O'Callaghan Westropp (*Member*) suggests that the well was excluded to preserve it from pollution.

S.E., and 12 hollows pit its eastern slope.[1] A circular fort, also in Caher-minane (100 feet), has a well-built wall, with two faces, 8 feet high and 9 feet thick. They are I think, hammer dressed[2] in places to take angles of other stones. The gate faced S.E., and had corner posts and lintels 7 feet long; near it, to the south, two steps remain in the inner face of the wall.

CAHERLAHERTAGH (130 feet), on a low hillock, near the road. About 5 feet of the finely built wall rises over the heaps of fallen blocks, its top level with the garth, which was divided into three by a T-shaped wall; an oval cloghaun stood in the north section. There is no trace of a gateway.[3] Beyond the road is a cromlech, the top slab now removed.

BALLYSHANNY (137 feet × 132 feet), much defaced, and standing on a rocky knoll to the west. The wall is 7 feet thick. There are some traces of a souterrain inside, and of steps, probably leading up to a gate, on the S.E.

CAHEREMON, near Kilfenora described by Petrie as 'a fine remain,' is now levelled with the field; it was of no great size.

DOON (296 ft. × 310 ft., or, with fosse, about 350 ft. each way, O.S. 16). A fine fort,[4] on a hill 450 feet above the sea; it is of pear-shaped plan, surrounded by a fosse cut in the shale, with a regular curve and batter to each side, 25 ft. to 20 ft. wide and 5ft. deep. A fence crosses the fort, and west of it the ramparts are better preserved, and in parts faced with stone, rising 20 feet above the fosse, and 12 and 15 feet over the field. They have three gaps: the middle one has a mound across the fosse; the southern faces a rectangular block of shale, probably for a plank. The only feature to the east is a flight of seven steps, cut in the rock; the entire circuit of the rampart is about 970 feet. From this bold outpost of the Old World we see Liscannor Cliffs and castle, and the boundless sea, with its fringe of dazzling foam; Kilfenora, one of the earliest villages of Clare, and Lisdoonvarna, one of the latest; the castles of Smithstown and Lemeneagh, recorded by the Four Masters; and the inland barriers of Callan and Glasgeivnagh, with Elva, the legendary battlefield of the Firbolg with the great King Cormac mac Airt, closing the view on the north.

---

[1] Possibly hut sites, as at Caherconree, Kerry (*Ulster Journal*, viii., p. 118); Eildon Hill (*Proc. Soc. Ant., Scot.*, 1895, p. 128, and 'Blackhill,' p. 143) and early British villages (*Brit. Archæol. Assoc.*, 1846. p. 155; Prehistoric 'Annals of Scotland,' and *Soc. Ant., Normandy*, 1835, p. 317). They also occur in Pen-y-ddinas above Llandudno and Penselwood on the borders of Dorset, Somerset, and Wiltshire, where many hundreds occur round a circular fort.

[2] I believe that traces of the hammer occur at Cahermore-Roughan, Ballykinvarga, and Caherminane, all border forts of the Burren.

[3] This is not uncommon in the forts of Clare, and even occurs in the ancient stone fort on a peninsula near Sebenico, in Dalmatia (*Land of the Bora*, p. 56).

[4] Mac Liag's poem, as translated by Ossianic Society (vol. v., p. 287), says: 'They placed Daelach at Dael. Aenach constructed a *dun* in his neighbourhood.' Two tributaries of the Daelach rise at the foot of this ridge, so perhaps this fort is the 'Tech nEnnach,' see *supra*, our *Journal*, 1896, p. 143 [2].

This Paper having far outgrown my original design, I must for the present omit the forts of more northern Burren, and conclude it by a brief statement of the facts which more especially forced themselves on me during my researches. (1) The key to the origin of our Irish forts lies as much in their congeners over the rest of Europe as in our own records. (2) The Firbolg legend, hitherto so unreservedly adopted to account for their origin, is (if not entirely mythical) only of value for two or three forts. It does not even touch on the cahers of Kerry, Cork, Mayo, and Ulster, still less on the British and Continental examples. (3) The evidence (so far as it goes) shows that such structures were built and rebuilt from a period long before the introduction of Christianity to (probably) the 14th century. (4) Very few of our forts were defensive in a military sense. (5) Their arrangement on lines and in groups also occurs all across Europe. (6) The question of masonry depends on geological, not racial conditions. (7) The features are stereotyped by the materials. (8) There seem to be traces of the work of the hammer but not of the chisel. (9) Wood was probably used for steps and lintels in a few forts.[1] (10) Water supply was deliberately excluded from the fort for sanitary reasons. (11) This and most other features existing in our forts appear in the body of Irish literature as commonplace phenomena of the buildings of the earlier middle ages.

It is greatly to be hoped that some of these cahers[2] may soon be vested as National monuments, not for rebuilding but for their preservation; this is of urgent need, for indescribable destruction is carried out every year. It is a reproach to us, as a nation, that we treat these priceless ruins as mere valueless jetsam of the sea of time. We make the forts our quarries and cattle-pens, the cromlechs our hovels and pig-styes, defacing and destroying for our sordid gains or mischievous pastimes. Would that we could utilise our pride in the past, whose glories we exaggerate, to the more practical purpose of preserving its relics, which we are helping, by direct injury or inexcusable apathy, to sweep with unsparing hands into the limbo of forgetfulness.[3]

---

[1] Cahermackirilla and Cahergrillaun, near Carran, have ancient gates too wide for stone lintels: and Mullach, in Dabrein, has recesses in its wall and terrrace only suitable for short ladders. See also *Journal*, 1896, pp. 153 [12] and 157 [15].

[2] Ballykinvarga, Ballyallaban, Caherahoagh, Cahercommane, Cahercuttine, Cahermacnaughten, Cahershaughnessy, Cashlaungar, Glenquin, Moghane, and Langough; all of the greatest interest.

[3] I here thank Dr. George MacNamara (*Local Secretary*), my sister, Mrs. O'Callaghan (*Member*) and the Rev. J. B. Greer, who never grudged giving their time, researches, or personal trouble to enable me to work up the Clare forts; Dr. W. Frazer (*Vice President*), Mr. Standish Hayes O'Grady and Mr. W. Borlase, of London, who gave me many valuable suggestions and references, and Captains Pery and Sloggett of the Ordnance Survey, who gave me tracings of the plans of the forts of Doon, Ballyganner, and Cahercuttine.

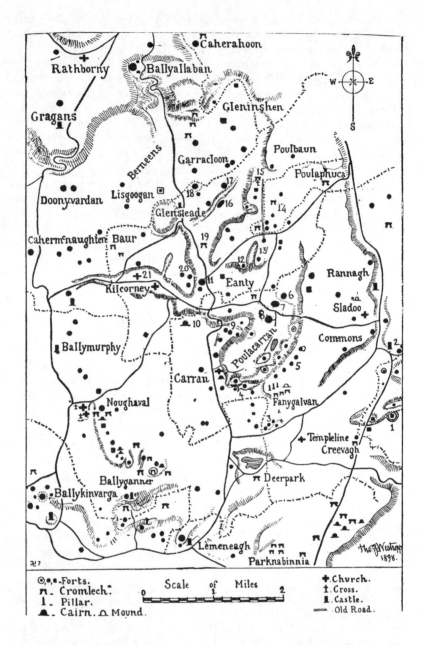

DIAGRAM OF ANCIENT STRUCTURES NEAR CARRAN AND KILCORNEY.

(Dotted lines represent Parish Boundaries, and thick lines represent modern Roads.)

1. Cahercommane.   2. Castletown.   3. Fanygalvan Forts.   4. Carran Ridge.   5. Cahermackirilla Ridge.   6. Moheramoylan.   7. Cahergrillaun.   8. Cahermackirilla   9. Poulcaragharush.   10. Poulawack Cairn.   11. Caherconnell.   12. Caherlisaniska.   13. Caherlisananima.   14. Cragballyconoal.   15. Ballymihil.   16. Cahercashlaun.   17.
Cahernamweela.   18. Caheranadurrish.   19. Poulnabrone.   20. Poulanine.   21. Kilcorney.

2

Ancient Burren - Carran
Kilcorney - Rathborney
Eastern Valleys

Burren Barony, a great upland of limestone capped in some places by shale, forms the north-western corner of Clare. On three sides it falls into those steeply terraced ridges which show so far across the bay and plains of Galway; on the south it sinks into the low green hills and heathy bog-land of Brentir and Corcomroe.

It lacks the towering height and noble outlines of the Kerry and Connaught mountains, but its weird grey ridges and valleys are very impressive in their suggestiveness of age-long loneliness and long vanished tribes. Some of its glens are even beautiful - hemmed in by cliffs, whose walls are varied by strange domes and buttresses, by clefts and caves. Its rocks are wreathed with ivy, ferns, and exquisite flowers, brightened by the gauzy sheets of little runnels and waterfalls: at their feet lie here and there a blue pool or deep thicket. We often get glimpses of the lowlands and the Atlantic from their summits. Wonderfully beautiful, too, are the lights and cloud shadows and the effects of the sunsets and slowly gathering gloom on the long ridges and valleys.

Over all these solitary places of old Thomond abound an amazing number of forts and cromlechs.[1] Some 400 cahers appear on the maps, though many are omitted or marked as 'sheepfolds'. Dozens are levelled to the ground, dozens are rebuilt and hopelessly modernized. Apart from human violence, natural causes combine to overthrow them: the filling bulges out the facing till it bursts the wall and pours out like meal from a torn sack; the ash and hazel tear the walls asunder, and waving in the breeze throw down the masonry; nevertheless numerous examples remain. Whence came the

---

[1] The terms 'fort' and 'cromlech' are used for convenience, not as implying the exclusively military use of the one class of remains, or the superiority of the other terms, to 'dolmen,' &c. In the same way 'caher,' and other anglicised forms, are used. The spelling of the names is that of the Ordnance Survey maps, except when (as at 'Tullycommon') the ancient name and modern pronunciation are both violated by following Petty's 'Name Lists.'

population that built and needed so many cahers? Even if their construction spread over many centuries, and if we consider the slighter ones to be mere cattle pens, enough remain to form an enigma. Burren is never named as very populous, and one may now walk for several miles across the crags and meet at most some solitary herdsman, but we sometimes find a caher in every few fields, or several very massive ones lying together.[1] Why did not fewer forts suffice? Were the older ones deserted for some superstitious reason, and, if so, did the 'tabu' extend even to their material? If not, did each townland possess several important men? So many 'strongholds' were scarcely needed, for, as we know that several[2] were the centres of villages, so they would evidently be available to the surrounding country as places of refuge in cases of sudden alarm. Indeed we seem to have a case of this in *The battle of Ventry*, where three duns destroyed by the King of Spain were crowded with people, horses, and dogs.[3] The time has not come for elaborate theories, still less for positive statements; we must for many years collect and arrange facts, a less brilliant but more useful task than theorizing on insufficient data. The present Paper is therefore only a survey (and not even a very complete one) of a district hitherto undescribed.

ANCIENT BURREN

A noteworthy fact is apparent in all our records: the Burren is practically unaltered from Pre-Christian times, the same families predominate, and we find the same rich pasturages and lonely crags. All this is much in favour of the survival of ancient customs and modes of building.

The history and early legends are of little consequence. The name Burren ('the great rock') is apparently of obvious origin, but the Dind Senchas finds the word 'not difficult' to derive from the name of an ancient hero. 'Boirenn, son of Bolcan, son of Ban, out of Spain, he came to Boirenn Corcomruad.'[4]

Then we hear of the settlement of the sons of Huamore - Bera at Finnvara, Irgus at Black Head, Daelach in Dael - and of invasions by the High-kings Fiacha and Cormac Mac Airt, but beyond the verge of written history the families which claimed descent from Rory, son of Maeve by the great Fergus mac Roigh, and which were named in later days the O'Conors and O'Loughlins, held these hills. The Dalcassians obtained at the most a cattle tribute, and there was probably a servile race of Firbolgic descent; the rest is vague and unreliable, or mere names of chiefs and dates of battles.

The later O'Briens invaded Burren in 1267 and 1317. John, son of Rory Mac Grath, the historian of these wars, gives us a picture true to nature after six centuries. 'The white-stoned hills,' 'the caher begirt tracks,' 'the

---

[1] The 1891 census gives, in the portion of Carran here explored, only 13 inhabited houses; in Kilcorney 20; portion of Rathborney 5. Total 38; against this we have noted over 100 forts. After the war (1641-52), the population of Burren is given as 823.

[2] *E.g.* Cahermacnaughten and Cahergrillane.

[3] The legendary nature of the poem does not alter the value of this fact, which possibly was based on the poet's own experience.

[4] *Revue Celtique*, xvi. (1895), p. 135.

close border paths and rugged margins of Dubhglen,' 'the long glen and widespread crags,' 'Burren's hilly grey expanse of jagged points and slippery grey steeps, nevertheless flowing with milk and yielding luscious grass,' and 'the dorsal ridge of the rough plain that showed its bleached face, varied with dark irregular seams,' are all named, and we recognize the (so to say) photographic accuracy of this ancient picture.

War, revenge, and the sea form the background of most of these records. When we recall the story of Liamuin 'fair robe' and her sisters with their ill-starred lovers, or the weird tale of Maelduin, son of Ailill, a native of these hills, going out into the 'great endless deep,'[1] we feel how much the life in strongholds and the perpetual presence of the mystery of the unexplored ocean affected the men of the Corcomroes. Indeed we probably owe a great chapter in the world's development to the attempts of our western boatmen to 'pluck out the heart of the mystery' of the unknown sea; for the Sagas of Brendan, Bran, and Maelduin went out into the world, and fostered a belief which no theological prejudice could destroy, that glorious islands lay beyond the untracked sea. These legends from Clare and Kerry never rested till they sent Columbus and his successors across the outer ocean to find islands and wonders such as the mind of monk or bard had never conceived.[2]

It is therefore far from improbable that this feeling and the kindred love of nature so deeply rooted in the Irish, led to the selection of sites, sacrificing commanding neighbouring positions for those with a distant glimpse of the sea or of some notable mountain.[3]

Whether the Clan Rory or the Eoghanachts or some earlier race built the forts of Burren is now impossible to decide. The finds are most equivocal, flint weapons, bronze ornaments, moulds for a bronze spear, iron coins of the Plantagenets and Tudors. The absence of kitchen middens and entire clochauns deprive us of other possible sources of knowledge.

Querns, so far as can be learned, have not been found in these forts; bullauns occur, and some consider these an older form of 'mill,' but, as these basins appear on upright or steeply slanting stones, we cannot be too sure of their use. In most cases the cahers rest on nearly bare crag, and in the case of the alleged finds of deer bones, nothing is proved. Venison must have been a staple food from the earliest times, and the Burren abounded in deer from the time when the 'Colloquy of the Ancients'[4] told how, in the bitter winter, 'the stag of Slieve Carn lays not his side to the ground, and no less than he - the stag of frigid Echtge's summit - catches the chorus of the wolves.' It is evident that these forts have been built and patched and rebuilt at very various dates.[5] The nature of materials, not the race or age of

---

[1] *Revue Celtique* (1894), p. 321, and (1888) p. 451. 'Voyage of Bran,' vol. i., p. 14. 'Thrice Fifty Islands.' The islands of Brazil and St. Brendan figure on most early maps.

[2] Columbus had at least one Irish sailor in his crew, a Galway man.

[3] As at Cragballyconoal, to command the one striking view of [Turlough Cairn].

[4] *Silva Gadelica*, vol. ii., p. 192.

[5] See our *Journal*, 1896, p. 148 [7]. We find records of forts built and repaired in later times, *e.g.* Grianan Aileach, 674, 973, and 1101. Dun Onlaig 'construitur,' 714. Forts built or repaired by Brian Boru, *c.* 1000. Grianan Lachtna, *c.* 840. Caher built by Conor na Cathrach O'Brien, *c.* 1120. Caisteal mac Tuathal, in Scotland, built by

the builders, determined the style, while the names, though in many cases at least mediæval, give us no reliable aid to the actual builders or earliest owners of these noteworthy structures.[1]

THE DISTRICT OF CARRAN AND KILCORNEY

In our examination of the Clare cahers,[2] we passed from the huge forts round Quin to the district round Inchiquin Lake, and then along the southern border of Burren. We now turn to the largest (if not the most interesting) group extending from Ballyganner and Tullycommane northward. We may define it as lying in the parishes of Carran and Kilcorney, west of the road from Castletown to Turlough, with some remains in the adjoining townlands on the northern and southern borders.

The district contains several shallow valleys in which lie the most massive and interesting of the forts, those upon the ridges being usually small, with slight and coarse walls, now nearly levelled. The cromlechs (with two exceptions) lie on the plateaux, and have not yet been described. In Mr. Borlase's valuable work a curious misapprehension appears with regard to this district. He writes, 'Blocks of the size and symmetry of those used by the dolmen builders would nowadays be far to seek.' On the contrary, blocks as regular, and of the size usually found in the cromlechs, occur over many acres of crag. Some of those employed in the existing structures are dressed to a straight edge. In Parknabinnia, in the field adjoining that in which four cromlechs stand, we find what was very probably a 'cromlech factory.' Two slabs have been raised from the rock bed, propped at one edge on rounded blocks, but otherwise *in situ*. They are practically rectangular, owing to the natural cleavage of the slabs, and measure 12 and 13 ft. long by 8½ ft. broad. Similar raised slabs occur at Ballykinvarga, Noughaval, and Ballymihil, all near cahers and cromlechs.

PARKNABINNIA (O.S. 17., No. 2, 25-inch map). - These curious remains, lying on the very border of Carran, have not hitherto been described, and are not marked on the maps of 1839. The four northern cromlechs lie in a field sloping northward. A long and very narrow old bohereen leads from

---

Tuathal, a chief, who died 865. Stone fort of Kincora, built *c.* 1000, demolished and rebuilt in 1062 and 1098. While Cahermore-Ballyallaban, Caherahoagh, and Cahermacnaughten, in county Clare, Cahercugeola, near Kilmacduach, &c. have late gateways; and Ballyganner and Cahercloggaun have mediæval castles.

[1] To give a few examples earlier than 1400:- Cathyrnachyne (Caherkine). 1287. *Inquisition*. Cahercrallaha (near Crughwill). 1317. Wars of Turlough. Cathair in daire (Caherderry), Cathair medain (Cahermaan), Cathair polla (Lismoran), Cathair mec ui ruil (Cahermackirilla), Cathair an Lapain (Caherlappane, *alias* Cahermackerrila in Killeany Parish), Cathair seircin (Cahersherkin), Cathair mec oilille sella (unknown), Cathair da con (Cahercon), 'Caitir' Urthaile (Caherhurley), *Trans. R.I.A.*, vol. XV., pp. 37, 38, all in rentals of 1380. Cahercottine, 1397, Tulla *Inquisition*. In Clare we nowhere find the tendency, so apparent in county Kerry, to call the forts after modern owners; even such names as Cahermurphy and Cahershaughnessy and these are at least pre-Elizabethan.

[2] *Journal*, 1893, pp. 281, 432; 1896, pp. 142 [1], 363 [17]; and 1897, p. 116 [23].

the direction of Roughan fort through Caherfadda, while a huge boulder, some 16 feet high, marks their position from a distance. The N.E. cromlech must have been a very fine example. The south side is 5 ft. 9 in. (at the west) to 2 ft. 3 in. high, 15 ft. 10 in. long, and 9 in. thick; a long 'plank' of the top slab leans against it, and the fallen north side has strangely regular natural channels across it. West from it is a small wrecked cist 6 ft. square; due south from it is a fine cromlech 17 ft. 10 in. long, tapering eastward from 6 ft. 4 in. to 5 ft. 6 in., with a curious angular gap in the west slab, as at Tobergrania, near Feakle. Here for many nights sheltered a well-known escaped prisoner, whose subsequent surrender occasioned no little interest at a recent assize. South-west from it is a small cist 12 ft. by 8 ft. nearly embedded in a mound, and surrounded by seven slabs 3 ft. high. Its west block has another example of a straight natural fluting set on end. Lastly on the summit of Roughan Hill, the older Reabacain, still in Parknabinnia, near a large low cairn, is a fine cist 13 by 7 ft., with parallel annexes to the sides and end embedded in a mound. The sixth 'labba,' recently disentombed from a cairn, is fully described in *Dolmens of Ireland*, vol. i., p. 77. 'Parknabinnia' is said to have been the 'cattle park' of Lemeneagh, as its neighbouring townland was the 'Deer park.'[1]

Creevagh Cromlech, from the North-west.

CREEVAGH (O.S. 10., No. 9). - Two nearly levelled ring walls lie near the Castletown road, between Glencurraun and the prettily wooded slopes and abrupt cliffs of the pass of Clooncoose, leading down to Kilnaboy. The southern ring contains a perfect and noteworthy cromlech, a chamber 14 ft. long tapering eastward from 4 ft. 5 in. to 3 ft. 10 in. It has a smaller cist at the east end, small triangular ones to each side and an irregular enclosure, about 7 feet across, fenced with pillar slabs 5 to 7 ft. high to the west. We have already described the cahers of Mohernacartan, and Cahersavaun on the borders of Carran Parish, while the cromlechs of Cappaghkennedy and Deerpark, will be found as fully noticed in *Dolmens of Ireland*,[2] so we may pass over the rest of south-western Carran by merely recording that it possesses very few cahers, and those few nearly levelled, the only mediæval ruin being the featureless roughly-built church of Templeline.

---

[1] These are probably the Rebechan cromlechs described in the Ordnance Survey Letters, MSS. R.I.A., 14. B. 23, p. 66. Despite discrepancies in measurements, the description seems to fit, and one is certainly the sixth Parknabinnia cromlech. The older name of Deerpark was 'Poulquillica.'

[2] *Jour. R.S.A.I.*, 1896, pp. 364, 365 [17,18]. *Dolmens*, pp. 70, 72.

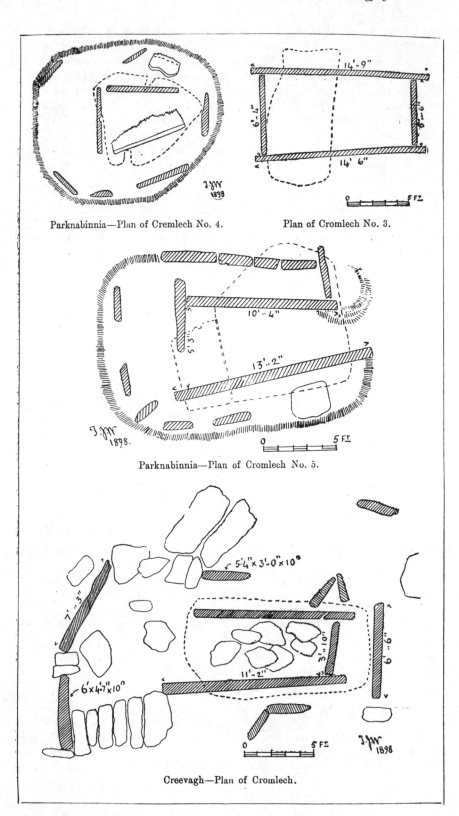

Parknabinnia—Plan of Cremlech No. 4.   Plan of Cromlech No. 3.

Parknabinnia—Plan of Cromlech No. 5.

Creevagh—Plan of Cromlech.

SOUTH RIDGE OF CARRAN[1] (O.S. 9., No. 12). - The country being greatly broken, the groups of ruins must be treated as they lie, rather than by townlands. Passing along the grassy though craggy ridges, famous 'winterages' for cattle, along the edge of Poulacarran valley, we find the following remains:- (1) A coarsely built, much dilapidated, irregular caher, close to the Carran road. It commands a grassy pass leading to the valley, and the well of Tobermacreagh; (2) A curious little cliff fort on a peak. It is just 40 feet across, all the eastern side gone, the wall clings to the west crags, one break being bridged with long slabs, and looking like a gateway as seen from the road; (3) A coarse thin ring-wall in a wilderness of low hazels, it is about 60 feet in diameter; (4) Another caher or ring-wall even more dilapidated than the last. These two are in Cahermackirilla townland, on the southern edge of which stand three gallauns; these lie in line N.N.E. (compass), the central one is over 7 feet high, the others about 4 feet.[2]

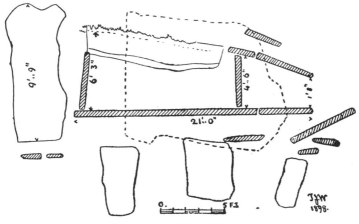

Fanygalvan – Plan of Cromlech

Eastward is a large though low green mound, and less than 80 feet away; three cromlechs lie in the townland of Fanygalvan - the *Fanadhgealbain* of the 1380 rental.[3] As shown in the 1839 map, there are three cists lying in

---

[1] The report on Noughaval and 'Carrune,' in Mason's 'Parochial Survey,' vol. iii., pp. 282-287 (1819), is disappointing. It states that there are three 'of what are called Danish forts' in Noughaval, and five in Carrune. 'There are no traditions with respect to any of these.' Under the head of 'Natural curiosities,' &c., a list of the clergy is given. The translations of the townland names are curious, *e.g.* Fannygallavan, Ring of promise; Clouncouse, perhaps cause of deceit; Glencullenkilla (Glencolumbcill), Glen of Hollywood; Cahergrillane, Dutch chair; and Mohermilan (Mohermoylan), Louse Park. The Ordnance Survey Letters dismiss these interesting ruins as 'the broken cahers and ruined church in Poulacarran.'

[2] They probably formed a mearing: see Cormac's Glossary, under 'Gall,' 'Boundaries of Pillar-Stones,' and the Book of Leinster, f. 78: – 'There went westward from the lake a great mearing. . . and he (Cuchullin) fared to a pillar-stone, and put his waist-belt round it, that he might die standing.'

[3] *Trans. R.I.A.*, vol. xv., p. 38. Similar groups of forts, cists, cairns, and mounds also occur at Tullycommane and Ballyganner, in this district; also in Bosnia, and in

line on the grassy hill which falls abruptly at their west end. Now there remain of the western only two small blocks 6 feet long. The central cist faces E.N.E., the fallen sides covered by the top stone, and about 10 ft. long. The eastern is a noble cromlech with two chambers. It is 23 ft. long, and from 6 ft. 3 in. to 2 ft. 8 in. wide; the north side has fallen. It is a conspicuous object, and its bleached stones shine like a red light at sunset, when seen from the road.

Down the slope stands a fantastic rock, somewhat resembling a human figure, and called Farbrega;[1] while, half a mile from the cromlech, along the road between Castletown and Carran, lie three very defaced stone forts. They are, respectively, in Sheshy, Moheraroon, and Fanygalvan, close together along the edge of a low depression, in which on an abrupt knoll are apparent the foundations and scattered stones of a fourth small caher.

CAHERMACKIRILLA RIDGE (O.S. 10., No. 5). - Starting from the cromlech of Fanygalvan, along the ridge, we find ourselves among many evidences of a once teeming population. Along this bluff, some 550 feet above the sea, lie three more cahers, which we may generally state to be from 70 to 100 feet in diameter and of fairly good masonry, though nearly demolished. Between the second and third, which are only about 350 ft. apart, are some singular slab huts of late date and a souterrain,[2] with built sides and four roof-slabs. The highest caher is of thin slabs, and contains the ruins of several late cabins and some lofty 'look-out' piers for herdsmen. It commands a view of the district from Tullycommane to Kilfenora and Moher, with a pretty glimpse of the sea and a bird's-eye view over Poulacarran. The last of these cahers, on the edge of Commons townland, is a circular ring, about 50 feet across. It has a large and curious straight walled enclosure about 150 feet

---

Scotland. Sir J. Simpson (*Archaic Sculpturings*, 1867, p. 47) sums up: 'The strong-holds were on elevated spots, the huts were lower down in shelter; along with these, circles, monoliths, barrows, and cairns occur. The cairns of the ancient dead interspersed among the hut-dwellings of the ancient living.'

[1] Farbrega rocks are common in Clare, especially on the hills near Broadford. A line of pillars at Carrahan, north of Quin, is locally said to represent the petrified robbers, who were thus punished for robbing the blessed bull of St. Mochulla as he carried provisions to that saint, who was building Tulla Church.

The notion of these 'false men' is old in Irish literature: see 'Battle of Moylena,' p. 31, for men petrified by fairies. In the Book of Feenagh, St. Caillin turns into pillars the Druids who 'did *corrguinecht*' against him (p. 123). See also Dr. Joyce's *Irish Names of Places*, 2nd Series, pp. 411, 412; and *Revue Celtique*, vol. i., p. 196: 'Fionn's Enchantment.'

[2] The typical souterrain in N.W. Clare is a passage 3 or 4 feet wide, and 4 or 5 feet high, straight, curved, or S-shaped in plan, with dry stone walls, or utilizing a rock cleft; the roof of stone slabs, level with the field. Domed chambers are practically absent, though a not uncommon feature in the S.W. district.

We may note that these structures hold a place in Irish literature. Two instances will suffice. 1. Cormac's Glossary (ed. Whitley Stokes), p. xxxix: 'Caer flies to the flagstone behind the fort, under which he is found by Nede's dogs.' 2. The demon-chariot of Chuchullain (our *Journal*, vol. i., 4th Series, p. 385): 'A pit in the dun belonging to the king,' which last was 'a seven-walled caher.'

out from the caher; the walls 8 and 10 feet high to the N.E. and S.E., in the intervening space is a small closed souterrain.

THE PLATEAU OF COMMONS &c. (O.S. 9., No. 8). The commonage is devoid of antiquities, save for a small circular fort on a cliff above the O'Loughlin's house, near Mougouhy, with a fine view of Cahercommane and Castletown Lough, but nearly levelled.

In Sladoo, *A Handbook to Lisdoonvarna* states that two uninjured cahers stand near the curious late church.[1] These, however, are not marked on the 1839 map; neither could Dr. George MacNamara and I find any trace or tradition of their existence. The only early remain seems to be a low mound of earth and stones, 36 feet across, its centre deeply excavated.

RANNAGH (O.S. 9., No. 1). - West of Sladoo and on the edge of a cliff, nearly as straight and regularly coursed as an ashlar wall, stands a rectangular caher; its northern wall is 7 feet high, 11 feet wide; the gateway faces the south, and is 4 feet 4 inches wide; it had stone gate posts on the inner face of a passage, 5 feet long and 5 feet 4 inches wide; the outer piers were built of large blocks, and 6 feet deep; the outer lintel was 7 feet 3 inches long. A steep old road leads from near it down to Poulacarran.

POULCARAGHARUSH (O.S. 9., No. 8). - This townland projects in a bold spur into the valley to the north of Carran Church, and east of the large and conspicuous cairn on Poulawack. Crossing a grass-grown old road, we find the following ancient enclosures:- (1) A finely-built but dilapidated ring wall, not far from the church. (2) A large irregular garth with straight reaches of wall, poorly built and levelled within a foot or two of the ground. (3 and 4) Two small forts which, by a strange effect of their position, look like a huge and lofty caher when seen against the sky. They lie north-east of the curious cup-like hollow of Poulcaragharush. The more northern is in parts nearly levelled, the eastern is on a knoll, and is in fair preservation. It is about 70 feet from the other fort, and nearly the same size, being 69 ft. over all. The gateway faces east and is in good preservation on the outer face, being filled up with stones. The jambs do not incline, the southern has a short corner post, the doorway faces the east, and is exactly 4 feet square; the lintel 6 feet 3 inches by 1 foot 9 inches by 1 foot 1 inch; the wall is 7 feet high to the west, and is 8 feet thick, built of rather good masonry, of most archaic-looking weather-beaten and channelled blocks. (5) A strangely small fort,

Gateway, Poulcaragharush Caher

---

[1] The description of the chapel, though elaborate, is most misleading, even to the statement of the existence of a stone roof; the account is probably given from hearsay.

scarcely 30 feet across, lies far down the slope, near the edge of Cahermackirilla; only portions of the wall are standing.

POULACARRAN (O.S. 9., No. 8). - This is a sort of 'bay,' running southward out of the large depression of Eanty. It falls abruptly almost, from the east gable of the plain old Church of Carran, near which we may note a cairn (not cist as in map), round which coffins are carried for burial in the graveyard. The valley is very divers- ified: it has tracts of cultivated ground and rich grass land, 'water splashes,' or shallow lakes, lesser glens overgrown with hazel and haw- thorn. In the spring it blossoms with such

Gateway, Poulacarran Caher

masses of primroses, anemones, ferns, violets, and deep blue gentians which make it a lovely garden. South of the swampy 'bleach pool,' named Toorleerahan (phonetically), is a ridge occupied by the caher of Poulacarran, a neat little oval fort 58 ft. north and south, and 70 ft. east and west. Like nearly all the forts of this district, it contains no remains of dwellings. Its gate faces N.E., and has jambs of single stones 4 feet deep and high. The lintel, as usual, has been thrown down; it measures 5 feet 8 inches by 3 feet by 1 foot 6 inches; the jambs have been pressed in from 3 feet below to 2 feet above; the wall is 4 feet thick, and 5 or 6 feet high, nor do many fallen stones lie round it. A second enclosure surrounds it, irregular in plan and faced with large and fantastic slabs. It is apparently of no great age, and contains a 'souterrain', formed by roofing a natural cleft, 10 feet by 4 feet 8 inches with lintels over 7 feet long. The south caher lies opposite the last, across the actual 'Poulacarran,' a boggy hollow and pretty little glen, overgrown with hawthorns. It is a little oval fort, of good masonry, and measures about 90 feet by 63 feet wide. It stands on the edge of a cliff and encloses green sward. A second enclosure, meeting the first at the cliff, and of inferior masonry, only some 4 feet high, lies on the crags. A 'pass' leads upward to the second fort on Cahermackerilla ridge.

The lower 'faugher' is irregularly continued along the east side of the valley; it has a row of small and nearly levelled cahers along its shelf. Two in Poulacarran, one of two concentric rings round a rock dome in Meggagh West, and one in Cahermackerrilla, while another, of only a few courses of masonry, lies on the slope under Poulcaragharush.

CAHERMACKERILLA (O.S. 9., No. 8). - This fort is so called by Petty, but is pronounced 'Carmackerrla,' and by the natives Cahermacrole. The name has been translated 'the fort of Irial's son,' possibly an O'Loughlin, with whom the name Irial was not uncommon. Strange to say, we find the name

'Macirilla,' the name of a Gaulish potter,[1] of one of the earlier centuries of our era. However, in the seventeenth century, some documents give the form Caher mac Connella (1624), and even in 1819 it was called Caher mac Connello.[2]

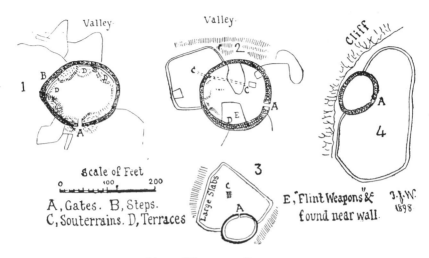

Plans of Forts near Carran

1. Cahergrillaun.   3. North Caher, Poulacarran.
2. Cahermackerilla   4. Cliff Fort, Poulacarran.

This caher is probably that called 'Cathair mec iguil' (or 'iruil') in the 1380 rental. It and the lands round it were held by the O'Loughlens, O'Briens, and O'Davorens, down to 1642, and by Brian O'Loughlin in 1659. It was occupied till about 1862 by a family named Kilmartin,[3] a member of whom lives just outside its ambit, and states that it has changed very little in his time. From having been so long inhabited the original internal arrangements are defaced.

It is a fine fort, a practically true circle of 140 feet external diameter; its masonry is large and very good, with a most regular straight batter, about 1 in 6, not the usual curve. The wall is 5 to 8 feet high and 15 feet thick, with small filling, the inner face being also battered and of smaller but good masonry. The gate faced E.S.E., its narrow passage running down a sloping rock. The large side stones remain parallel and 8 feet apart all their length, implying from their unusual width the use of wooden lintels.

The remains of modern houses and of cultivated garden plots occupy the garth; in these plots were often found 'sharp flints that you could strike fire out of,' and base metal coins 'about as big as sixpences, with a cross and a head,' but none were preserved.

---

[1] *Revue Celtique,* vol. xiii., 1892, p. 317.
[2] Inquisitions of Donat, Earl of Thomond, 1624, and Morogh O'Cashie, 1623: Mason's 'Parochial Survey,' vol. iii., p. 287.
[3] This family has evidently been long settled in the Burren. We find a Ballykilmartin in Killeany, in Petty's Survey, 1652.

A long narrow drain or 'souterrain' formed by roofing a rock cleft ran westward under nearly half the garth to the wall and into an outer enclosure. Though the ends are now stopped it is open all the way, for dogs have been sent through it.

The western enclosure is of equally good masonry, its wall is only 5 feet thick, but it is nearly 8 feet high. A low green valley runs east and west along the north of the fort.

CAHERGRILLAUN (O.S. 9., Nos. 4 and 8). - The name is rendered 'Dutch Chair' in Mason's Survey.[1] This is an oval caher, 120 feet north and south by 154 east and west, on a grassy hill north of the last. It is much overgrown by hazels, and encloses smooth green sward; the foundations of many late houses and enclosures adjoin it to the north and south. The rampart is 15 feet high to the north, and 9 feet to the east and west. It is of fine uncoursed masonry for 8 feet of its height, above which much smaller stones appear; perhaps many other cahers (we shall note another not many miles away) had inferior upper walls which have entirely fallen. The stonework to the west is of very large blocks and Cyclopean in style. It is noteworthy that the somewhat ruder and longer masonry (supposed by some to be of an earlier age than the larger and better-fitted blocks) occurs above the 'Cyclopean' masonry. Nay more, the masonry without spawls occurs above that with them. This is not a solitary case, nor confined to Ireland, for Dr. Christison notices it in the forts of Lorne.[2] We have this further proof of the doubtfulness of all attempts to date or group forts by their stonework. The rampart is 9 feet 6 inches to 10 feet at base, and 6 feet 7 inches to 7 feet at the top. It has the usual curved outline which was probably a regular batter which got bulged out by the settlement of the filling, which, like the facing, is large for some 8 feet high and small above.

The only internal features are a plinth or very narrow terrace, 12 inches to 18 inches wide (as at Cahercottine), and a flight of five steps to the west leading from the 'plinth' to a platform from left to right, and they measure (ascending) 12, 12, 15, 10, and 10 inches high, 23, 16, 13, and 12 inches tread, and 18 inches in depth. There are traces of a similar flight leading from right to left up to the same platform. This feature, though not unknown in the Kerry forts, seems unique in Clare. The gate faced S.S.E., its sides are parallel and of massive 'stretchers.' The passage is 8 feet 5 inches wide and 10 feet long, and if roofed, must, like Cahermackirilla, have required beams of wood.

MOHERAMOYLAN (O.S. 9., No. 4). - A defaced caher, possibly the Moher O'Loughlin in Eanty (1655) about 120 feet across, and so nearly levelled that it is only distinguishable on the new maps by the modern enclosures; lies on a craggy hill to the N.E. of Cahergrillaun and is circular in plan. Its gate faces south, and seems on the point of falling, as the east pier was distorted, the back stones having been removed. It is 6 feet high, 4 feet 4 inches wide (the exact width of the gates of Rannagh and Caherahoagh). It has two lintels, the outer and larger being 6 feet by 2 feet 10 inches, the

[1] Vol. iii., p. 287.
[2] *Early Fortifications in Scotland*, pp. 146 and 147.

passage behind it was 5 feet 3 inches wide, the wall 9 feet thick. The masonry seems to have been of very thin slabs, 5 inches to 8 inches thick, which accounts for its thorough dilapidation.

In the garth there are some late enclosures and a straight souterrain lying N.N.W. and S.S.E.; it is of the usual type, parallel walls of small stones 4 feet apart, roofed at the ground level with slabs, 5 feet 6 inches long. The term 'Moher' is used by the peasantry in the sense of enclosure rather than fort. This was the case even early in the last century, for we find leases of 'the mohers of Ballymahony in Burren' granted by the O'Brien's to the England family.[1]

Gateway of Moheramoylan.

A cromlech stands on a green hillock 2000 feet westward from the fort. It has fallen towards the north, the sides were only about 3 feet high, including the part set in the ground; the massive top slab is 14 feet 5 inches east and west, and 9 feet 7 inches north and south by 8 or 10 inches thick.

KILCORNEY AND THE EASTERN VALLEYS

Kilcorney Parish is intersected by three valleys - Eanty, an extension of Poulacarran, Glensleade, a small abrupt basin at the end of a depression, and Kilcorney, a long irregular glen, bounded by picturesque cliffs. The name has been retained unaltered since, at any rate, 1302. Windows, probably as old as the eleventh or twelfth centuries, remain in its ancient church, one with a carved head in the style of that at Inchicronan, but no records or traditions of its founder seem to exist. The primitive structures appear to have hitherto attracted no attention, though Kilcorney Cave, with its 'outputs' of water, fish, and fairy horses,[2] has received notice since the middle of the last century.

Gough, in his edition of Camden's *Britannia* 1789,[3] after enumerating some of the plants of the district, describes Kilcorney as 'a pretty low valley entered at the east end. On the north side of a small plain of an acre, under

[1] Dublin Registry of Deeds, B. 51, p. 378, and B. 94, p. 445 (1725-1726).
[2] I have heard locally strange stories of the untameable recklessness and savage temper of alleged descendants of the fairy horses.
[3] Vol. iii., p. 579. He seems to have confused the points of the compass.

steep rugged cliffs, lies Kilcorran Cave, the mouth level with the plain, about three feet diameter, part blocked up.' 'The cave pours forth occasional deluges over the adjacent plain to a depth of about twenty feet. Sometimes, once in a year or two, commonly three or four times a year, preceded by a great noise as of falling water. It flows with great rapidity for a day or two.'[1]

Gough, however, mentions none of the antiquities, and, as he states in another place[2] 'of the ancient cathairs we have now no remains but the duns,' his information must have been defective.

Of the forts, the Ordnance Survey Letters of 1839, and later writers, give only a few names. Mr. J. Foote, of the Geological Survey (in a letter to George V. Du Noyer, January 8th, 1862), wrote enthusiastically of the ruins, but neither he nor Du Noyer published any description.[3] He writes:- 'There are no less than seven cromlechs, sixteen beautiful stone forts, some having caves, and all walls of great thickness, an old castle, and a stone cross. Here is ground for the antiquary! The place must have been creeping with druids. I never saw such beauties (of cromlechs). Here is one (Poulnabrone) I sketched yesterday. The end stone and some of the sides are down: the front stone 5 feet high (he gives the top slab as measuring 9 feet north and south, 12 feet east and west, with a slope to the S.S.W.). All stand on little green mounds of earth, surrounded by bare sheets of rock, and some slope to the east.' By a plan he shows that Ballymihil cromlech and the second at Berneens were then still standing, and that the top slab still rested on the south cromlech of Cragballyconoal. He locates the 'stone cross' where 'monument' is marked on the Ordnance map and where it still remains.

The place has little or no history. Glensleade (*Gleana Slaodh*) appears in the 1380 rental and the 1569 map. In 1641, Caherconnell and Poulanine were held by Donough O'Brien, Lysagh O'Loughlin, and Mac Loughlen Roe O'Cullinan: Ballymihil and Glensleade by William O'Neylan and Teige O'Loughlen. After the war, several of the Hogans, Comyns, and Macnamaras were settled in the parish, and at a still later period a branch of the Lysaghts (Gillisaghta) settled in the Kilcorney Valley.

KILCORNEY VALLEY AND RIDGES (O.S. 9., Nos. 2 and 3)

The Kilcorney Valley (save for its venerable church and the alleged site of Kilcolmanvara) only possesses an earthen tumulus 53 feet in diameter and 9 feet high, with a slight bank round the top. It lies to the south-west of the church, and commands a fine view of the cave-pierced cliffs.

The conspicuous cairn of Poulawack stands on the southern ridge near Poulcaragharush. It is a shapely pile of flat stones, about 200 feet in girth and 12 feet high, in good preservation. A kerbing of slabs set on edge girds its base; and an attempt has been made to break in on the northern side. The sea is visible from its summit; this, with the bright, fresh outlook, and

---

[1] Gough cites Dr. Lucas in *Phil. Trans.*, No. 456, p. 360.
[2] *Britannia*, iii., p. 483.
[3] Du Noyer's 'Sketches,' R.S.A.I. Library, vol. xi., pp. 85, 87.

its contiguity to Eanty, the probable site of ancient fairs, recalls the legend of Amalgaid,[1] who 'dug' tumuli and made his cairn, 'to make round it an annual meeting place for the clan,' 'to watch there for his vessels,' and eventually to make it his resting-place. Gloom seldom surrounded the ancient chieftain's grave; it lay on a fair site, and was regarded as a place of repose and comfort, so that a pagan king could sing:-

'My mound - my protection after parting with my army,
My pure, bright haven, my tomb, and my grave.'[2]

From the west end of the valley, a long ascent through rocks covered with mountain avens brings us to Lissylisheen caher, a small ring wall, 8 feet thick. The gateway faces the east, has doorposts at the inner corners, and is only 3 feet wide. The neighbouring castle still shows a large well-built rectangular court and a lofty block of masonry. From its grassy summit we get a most extensive view: the huge peaks of the Galtees and Mount Brandon rise to the far south. A pretty range of cliffs stand out against their belt of foam in Liscannor Bay; behind us rise the great hills of Slieve Elva and Northern Burren; the church and forts of Noughaval, seem very near; and Cahermacnaughten[3] lies about a mile to the north.

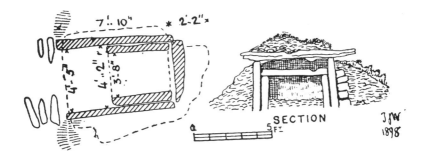

Plan and Elevation of Cromlech, Baur South.

BAUR - On the north cliffs of Kilcorney two cromlechs lie among heathy tussocks in the townlands of Baur, beside the steep road leading to Glensleade. Neither of these are marked[4] even on the new Survey. The one stands in the west boundary wall of Baur North and was once a noble specimen; but its cracked blocks bear marks of fire.[5] The top has collapsed, and only the south side is fairly perfect, being 16 feet 3 inches by 5 feet 10 inches. The upper edge was hammer-dressed. The cist tapers eastwards from 9 feet to 5 feet 9 inches, and had low stones at the west ends, as at

---

[1] 'Dindsenchas' (*Revue Celtique*), 1894, p. 141.
[2] Verse attributed to Art Aeinfer, *Proc. R.I.A.*, 3 Ser., vol. iii., p. 535.
[3] *Journal R.S.A.I.*, 1897, p. 120 [27].
[4] Unless a slight oblong at the wall be intended for the northern dolmen.
[5] See *Dolmens of Ireland*, vol. i., p. 74, for fires lit on cromlechs in Sligo on June 23rd, and in Spain on April 30th.

Tobergrania, &c. The other cromlech lies in Baur South, in the S.W. corner of the field marked 12.543 on Sheet 9, No. 3 of the new Survey: it is a very perfect little cist, covered with a low mound. The dimensions are given in the plan.

It is noteworthy for having an internal cist, 3 feet from the west end, and about a foot lower than the outer box. A somewhat similar arrangement existed in the huge cromlech of Derrymore, near O'Callaghan's Mills in this county, and other internal cists were found by Mr. Borlase at Tregaseal in Cornwall, where a layer of charcoal, human bones, and broken pottery lay on the ground, and little heaps of bones on the shelf. Several such cists occur in the dolmen of Karleby in Sweden, and contained crouching skeletons.[1] The Baur cromlech, however, has long been open and a shelter for goats. There were, at least, five defaced cairns along the edges of Baur and Poulnaskagh, and one near the end of that deep gully occupied by the glebe of Kilcorney. They average about 20 feet across, and are seldom more than 4 feet high.

CAHERLISCOLMANVARA lies in Poulnaskagh; its wall is levelled to within 2 feet of the field. The descent to the valley near this fort has three waterworn loaf-shaped rocks, about 8 feet high, across its pass. East of this, on the ridge near Caherconnell, are three very defaced cahers in Poulanine. Caherlisnanroum, on the cliff edge, is of good masonry, and has long lintel blocks and a side enclosure; its name (like that of Lisnanroum[2] on the southern hill near the road to Noughaval) is said to have been derived from the 'drum' or long ridge on which the cahers stand.

EANTY VALLEY (O.S. 9, No. 4).

From the ridge of Poulcaragharush, we look over a square valley. To our left lies the large fort of Caherconnell, to our right that of Cahergrillaun, and, far away to the north, shines the white cromlech of Cragballyconoal. The valley, with its north-eastern slopes, is mainly occupied by the four townlands of Eanty, Eantymore, Eantybeg North, and Eantybeg South, the Eanaghbeg of 1380. They seem, from the name, to have been the site of some important fair in early times, and retained the older name, 'Enogh,' even in the Books of Petty's Survey, 1655, in which we find[3] 'Enogh' as containing a number of sub-denominations. Among these we find the fort names Lissananamagh, Moher O'Loughlin, Drumliseenysiyack (Drum Liseeniska), and Lisnagleyragh, one of the other divisions being Enoghbane.

A precipitous gorge cuts into the northern hill; at its mouth is a small lake, while two forts stand one on either side. That to the west (1) is called from

---

[1] The interesting dolmen at Derrymore is not on the maps, and was only recently pointed out to me by Mrs. Gore of that place. For others, see *Dolmens of Ireland*, vol. ii., p. 442, and M. Du Chaillu's *Viking Age*, vol. i., p. 75, and *Ancient Swedish Civilisation*, by Dr. Montelius, p. 35, figures 35 and 36.

[2] A very small and featureless angular enclosure.

[3] Book of Distribution, vol. ii., p. 68 (Clare). It is regretable that the new Ordnance Survey has systematically omitted numbers of most interesting field and hill names, in many of which alone the older townland names survive.

the pool Caher-lisaniska; that on the eastern bluff (2) is called from some haunting spirit Caherlisananima.

Neither calls for much notice; they are small and oval, about 87 by 50 feet, the western being much gapped. A larger stone enclosure (3), diamond-shaped in plan, and (4) a small oval fort, both greatly gapped, lie near the Carran road in Eantymore. Two more (5 and 6), one a fairly square fort, 110 feet across, the other oval, and both nearly levelled lie east of the bohereen from Moheramoylan. Near these forts, in Eantybeg North, is a slight little ring-wall (7), called, like its neighbour, Lisananima. Its walls are only 5 feet high and thick, of thin slabs and poorly built. The gateway is perfect, and faces S.E., being 5 feet 6 inches high, with inclined jambs, and from 3 feet 10 inches to 3 feet 6 inches wide; the lintel measures 6 feet 9 inches by 2 feet. The neighbouring farmers deny that any 'spirit' has ever been seen in it; so its name was possibly transferred from the lower fort.

Gateway of Lisananima

THE RIDGE ABOVE GLENSLEADE (O.S. 5., No 16).

CRAGBALLYCONOAL. - We leave Lisaniska, ascend the stony pastures, cross the bohereen from Caherconnell to Poulaphuca, and enter this townland. Though it is in Oughtmama Parish, it so closely adjoins and is so nearly surrounded by the forts of Kilcorney, while so many miles of mountains, nearly devoid of antiquities, lie to the east, that we must describe its forts along with those of Ballymihil. It appears as part of Oughtmama in Petty's map of 1686; but the name is not given.

The ridge is about 700 feet above the sea. It slopes southward to Eanty, and falls westwards in steep bluffs into Poulgorm. Eastward extends a bleak and featureless plateau to the valleys of Turlough and Rannagh. Nearly all the forts are small, oval, of light masonry, and nearly broken down to within 3 to 5 feet of the ground.

An ancient disused road runs along the ridge in a nearly straight line, north and south, from Ballymihil cromlech to Lisananima: this forms the bounds of the parishes and townlands for most of its course. In Cragballyconoal, on the very bounds of Ballymihil, we find (1) a cromlech in a green mound; the top has been removed since 1862; the sides are about 6 feet high to the west; the top edges have been hammer-dressed; they slope towards the east, and, being coated with white lichen, form a conspicuous object across the valley.[1] (2) A circular stone fort lies behind the Mackies' house, lately the scene of a night attack; the southern segment has been destroyed, and the house built on its site and with the material; the rest is mostly about 8 feet high, and a souterrain forms an S-curve under the wall. This 'cave' is of the usual type, with side walls 3 feet apart, and roof slabs level with the ground. (3) Northwards lies a larger fort, D-shaped in plan, with the straight side to the south. It measures 120 feet internally, and contains a defaced circular cloghaun in the centre of the garth and measuring 12 feet internally, and a straight souterrain, 3 feet wide, leading under the wall. The gateway faced S.S.E., and had three lintels, 7 feet 3 inches, 7 feet 4 inches, and 9 feet long, and from 3 feet to 2 feet broad, and 9 inches thick; one side-post still stands, but the width of the entrance cannot be accurately fixed. (4, 5, 6) Three nearly-levelled cahers lie a short distance to the east. This close grouping recalls the 'grianans and palaces' outside the royal dun, or the groups of 'caher, courts and castles' seen by Ossian in Tir-na-nóg.[2] (7) A second cromlech lies in the remains of a mound on a heathy moor. It is made of three very thin slabs, 3 inches thick, and scarcely 4 feet high; the ends are removed; the dimensions are given on the plan; it slopes and narrows eastward. Near it, in Ballymihil, is a craggy field, set with upraised slabs, small stone 'piers' and heaps; a slab, rudely shaped like a cross, is set in one wall; another rude cross, of greater size, lies southward down the slope. (8) Farther, to the N.E of the cromlech, is a small circular caher, 59 feet internally. The gateway faces the south, and is 4 feet 6 inches wide, with two pillars on each side; the lintels have been removed, and the wall is only 4 feet thick and high. This fort commands, through a depression in the ridge, a striking view of the summit of Turlough Hill, rising to the N.E in three terraces, and crowned with its conspicuous cairn - another instance of the sacrifice of a more commanding site to a more attractive or extensive view.

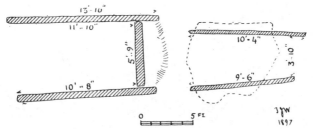

The Southern and Northern Cromlechs, Cragballyconoal.

Passing into Poulbaun (9) we find a caher on a rising ground, with a fine outlook over Glensleade to the sea; the round castle of Doonagore and the cliffs of Moher in the distance. The defaced gateway looks to the S.W., and is 4 feet 10 inches wide, with parallel sides of coursed masonry. The garth only contains a curved souterrain, 3 feet wide, lying to the N.E. On the crags below it, lies a heap of large slabs (10), most probably a fallen

---

[1] The dimensions are fully given on the plan.
[2] *Fenian Poems*, Ossianic Society, iv., pp. 249 and 259.

cromlech; the top and largest slab measures 12 feet from east to west, and is 8 feet wide.

We now enter Ballymihil, and find a fallen cromlech (11) on the bluff overhanging Poulgorm; the top is 11 feet 6 inches long, tapering eastward from 7 feet 7 inches to 6 feet, and 10 inches to 12 inches thick. The sides lie under it where they fell, and a rude dry-stone pier has been erected on the top to support a flag shaped like a round-headed cross, or rude human figure. We could learn nothing of its age or object; but a somewhat similar, though smaller, slab lies in the cist at Coolnatullagh.

Southward lies a straight-walled garth (12), only 3 feet or 4 feet high, enclosing a curious rock; still farther south is a ring-wall (13), quite levelled in parts, but with sections to the N.W. and S., still 9 feet to 11 feet high; and, like Cahergrillaun, it shows smaller masonry on top from about 8 feet above the ground. Near it is a circular modern enclosure on the edge of the slope. In a valley far below the level of the plateau, but still in Ballymihil, a small ring-wall (14) lies on a projecting spur; its wall is much gapped, and it only contains a modern sheep-fold.

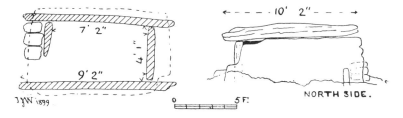

Plan and Northern Elevation of Cromlech, Poulaphuca.

POULAPHUCA. - Following the bohereen eastward from the Mackies' house, we find, in a field at the highest point of Poulaphuca[1] townland, a fine cromlech. It forms a cist of four blocks, with a massive top slab, 10 feet by 6 feet, and 10 inches thick; the interior is irregular, 8 feet 9 inches long, and tapers slightly eastward (4

Cromlech, Poulaphuca, from N.W.

feet 4 inches to 4 feet 1 inch). It stands in the remains of a cairn or mound. A small overthrown cist, 3 ft. square, lies in a green mound, 30 feet north of the large dolmen.

---

[1] It is noteworthy that the 'pooka' on not a few occasions gives its name to sites where prehistoric remains occur. We find in Clare, besides this dolmen, another at Caherphuca, near Crusheen. In Kerry we find a Cloghaunaphuca, and even the pooka's footmark, among the Fahan ruins. In Kilkenny 'The pooka's grave,' a dolmen. In Cork Carrigaphucha, which Borlase says is a pillar near an encircled cromlech. In Queen's County the 'Dun of Clopoke.' These show how widespread was this association of the 'pooka' with ancient remains.

The site commands a very fine view up the Turlough valley[1] to Belaclugga Creek, Galway Bay, and Corcomroe Abbey. Opposite lie the dark Slieve Carn and the finely terraced, cairn-topped mountain over Turlough. Near rise the dark and steep cliffs of Deelin, at the foot of which lies a large and fairly perfect caher, also in Poulaphuca. It is nearly circular; much of the wall is standing to a height of from 6 to 9 ft. It seems to have traces of a terrace, but there are no other features.

The old road drops from near the cromlech in steep curves to the pass from Rannagh to Turlough, one of the most beautiful glens of the Burren.

Descending from Cragballyconoal westward, by the very rough bohereen, we pass three forts in Poulgorm. One is a ring-wall of good masonry, over 9 feet thick; the second lies a short distance to the north, and is a straight-walled enclosure; the third is a small fort named Lishagaun. We then see before us a massive caher (which was seen first from Poulcaragharush) on the opposite ridge, though overhung by greater heights, between the valleys of Eanty and Kilcorney.

CAHERCONNELL (O.S. 9, No. 4) is a large and perfect fort, 140 feet to 143 feet in external diameter, nearly circular in plan, and girt by a wall with two faces and large filling; it is 12 feet thick, and from 6 feet to 14 feet high, being most perfect towards the west. The masonry consists of fairly large blocks, many 3 feet long and 2 feet 6 inches high, with spawls in the crevices, and a batter of 1 in 5. The inner face is nearly perfect, and had neither steps nor terraces. The gateway faced the east; it was 5 feet 8 inches wide, and had external side-posts. The garth is divided by a long wall running north-west and south-

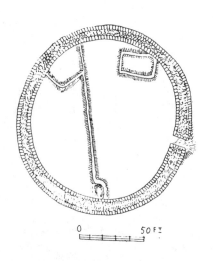

Caherconnell

east; at its northern end are two house sites, one 30 feet long, and at its southern an enclosed hollow, possibly a hut or souterrain. The names Caherconnell and Cahermaconnella (Cahermacnole) suggest the Ardconnell and Ardmicconnail of the Book of Rights, which appear with names of other places in this district.[2] Perhaps we may also connect it with the legendary Connal, son of Aenghus, of Dun Aenghus; but, like most other early names and legends in Burren, the subject is too misty to justify any positive statement or even a strong theory.

---

[1] This valley is so denuded of antiquities that, though I have examined it, I must entirely omit it from this Paper. I also reserve the Finnevarra group of forts to a later occasion.

[2] See, however, a note by Mr. P. Lynch, in the *Journal R. S. A. I.*, 1892, p. 80.

GLENSLEADE (O.S. 5, Nos. 15 & 16; O.S. 9, No. 4).

POULNABRONE (O.S. 9., No. 4). - In a rocky field lying east of the main road is a beautiful cromlech (*vide*, p. [56] plan,), noteworthy for the airy poise of its great top slab, which, contrary to the usual practice, slopes towards the west. This measures 13 feet long, from 6 feet to 10 feet wide, and a foot thick, and rests on three stones 5 to 7 feet high, the others having fallen. The structure forms a chamber, 9 feet 3 inches long, tapering eastwards from 4 feet 3 inches to 3 feet 9 inches internally; it stands in the remains of a mound, and is unaltered since 1862.

Not far north from this cromlech there is a long grassy glen very suggestive of a river-bed, and running back into the plateau under the ridge of Cragballyconoal from near the grassy mound and fragments of wall which mark the O'Loughlin's castle in Glensleade. If we follow up this glen by a painful walk along very broken crags, full of avens, gentians, and long hartstongue ferns, we pass a well-built, small, and low ring wall, about 60 feet in diameter; it lies on the north crags, and the adjoining enclosures are all modern. We then come in sight of two lofty knolls, crowned with cliff forts, and forming a striking view as seen from the glen.

CAHERCASHLAUN (O.S. 5, No. 16) in Poulnabrone is a natural tower of regularly stratified limestone rounded to the west, and falling in jagged cliffs towards the north-east. This rock rises 70 to 100 feet from the glen in even a bolder mass than does Cashlaun Gar.[1] The top is roughly oval, and is girt by a dry-stone wall, 4 to 5 feet thick, and at the most 6 feet high, most of it being nearly levelled, and clinging to the very edge of the crags with needless care. The garth measures internally 152 feet east and west, and 75 feet north and south; and contains a souterrain 80 feet from the west. This cave is formed out of a cleft about 7 feet deep, 27 feet long, and 4 to 6 feet wide; five long roofslabs remain over the middle. The gap of the ruined eastern gateway leads down into a second and lower enclosure,[2] surrounded by a coarsely built wall of much larger blocks than the upper fort, many being 5 and 6 feet long; in parts the wall is 5 and 6 feet high. The enclosure is 70 feet deep, making the entire length of the fort 240 feet from east to west. The entrance was through a regular cleft, sloping upwards through the crag-ledge; it was about 4 feet wide, and roofed by lintels, now fallen; it must have resembled the cleft under Carran cliff fort. This second wall was intended to protect the only easy ascent, and resembles one I recently found hidden in hazel scrub on the north slope of the knoll of the similar, though more massive, Cashlaun Gar.

---

[1] *Journal*, 1896, p. 152 [10]. Such rocks are sometimes called 'doonaun' by the peasantry.

[2] These outworks occurred in ancient Gaulish forts: for example, the dry-stone rampart made by order of Vercingetorix, on the hill slope of Alesia, 'maceriam *sex* in altitudinem pedum preduxerant' ('De Bello Gallico,' vii., c. 69), and the great fort of the Beuvray, near Autun (*The Mount and City of Autun*, Hamerton, p. 64).

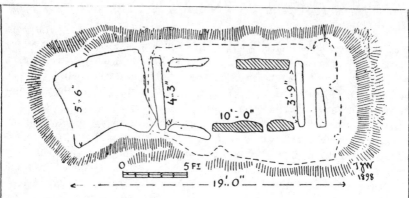

Plan of Poulnabrone Cromlech.

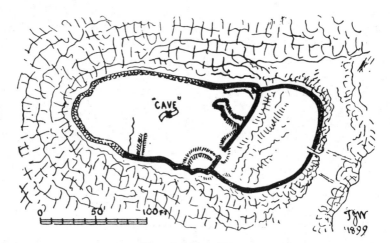

Plan of Cahercashlaun.

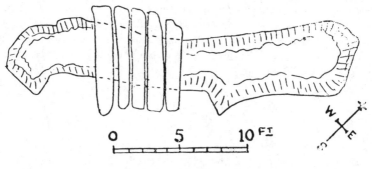

Souterrain in Cahercashlaun.

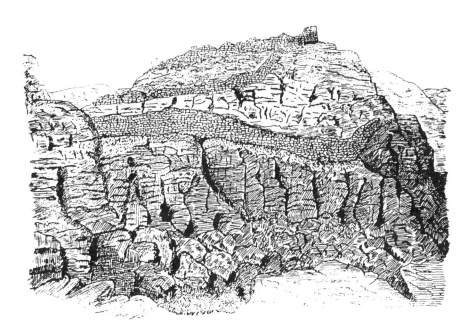

Cliff fort of Cahercashlaun, from the North

POULGORM CLIFF FORT. - On the opposite cliff overlooking, and about 300 feet to the S.W. of Cahercashlaun, is a rude ring-wall 60 feet across; it has a side enclosure, and has been much rebuilt, and used as a fold.

CAHERNAMWEELA. - This fort, and the large enclosure near it, seem also to be called Cahernanebwee. It is a ring of good masonry, 50 feet internally, 5 feet thick, and at most 6 feet high. The nearly levelled gateway faced S.S.E., and is 3 feet 4 inches wide; the sides are parallel, made of large blocks running the whole depth of the wall. The mossy garth only contains a hut-foundation near the gateway. The site is overlooked by a ridge scarcely 50 feet away, and slopes abruptly to the east and south. There is a side enclosure to the S.W. at a lower level, but joining the caher wall.

ENCLOSURE. - About 300 feet to the N.W., on the summit of the ridge, is an old enclosure. It is a most disappointing object, seeming to be high and large and imposing, especially as seen from Caheranardurrish. It is actually a rough wall, 3 feet thick and 7 feet high, enclosing an irregular space 110 feet across. There are no foundations in the garth, and it was probably a mediæval bawn.

Going westward by a difficult way across waterworn and loose crags (full of fossil corals) and a level-floored depression, we ascend the opposite ridge, and find two other cahers.

CAHERANARDURRISH (O.S. 5, No. 15). - The eastern fort of the name (the other lies on the crest of the hill-road behind Rathborney Church) stands on a knoll above the deep basin-like hollow of Glensleade, some distance to the N.W. of the castle. Though surrounded by crags, there is abundance of coarse rich grass both in and around its wall. The name is taken from the gateway which faces E.S.E., and is very perfect; it has sloping jambs, and is from 4 feet 10 inches to 4 feet 7 inches wide, and only 5 feet 3 inches high. As there is very little fallen rubbish, it suggests either that 'Fort of the high door' is an archaic sarcasm, or that high doors were rare in ancient Burren. The gateway has three lintels; the middle has slipped, and the outer measures 8 feet 2 inches by 1 foot 6 inches by 9 inches; it has two long slabs above it to spread the weight of the upper wall. The fort is oval, from 110 feet to 116 feet internally; the wall 7 or 8 feet thick, and 5 feet to 8 feet high, of good long-stoned masonry.

In the centre of the garth used to be a heap of stones suggestive of a fallen clochan. This is now cleared away, and only a small cist remains, 3 feet wide, and at least 9 feet long, with a partition of slabs in the middle. This may have been one of those strange little slab enclosures to be seen in the floors of several Irish and Welsh forts and Scotch brochs. The filling of the wall has been much dug up by seekers after imaginary treasures, or more practicable rabbits. Unfortunately such gold dreamers abound; all agree that nothing but a few coins of the 'cross silver' have ever been found (and that very rarely); but these discouraging 'modern instances' never save our venerable buildings from these foolish and destructive attempts to discover fairy gold. Even in the last three years the right jamb of the gateway of this caher has been tampered with, and the pier is in considerable jeopardy.

On the south slope of the knoll is a very small circular fort 47 feet internally, with walls 5 feet thick, and barely 3 feet or 4 feet high; the gateway faced the south. A well-built bawn, lined on the inside with upturned slabs, runs down the slope near this little ring-wall.

RATHBORNEY GROUP (O.S. 5, Nos. 7, 11, 12).

Part of this parish extends up to the central plateau; therefore we must briefly note its forts and cromlechs.

Garracloon has two old enclosures, fairly built, but much broken. A third, farther eastward, somewhat D-shaped in plan, bears the townland's name. Lisgoogan, the *Lessaguagain* of the 1390 rental, contains a square caher about 100 feet across with traces of an irregular, somewhat circular outer ring, 260 feet in diameter, to the west of the main road. The survey of 1655 names two cahers,[1] Kaheriskebohell and Kaherballyungane, or Kaherballyvanghane, lying between Lisgoogan and Caherwooly (Caher-odouloughta, near Cahermacnaughten), these I cannot localise unless they be the forts at Doonyvardan. Berneens is a long, straggling townland. It has a cromlech at its western end on the summit of the hill, and another on the hillside near the Gleninshen group, described below: a very dilapidated little ring-wall, less than 50 feet in diameter, on its southern edge is called Caherberneen. Gleninshen, a bare craggy upland, with no trace of the ash trees which gave it its name, has the remains of a small well-built circular caher in the fields close to Caheranardurrish. There are five other forts: two circular, two rudely square in plan, the southern being Gleninshen caher; the

---

[1] Book of Distribution and Survey, Co. Clare, vol. i., p. 474.

fifth, much rebuilt for a sheep-fold, lies near the southern cromlech. In the western portion, close to the main road, are two cromlechs; the first is nearly perfect, and has been described and figured by Mr. W. Borlase under the name of Berneens.[1] His description is, as usual, very accurate. 'This dolmen lies E.N.E. and W.S.W. The roofing stone measures 10 feet 11 inches long, and 7 feet 6 inches broad. The sides are respectively, 11 feet 5 inches and 11 feet long.' It tapers from 4 feet 5 inches to 3 feet 2 inches, and was surrounded by a small cairn. The initials 'J. O'D.' are cut on one of its slabs, but we can scarcely attribute them to our great Irish scholar, though he and Eugene O'Curry carefully examined the district. Of the second only the ends and south side rise above the avens and cranesbills. The side measures 13 feet 6 inches by 4 feet 3 inches by 10 inches; the ends show that the cist tapered eastward from 5 feet 2 inches to 4 feet 4 inches: it was perfect in 1862. A third cromlech lies N.N.E. from, and in line with the two last up the slope of the hill in Berneens. Its south side has collapsed since 1862; it is otherwise fairly complete. A more desolate region than exists to the east of these remains is hard to imagine. 'Silence broods over the dead grey land'; and the absence of all antiquities show that its loneliness is of no modern growth. The lines of habitation and traffic across these uplands seem always to have been the same, namely from Belaclugga to Turlough and Tullycommane, from Glensleade to Lemeneagh, and from Cahermacnaughten to Ballykinvarga, all three meeting the road from Kilfenora, which ran eastward to the 'Bohernamicrigh,' 'the stone road,' which led to the ford of Corofin, the pass to central Thomond.

EASTERN VALLEYS (O.S. 6).

Very few prehistoric remains of interest lie east of the central plateau. The caher of Turlough, '*uamhainn na Turlaige*,' has been destroyed since before 1839. There are several noteworthy cairns. Carnbower on top of, and giving its name to, Slieve Carran, stands 1075 feet above the sea and is of considerable size. Two others are nameless, and stand on Turlough and Knockycallanan mountain; one is on the summit,[2] 945 feet above the sea. We have already noted Cappaghkennedy cairn,[3] with its fine neighbouring cromlech. Not far behind the darkly picturesque glen, bearing the unmelodious name of Clab ('clob' as pronounced), on top of Gortaclare Hill (907 feet) is a spot called Creganaonaigh, the site of some ancient 'fair' marked by several small circles of stones. Mr. Borlase states that there was a tradition of a battle fought on the hill top.[4] But I could get no definite information about the site.

---

[1] *Dolmens of Ireland,* vol. i., p. 66. The Gleninshen dolmen was not marked on the 1839 map, so I, in *R. S. A. I. Journal,* 1894, identified it as the Berneen Cromlech, and was followed by Mr. Borlase.

[2] See illustrations of Poulaphuca cromlech, *supra,* p. [53].

[3] *Journal,* 1896, p. 364 [17]; Borlase's *Dolmens of Ireland,* vol. i., p. 73.

[4] *Dolmens of Ireland,* p. 809.

Cromlech, Coolnatullagh, from N.E.

RANNAGH EAST and COOLNATULLAGH have three small cromlechs. The former townland contains two of these. One has fallen; it lay in a field below the highest turn of the Castletown road, and is not marked on the new maps. It was a cist, 4 feet 6 inches wide at the west end, and 6 feet 3 inches long internally; it seems to have tapered to 3 feet 6 inches, and the south side was 8 feet 6 inches long.

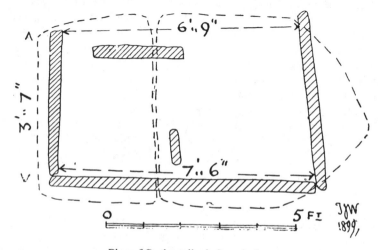

Plan of Coolnatullagh Cromlech.

The perfect cromlech lies further to the north-east beyond a low rocky valley. It is a small cist, nearly buried in the ground. The north and south slabs (respectively 9 feet and 9 feet 9 inches long) support an irregular top block. The chamber tapers from 3 feet 3 inches to 2 feet 3 inches. Coolnatullagh cist was recently found by Dr. G. Macnamara; it lies half a mile east of the 'kill', or old burial-place of Kilnatullagh, near the corner of a regular oblong plateau overlooking the valley from Coskeam to Castletown. It is a small cist of thin slabs; in it stands a curious little stone, shaped like a rough cross. There are remains of a grass-grown cairn in this townland, perhaps the 'tullagh' which gave it its name. A caher stood on the hill of Coskeam; but it appears to be nearly levelled. The peaks of this hill are called Doonmore and Doonbeg. To sum up, the few forts in the valleys from Turlough and Sladdoo to Kinallia and Glencolumbcille are small, and defaced past all description.

This Paper being confined to the third section of the district (the eastern and central ridges of Burren), leaves the forts of Ballyvaughan and Lisdoonvarna for another occasion. The interesting character of the hitherto undescribed uplands about Carran and the damage done to their antiquities in the last twenty years rendered it necessary to secure as far possible a permanent record of 'the waste dwellings and desolations of many generations' for future scholars who may hereafter find so much to censure in the apathy and destructiveness of the vast majority of the present occupants of ancient Burren.[1]

---

[1] In Carran about 67 forts and 8 cromlechs remain. In Kilcorney about 28 forts and 4 cromlechs. On Rathborney border, 11 forts and 4 cromlechs. Cragballyconoal and Poulaphuca, 11 forts and 4 cromlechs. Parknabinnia and Glasgeivnagh, 17 forts and 16 cromlechs - in all about 134 forts and 36 cromlechs, 5 gallans, and uncounted cairns. The *Dolmens of Ireland* having omitted to give plans and descriptions of so many of the cromlechs in this district, I have felt it to be all the more necessary to supply the omission.

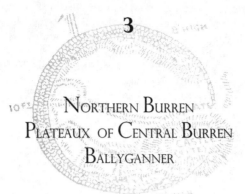

3

Northern Burren
Plateaux of Central Burren
Ballyganner

Embarrassed by the wealth of ancient remains, we have examined Inchiquin and the eastern districts of the ancient Corcomroes;[1] to complete our survey of the principal cahers of Burren it only remains for us to explore that section 'in the arms of the sea.' A fresh bright district of warm limestone - 'the land of the green and the grey' - lies along the ocean. Its rocks are tufted with samphire and maidenhair, with countless flowers and ferns, and its hills are broken by deep valleys and bright brooks. It ever grows in fascination, whether its terraced hills reflect 'the glowing embers of the sunset' or lie shimmering beneath unclouded noon. Its great bluffs look across miles of waves to the Isles of Aran, 'poised in the golden west,' beyond which some writers fixed the garden of Hesperides 'on the west side from Aran, where goes the sun to its couch.'[2] 'Above, free winds and clouds, ranging at their will; brightness out of the north and balm from the south, clear in the limitless light of arched heaven and circling sea.' The ancient inhabitants felt this beauty and sang of Aran in words equally descriptive of the Burren - 'The sea impinges on her very shoulders, skittish goats are on her pinnacles, soft blackberries are on her waving heather, blueberries and sloes of the dark thorn; her nuts hang on her forest hazel boughs, and there was sailing of long galleys past her; the seagulls, wheeling round her grand cliffs, answer one the other.'[3]

In this beautiful district an important series of early settlements lay; the cahers and middens alone remain with a very few cromlechs, and the buildings form the subject of this Paper. Few of the cahers equal in interest or preservation those of our former explorations, but many are most instructive and several of importance to the general result of our

---

[1] Previous Papers in this *Journal*, 1893, p. 281, Bunratty Baronies. 1896, p. 142 [1], Inchiquin. 1897, p. 116 [23]; 1898, p. 353 [35]; 1899, p. 367 [47], Eastern Burren and Corcomroe. 1898, p. 409, Loop Head.

[2] *Giolla-an-fhiugha* (Irish Text Society), p. 21.

[3] *Silva Gadelica*, vol. ii., p. 109.

conclusions. We commence our survey at the extreme north-eastern promontory of Black Head, and then explore valley by valley eastward till we meet the field of our former work at Berneens. Thence we purpose following a westward line till we return to the sea near the cliffs of Moher.

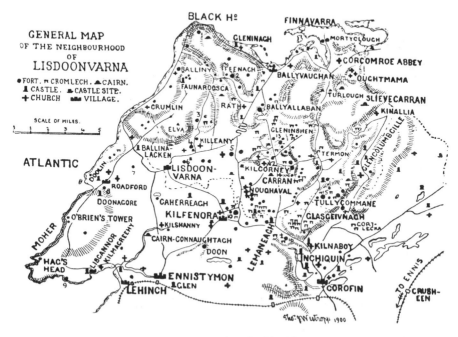

References to Forts described in this paper.
1. Caherdooneerish.   3. Caherbullog   6. Lissafeeaun.
2. Lismacsheedy and   4. Chercloggaun.   7. Knockastoolery.
   Caherfeenagh.   5. Cahermoyle.   8. Cahernafurresha.

BLACK HEAD (O.S. 1 and 2).

CAHERDOONEERISH[1] (Caherdoonfergus on the O.S. map). - The almost impassable mountains near Black Head[2] were not untenanted in early times. In the misty and dark reaches of Irish prehistoric legend one of the most definite statements locates a Firbolg chief Irghus, of the clan of the sons of Huamore, at Rind Boirne (the Headland of Burren), and as we shall see, his name is still preserved in the fort on Black Head. Of other early tribes in the district we seem to catch a glimpse of a section of the far-reaching Ua Cathba and Ua Corra in the farthest point of legend, and later of the Eoghanacht clans (who gave to Aran and Burren the names of Dun Onacht and Eoghanacht Ninuis), who, along with the race of Rory, were located in

---

[1] Lord Dunraven's 'Notes,' vol. i., p. 17; this *Journal*, 1900, p. 425; *Limerick Field Club Journal,* vol. i., pt. IV., p. 40.

[2] 'The great wast rock of Kaneborny.' Cromwellian Survey – Book of Distribution, p. 480.

the Corcomroes, at any rate before the fifth century. The name of the fort, as fixed by O'Donovan and O'Curry in 1839, is Caherdoonfergus, but the older natives of the district say positively that the name Fergus does not occur in it, and give such forms as 'Caherdooneerish,' 'Caherdooneerus' and 'Dooniriras,' the first being the most common. The very fact that the people are utterly ignorant of the existence of such a legendary hero as Irghus (Irghuis=Eerish) favours their tradition, while O'Donovan and O'Curry were saturated in the legends of Fergus, son of Roigh, and were evidently eager to find his name and give him a local habitation in the land of his descendants, the O'Conors and O'Loughlins, thereby running the risk (that so closely besets the incautious inquirer) of supplying leading questions and extracting false legends.   This treatment of genuine place-names and traditions is unfortunately on the increase, and many definite instances may be given where the Ordnance Survey and tourists have unconsciously foisted modern stories into the mouths of the too acute witnesses they cross-examined, or too enthusiastic Celtic scholars have revised the traditional name 'out of honesty into Irish,' *i.e.* such Irish as was conceived by themselves.[1]

Caherdooneerish (from the North-east).

   The place in 1839 was said to be enchanted (*i.e.*, 'haunted') 'by Fergus, son of Roigh, and his companions.' Doubtless it was, like many another fort, reputed to be haunted; but, we fear, that Fergus was projected on to the minds of the natives from too zealous inquirers, and expelled the real hero from our place names as ruthlessly as the heroes of Tara, in the older legend, expelled him from the district. The headland was also haunted, men said, by that hideous and demonic banshee, Bronach, the sorrowful, 'who abode in the green fairy mounts of Erin, but had her dwelling in Hell,'[2] as well as by gentler and more human spirits. It was no unpoetic or ignoble belief that

---

[1] A 'restored' name is of less value than a 'restored' caher; each should be 'conserved.'
[2] Wars of Torlough, under year 1318.

fancied the lost and weary spirit of the pagan chiefs - unshepherded, uncomforted, outcast - clinging to the shattered ruin of their fortress, in that solemn solitude of rock above the melancholy, wrinkled ocean, even if we cannot accept as a genuine legend that Fergus appeared through the mist wreaths as he did to Murgen in Ferguson's weird poem of *The Tain Quest*: -

> 'Fergus rose, a mist ascended
> With him, and a flash was seen,
> As of brazen sandals blended
> With a vestments wafture green.
> But so thick the cloud closed o'er him
> Eimena, returned at last,
> Found naught on the field before him
> But a mist heap grey and vast.'

and such a mist heap hides from our research the true origin of this as of other cahers.

The Caher stands on a lower brow of Black Head where the juniper, not daring to rise against the cruel gale, creeps upon the rocks. To the south-east rise the cliffs of Doughbranneen higher up the hill. To the south is seen nearly all the shore of Killonaghan. On the other sides lie the broad bay of Galway, and the ever-complaining sea, boundless save for the long low grey Isles of Aran. The fort is an irregular enclosure, D-shaped in plan, forming almost a right angle at its south-west corner - an actual *corner*[1] such as we only see elsewhere in the presumably late rectangular forts or mohers - this, with the poor and small masonry adjoining, suggests a rebuilding of the older fort. The garth measures internally 65 feet, north and south, and 69 feet, east and west. The rampart is, indeed, for the most part of that inferior masonry found above the 'cyclopean' stonework in some of our forts. There is a large breach to the south-east, and another to the east, where the old gateway is still to be traced; between these gaps stands the highest piece of wall. I have failed to get an accurate measurement; but it may be 15 or 16 feet high; the masonry in the lower part, to the north and east, is better and larger than the upper part, and, perhaps, may mark a much older foundation, though it is equally probable that the larger and better stones may have been reserved for the lower, and the smaller and more portable blocks for the upper wall. The gateway was only 32 inches wide, the smallest I have measured in Clare (the next smallest being Ballyelly, 34 in., lying a few miles to the south, and Cahercommane, 36 inches). It had no corner posts, only one stone, 39

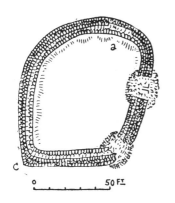

Plan of Caherdooneerish.

_____

[1] 'c' on plan.

inches long, lies in the *débris*. A wider passage runs through the thickness of the wall and terrace from the gateway (as at Doon Aenghus, and Ballykinvarga). The outer section of the wall measures about 6 feet, and the terrace 5 feet; but the wall is often 13 feet thick. The masonry is irregular and poor, laid as headers, with no structural batter and leaning out in parts. Traces of distorted upright joints seem to remain, one to the north-west, and at least three others, for about a third of the height of the wall, along the northern segment; two of these diverge and are about 10 feet apart, as if built by a small gang; they all begin above the large stonework, and have unjointed masonry above them, as if more than one rebuilding had taken place. There is a short joint running for 4 or 5 feet up the wall to the south, and two more to the west, but wavy and distorted. I call these 'upright joints' with reserve; they are not as well marked as those in Dun Conor, Cahercommane, Ballykinvarga, Staigue, and other forts, and we shall see in the far better masonry of Caherdoggaun how careless the old builders were about breaking joint. Between the western joints, the stones are larger; but have been in some cases set on a steep slope, as at Cahercommane,[1] which doubtless (as there) implies a hasty rebuilding. In short, the masonry is far inferior to the usually excellent coursed and 'cyclopean' stonework of other forts in the limestone districts.

A terrace, 3 to 4 feet high, runs round the inside of the wall; there is some appearance of a flight of steps, rising from the left and the right, to the summit of the wall from the terrace.[2] Lord Dunraven found them to be 2 feet 6 inches long; but I found no indisputable trace. There are no old structures in the fort or on the crags near it. The approach from the north is so steep as to be practically inaccessible; indeed, it seems wonderful that anyone took such a wind-swept, waterless brow for a residence, or, having done so, took pains to strengthen almost impassable crags and grassy slopes of rock, with a wall 12 feet high, on a ridge 647 feet above a harbourless and stormy shore.

OTHER REMAINS. - Eastward, along the higher plateau, are other traces of occupation. A small cairn called Doughbranneen, 1040 feet above the sea; on a lower shoulder is another cairn nearly levelled, and called Seefin, Finn's seat, no uncommon name for prominent brows in Ireland; below is a fine range of land cliffs. Farther eastward, on the next summit, in Aghaglinny townland, 1045 feet above the sea, is a long, oval caher; its wall is much overthrown, and measures about 230 feet from east to west, and 100 feet across; a path leads past it from Feenagh to Gleninagh. Down this path, to the south-east, lies a caher in Gleninagh south; it is about 150 feet in diameter, with rather flat curves in the wall to the north and west; the rest much defaced and overthrown.

Among these hills lies also a beautiful natural amphitheatre, its regular curving seats capable of seating some thousands of spectators, the arena covered with rich green sward.

---

[1] This *Journal*, 1896, p. 55 [13].
[2] 'a' on plan

A small circular fort is marked on the 1839 map down the steep slope to the north of Dooneerish. I believe I have been close to the site, without finding any trace, but a ruined modern house near it may have abolished its ancient neighbour, which must have been as small as the little ring walls at Glensleade and Poulcaragharush.

CAHERDOONTEIGUSHA (O.S. 1). - Stands on a ridge south from the Head and near an old road; it is greatly gapped, but some large reaches of the wall are standing.

CAHERBANNAGH (O.S. 2). - Up the Caher river, after passing the great sandhills of the Murroughs and Fanore, in which flint scrapers, pottery, and hut sites have been discovered, with heaps of shells, and (it is said) deer bones,[1] were a group of forts. Two circular cahers and two 'mohers' or straight-walled enclosures lie on the rocky hillside, just within the bold gorge known as the Khyber Pass, between the nearly defunct village of Caher and the high fort of Caheranardurrish (the western of the name) above Feenagh. The 'mohers' have nearly vanished since 1839, and the cahers were even then broken down and greatly dilapidated. In that year Caherbannagh, 'the fort of the pinnacles,' gave no proof of the fitness of its name. Caher ought probably to be called 'Caheragh,' as it appears as 'Cathrach' in the rental of the O'Briens, in *c.* 1390, along with townlands Liss na h'Aba and For Maol. They reappear in 1624 as Formoyle and Cahera Lissyniagh in the Inquisition taken on the death of Donough, 'the great Earl' of Thomond. In 1317 Formoyle and Letterconan appear as the muster place of the army of Prince Donough O'Brien on its way to assail their rivals at Corcomroe Abbey. The places were then called Cil Litire and Maol Odhrain. Another fort which I was unable to visit lies in a rather inaccessible spot to the north of the Caher river, and not far from Fanore Bridge, and there are two others in Fanore, both nearly destroyed, and one having only part of the northern segment remaining.

With regard to Caherbannagh, it is noteworthy that Hugh MacCurtin wrote a pretty poem on some 'pinnacled' fort in O'Loughlin's country: -

'Thou melancholy singing dove on yonder blackened 'doon,'
Dismal and defenceless is the ruin on which you perch,
The ruin of the noble pinnacled house of the descendant of Roigh.'[2]

---

[1] See Miss Knowles' Paper in the *Journal of the Limerick Field Club*, vol. i., Part 4, p. 39.
[2] MSS., R.I.A. Library, 23. A. 17.

KILLONAGHAN (O.S. 4).

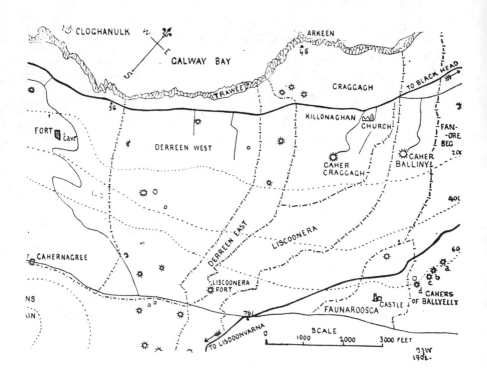

Map of Killonaghan Parish.
(The lightly dotted lines are heights above the sea.)

Turning southward along the shore we find ourselves in a long 'one-sided valley' between a table-land and the sea, forming the greater part of the parish of Killonaghan and the old merged parish of Crumlin. Of later antiquities there are two venerable churches - Crumlin, the older, being attributed to St. Columba in the year in which he left Aran. The curious round castle of Faunaroosca stands on the higher slopes of the hill, and, like all the 'valley,' commands a noble sea view, with the Isles of Aran plainly visible, and the giant peaks of Connemara far away to the north-west.

BALLINY[1]. - We first find the large caher of Balliny resting on a knoll of crag projecting from the hill-side to the east of Killonaghan church. It was occupied, and partly buttressed, by a small hamlet in 1839, which on my first visit I found subsisting, though the houses in the garth were then unoccupied. Three years later they were inhabited, and, as the house leaning

---

[1] Lord Dunraven's 'Notes,' vol. i., p. 18.

against the wall had never been deserted, we may consider Balliny as the interesting survival of an inhabited caher, which may very probably have been occupied with scarcely a break from early times.

It is a circular fort, 118 feet in internal diameter, the wall 10 feet thick and from 5 feet to 8 feet high. Segments to the south-west and east are built of large blocks, the most massive being on the eastern side, where the caher was undefended by the ground; most of these blocks are 4 feet long, one nearly 7 feet, and several over 6 feet long, and about 18 inches thick and wide; the smaller stones are mostly used as headers. The wall has a slight and variant batter, and has the appearance of a terrace which was formed (as at Ballyallaban) by the removal of the inner face and the filling, leaving the outer facing as a parapet. I found no traces of steps, upright joints, or old enclosures. So much has been patched, rebuilt and overgrown, that the fort is of little antiquarian value, though it has gained in picturesqueness. There are two gaps, one to the east, probably on the site of the gateway, the other in the north, to let in a bohereen. Lord Dunraven has briefly described this caher.[1]

Caher-Balliny (from the East).

CRAGGAGH. - Between the road and the sea is a large rock called Dermot and Grania's bed, under which is an artificial cave not a dolmen.[2] Not far away are the foundations of three nearly levelled cahers. The caher of Craggagh, near the foot of the hill, occupies (like Balliny), a low craggy knoll, and is defaced by the neighbourhood of modern houses. Its walls are much gapped and overgrown. An old-looking bohereen leads from it to Killonaghan church.

BALLYELLY. - A group of cahers stands far up the hillside, behind Balliny and near Faunaroosca. The first and most northern fort is a circular caher nearly levelled; it measures 57 feet externally, and its wall is only 4 feet

[1] Lord Dunraven's 'Notes,' vol. i., p. 18.
[2] Borlase's *Dolmens of Ireland*, vol. i., p. 65.

thick, carefully built without filling. The second caher is circular, 78 feet externally, and has no gate; the wall is well built, and best preserved to the south. The third caher is a ring-wall of coarse, large masonry, 77 feet internally; the wall 8 feet thick and high; the jambs of the north gateway remain, the opening being only 34 inches wide, with parallel sides. The foundations of a late oblong building and an ancient circular hut lie in the garth; the latter lies to the south-west side. The fourth caher lies 60 feet to the west of the last down a steep slope. It is a scarcely traceable ring of small filling and mossy stones. The fifth caher is gapped and much defaced; it lies farther up the slope. Finally, the baun of Faunaroosca castle appears to be a straight-walled 'moher,' being of massive dry stone-work; the walls 5 feet thick. It was probably much modified when the later turret was built at its south-east corner.

DERREEN. - This now treeless slope once possessed among its oak trees thirty-three forts, of which twenty were in the two townlands of Derreen - 'numerous its cahers, unnumbered its raths and fortified strongholds'[1] - but all that I have examined or seen are in the last stage of ruin. A fort named Liscoonera lies up the hill, 730 feet above the sea. There is a nearly levelled fort, D-shaped in plan, near the lower road in Derreen East; three are nearly levelled, five more 'rings' have been more or less rebuilt as folds, but I think are of ancient origin, and three sides of a rectangular 'moher' also remain. Above these, beyond the upper road, four ring-walls, about 100 feet in diameter, lie in the townland of Knockauns, three have been levelled; the fourth, near the road, is nearly gone. The 1839 map shows two others, which seem to be only late folds.

CRUMLIN. - This townland, besides the venerable church of St. Columba, possessed five cahers; the first is oval and overthrown; the second is a small and, I think, a late 'ring.' To the east of these a straight walled enclosure, measuring from 160 to 200 feet long, and about 140 feet wide. An old bohereen leads past it to the upper road, and a 'cave' remains outside, and near its northern angle. On the hill south of the church is Caherduff, possibly so named as being on the shady side of the hill, while Caher na Grian lies on the opposite slope; these belong to Killilagh parish, and are reserved for further notes.

The upper road passes through (and of course defaces) the ring of Cahernagree ('the fort of the herds'), on the borders of Crumlin and Knockauns mountain. The fifth site in Crumlin lies to the south-west of the last, and not far from the road; it is, as usual, almost completely destroyed. The road past Faunaroosca branches to the south-east, from a point lying to the north of these forts, and leads by a steep and difficult way across deep gullies and a boggy plateau. The latter is devoid of antiquities, and extends from Knockauns mountain to Elva. The deep-cut streams, rich marsh plants, and fine open view southward over Lisdoonvarna to the hills of Inchiquin and Callan and the bays of Liscannor and Bealaghaline alone give interest to this road till we pass the venerable church of Kilmoon and emerge on the main road from Lisdoonvarna to Ballyvaughan.

---

[1] Irish 'Nennius,' p. 29.

KILLEANY AND CAHER VALLEYS (O.S. 4 and 5).

It is passing strange that of the hundreds of visitors who stay in Lisdoonvarna none have attempted to describe fully the many objects of interest in the neighbourhood.[1] Taking the road from this watering place to the south of Slieve Elva we see through a break the long side wall mortuary chapel and holy tree of Kilmoon church. East of these, on a grassy rise, is the lofty pillar stone called 'the Cross.' It is a plain crag block, 11 feet 6 inches high, 13 inches wide, and 8 inches thick, and may be of ecclesiastical not prehistoric origin.

CAHERBARNAGH, 'stone fort of the gap,' is now nearly gone. Its green ring and a few stones barely rise above the field on a low knoll beside the road. It had a shallow fosse, and the name is cognate with Lisdoonvarna 'earth fort of the gap.' It is doubtful whether this 'gap' was the deep river bed at the foot of the slope or not. Lissateeaun, a bold encircled earth fort, apparently carved out of a natural knoll, rises in this valley, and is regarded as the 'Liss' in the place-name. We have already noted the curious doubling in some of our forts, as, for example, 'Caherdoon' which is also found in Scotland and Wales, as Catherton, Caermarthen (Caer Maridun), &c., Lisdoon, and Caher-lis. This probably springs from the old use of 'cathair' for city or monastic settlement, and its appendage to the word 'dun,' which, from its occurrence in place-names (dounon) in Ireland, Britain, and Europe, in remote times and in fort names (duna)[2] in Bosnia, we may probably regard as the oldest name for fort among the Celtic tribes. The process of 'doubling' has not ceased; for we find that between 1878 and 1895 the name of the 'Black Fort' of Aran had been expanded into 'Doon du' 'hair,' 'the dun of the Black Cathair.'

A long valley lies to the east of Slieve Elva - a great brown bluff, 1109 feet high, 'with its brow to the land,' and a belt of trees on its sheltered face. Elva was the legendary scene of seven battles of King Cormac MacAirt, and overlooks the whole reach of Burren to Berneens, Cragballyconoal, and Tullycommane. On the south-eastern slope, above the little valley, where stands the interesting church of Killeany, founded by the evangelizer of Aran, lie two large cahers on a craggy ridge.

CAHERCLOGGAUN. - The name is locally understood to mean 'fort of the silver bell' but I found no legend to explain the name or account for the metal. A stream to the west is named Owencloggaun, and one might be tempted to fancy there was some legend of hidden bells of Kilmoon or Killeany, as there is at Kilnaboy and Dromcliff in the same county.

---

[1] The ruins are slightly noted in P. D.'s *Guide to Lisdoonvarna*, 1876. O'Hanlon's *Lives of the Irish Saints*, vols. iii., pp. 180, 915; vii., p. 388. 'Churches of County Clare,' *Proc. R.I.A.*, vol. vi., Ser. III., p. 132; this *Journal*, vol. xxx., pp. 279-306; 420-426. Unpublished material occurs in Ordnance Survey Letters, MSS. R.I.A., Clare, vols. 14. B. 23; 14. B. 24.

[2] So usually alleged, but 'duna,' in Hungary and Russia, is taken from the Danube (locally 'Duna'), and the river Duna at Riga.

Cahercloggaun (from the North-east).

The fort stands on a craggy knoll, with a fine open view to Callan and Moher, and overhangs the valley of Killeany, where a stream breaks out of the rocks not far away. The fort was an ancient residence of the O'Loughlins, who, probably in the fifteenth century, built a peel tower in its garth preserving the ring-wall as a bawn, as was done at Ballyganner and Ballyshanny. The place is named 'Kaercloghan' on the Elizabethan map of Munster, *circa* 1560. Hely Dutton ingeniously revises its name to 'Cahercallaghan.' Its inhabitants seem to have been in constant trouble with the Government; in 1570 Brian O'Loughlin of this place needed a pardon; the next year another inmate, Donough Mac Rorie O'Loughlin, needed another, and in 1585 a large group of its inmates received pardon, Donough appearing again with his tenants or retainers, Edmond and Owen Mac Swyny, Teige Mac Brien and Teige O'Tyerney.[1] It subsisted as a castle till 1652, when it was allotted to the transplanted Pierce Creagh of Adare, county Limerick, who eventually settled at Dangan, near Quin.

The caher is a strong ring wall of 99 feet internal, and 119 feet external diameter, and nearly circular in plan. The wall is 8 feet to 9 feet high to the north, and at least 16 feet or 18 feet to the south, where it arises out of a deep hollow to several feet above the level of the knoll that formed the platform. It is of large, well-shaped blocks, laid in courses, and from 3 feet 6 inches to 5 feet long and 3 feet high in many instances; the masonry is of unusual character, for it is laid as if the builders strove successfully to avoid breaking joint, producing a close series of upright joints which, while allowing for settlement must have greatly weakened the wall. It was fairly perfect when I first saw it in 1878, and, indeed, even in 1885, but in 1896 much had been demolished, and a large heap of road metal indicated the destroyers and possible doom of this fine fort. It is some slight comfort that

---

[1] Annual Report of the Deputy Keeper of the Records (Ireland), Fiants, Nos. 1641, 4753, see pages 21 and 38.

when the Society visited it in 1900 the demolition had evidently ceased for some time. It would be a disgrace to the people of Lisdoonvarna if they took no steps to preserve an interesting antiquity in their neighbourhood from destruction by sordid individuals and road contractors, who have abundant limestone all round. The gate-way faced the S.E. It had been demolished long before 1878, and, indeed, probably before 1839. To the left (south) of its gap heaps of grass-grown masonry, with traces of an ambrey and steps, mark the site of the castle. In the garth are the foundations of four regular curved enclosures, three to the south and one to the west.

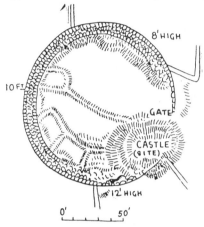

Plan of Cahercloggaun.

CRAGREAGH. - Cahermore, a ring wall of large blocks and exceptionally good and regular masonry, lies in this townland, a short distance to the N.E. of Cahercloggan, on the edge of abrupt crags. The garth is 99 feet in diameter, and the wall 5 feet or 6 feet high apparently without small filling. The defaced gateway faces the N.E. on the edge of a steep descent.

We pass above the valley, through rich grass and low hazel scrub to a high point on the western road, whence the descending valley of the Caher river can be seen nearly to Caherbannagh. The low walls of a small rectangular fort of good masonry, and another well-built 'ring' lie below the road in Lisheeneagh and Lismorahaun. In the latter townland is also a very small stone fort, barely 50 feet across, perhaps the Lismoran or Cathairpollo of the 1380 rental and other documents, which was granted, in 1665, to Murrough 'of the burnings,' Earl of Inchiquin.[1] It may be noted that another Caherpollo, *alias* Fahassane, lay close to Noughaval, perhaps at Caherwalsh, and that record remains of a fort, Cahirelany, adjoining the southern edge of Caherbullog in 1711,[2] which, perhaps, corresponds to Lisheenagh.

COOLEAMORE. - Below the eastern road on the opposite side of the valley from the last is a cromlech. It stands on a long grassy mound near a low cliff. Part of the north side and east end remain with enough of the broken bases to give a complete plan. The remaining north slab is 10 feet 7 inches long, and slopes eastward from 6 feet 8 inches to 4 feet 9 inches high, being probably hammer-dressed. The cist tapers eastward, from 6 feet 8 inches to 5 feet, but extended farther westward for 8 feet, and is therefore about 20 feet long; its axis lies N.E. and S.W., and a small pillar, 5 feet high, stands at its N.E. corner. Not far to the northeast 'Cahernateinna,' 'the fort of the fire,' is marked on the maps of 1839 and 1893; it is also described as a caher

---

[1] Roll. 19 Car. II., p. 2; MSS. R.I.A., 14. B. 19.
[2] Registry of Deeds, Dublin, 1711, Book 9, p. 35.

in the Ordnance Survey Letters, and Mr. Frost's *History of Clare,* but when we, with Dr. Wright, and Dr. Munro, examined it, we found that it was only a modern sheepfold, loosely built, with no ancient foundations; we searched carefully and found no remains either at it or in the fields for some distance around. It is difficult to discover how this non-existent fort got its curious name, and was placed on the maps and in a local 'History and Topography'; this shows the endless distrust necessary in revising our lists of mere 'map-names' and antiquities derived from published sources.

Cooleamore Cromlech from the North-east.

CAHERBULLOG. - This townland possesses two cahers, 'the two Caherbollucks,'[1] which were surrendered to the Government by Sir Tirlagh O'Brien, to whom they were regranted in 1583. The lower fort bore the townland name in 1839, but is now known as 'Cahermoyle'; this name, and that of 'Cahermore,' as already noted, are so general as to have ceased to be proper names in Clare. The upper fort is now 'Caherbullog'; the name is variously rendered 'fort of the leathern bag' or 'fort of the wind gap (bellows).' The latter term is certainly very appropriate in this valley, along which the hemmed-in gale rushes at times with the greatest violence, but the former is elsewhere accompanied by legends (resembling those of the wooden horse of Troy or the oil jars of Ali Baba) in which soldiers are introduced into a fort concealed in leathern bags. We find also that Ptolemy mentions a camp named Blatum Bolgum in ancient Britain in the first century of our era, which may suggest the same idea.

CAHERMOYLE. - This fort is featureless and much dilapidated, though it looks well from either of the roads, between which it is nearly equidistant, being near the bottom of the valley. It is a slightly oval ring, 91 feet north and south, and 96 feet east and west. The wall is 7 feet thick, 8 feet high, and coarsely built; the garth is level with the top of the wall save where the southern section has been raised by a modern wall. Wherever the outer face has fallen the clean built face of a second section appears as at Caher-screbeen, and, perhaps, implies an enlargement of the original fort by building a new rampart round it. There are no ancient foundations apparent in or around the fort.

---

[1] Grant, 1583, to Sir Tirlough O'Brien.

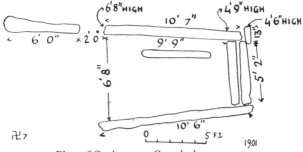

Plan of Cooleamore Cromlech.

CAHERBULLOG, the upper caher, is found near the conspicuous modern house of that name. It lies up the western slope between the old and new roads, and is a ring wall 75 feet internally, and measuring almost exactly 100 feet external diameter. It is coarsely built with two faces and small filling; it is 6 feet and 7 feet high and 11 feet thick. There are two looped enclosures in the garth, and two of those puzzling little huts, 3 feet to 5 feet internally, supposed to be kennels. Mr. R. Macalister[1] contests this view, and found that some of the natives of Fahan agreed with him – but, leaving out of the question the greater hardihood of men and dogs in those early days many valuable and well-bred dogs are still kept in even more open kennels even more exposed to the

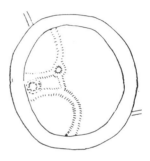

Diagram of Upper Caherbullog

inclemency of the same enemies, 'winter and bad weather,' than an animal in these small huts could well have been. Indeed we read of 'a fosse (? souterrain) in the middle of a courtyard among the dogs' in 'Bricriu's Feast,' and of the cries of the dogs and horses in the burning forts near Ventry.[2] In the field to the south of the fort is the great pit called Poulna-gollum, after the doves that once hid in its leafy sides; it leads down to a hidden river.

DERRYNAVAHAGH. - This townland has near its southern end, on the slope near the eastern road, a well-built caher of large blocks on a steep knoll; the garth is level with the top of the wall, which is from 5 feet to 7 feet high, but much gapped and defaced as a modern house and enclosure stand beside it. I failed on three occasions to find a larger caher marked to the north of the last. Still farther to the north a steep and nearly lost road leads past Caheranardurrish to the Feenagh Valley.

In dealing with the forts in their order we have had to neglect the arbitrary divisions of the long extinct parishes, so we may note that Cahercloggaun, Cragreagh, Lisheeneagh, the Caherbullogs and Derryna-

---

[1] *Trans. R.I.A.*, vol. xxxi., p. 290.

[2] 'Bricriu's Feast' (edited by Henderson), p. 31; 'Battle of Ventry' (edited by Kuno Meyer), p. 290.

vahagh are in Kilmoon, Cooleamore and 'Cahernateinna' in Killeany and Lislarheen in an intrusive angle of Rathborney.

The topographical treatment of the remaining portion of central Burren is difficult. The only well-marked natural divisions are the Aghaglinny valley and the Glenarraga valley south of Ballyvaughan; the rest is a range of nearly level plateaux, divided by the Kilcorney valley and its heights, which have already been described. It may therefore be best to describe the portion west of Carran and north of Noughaval up to Lissylisheen, and then the part from the Corkscrew Hill to Cahermackirilla, near Killeany, which (except for Mortyclough) practically completes the prehistoric remains in Burren. The shore district of Killilagh must then be described. Outside these tracts the cahers are few and far between in the other parts of Clare. The word 'complete' must, however, be taken as only implying approximate completeness, for it is scarcely possible to go a second or even a third time over one of these wild crag-lands, even after a previously careful examination, without finding the remains of forts, dolmens, 'caves,' and hut-circles, which, among the endless blocks and ridges of shimmering grey crag, can scarcely be identified (even when previously known) from a distance even of a hundred yards.

AGHAGLINNY (or FEENAGH) VALLEY (O.S. 2 and 5).

Derrynavahagh extends nearly down to the bridge at which the roads along the sides of the Caher valley unite, not far to the south of Caherbannagh. Between its termination and the bridge, but closer to the latter, an old grass-grown road may be found to the east of the present one ascending the steep hillside and forming a continuation of the old bohereen from Ballinalacken, through Cahernagree, and past Faunaroosca Castle.

This road is very steep and, naturally, out of repair, crossed in places by abrupt ledges of crag washed bare by the rains of some sixty years. It ought on no account to be attempted on a car. Our party, on the occasion of our first visit, went up too far to retreat through our driver having 'heard it could be crossed easy,' so we had to push the car, and lift it up ledges and out of gullies, holding it back with equal exertion, while the driver buttressed the horse, on its precipitous descent.

It was most probably up this pass, long before the dawn of an August morning in 1317, that Prince Donchad O'Brien marched from the muster place at Formoyle and Lettermullin below us down the long valleys, past Rathborney and banshee-haunted Lough Rask, followed by wolves and birds of prey, to the deadliest and most savage battle of that savage civil war. Prince Dermot O'Brien and his army met their rivals on the crags to the west of Corcomroe Abbey, and heaped Drom Lurgan with their dead bodies, slaying Donchad and most of his kinsmen and chiefs.

Creevagh Dolmen

Thomas J. Westropp and Friend

Cappaghkennedy Dolmen

Ballyganner Dolmen

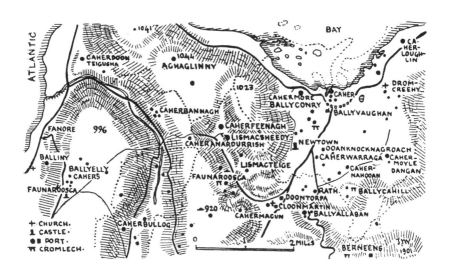

Forts near Ballyvaughan.

CAHERANARDURRISH (O.S. 5, No. 1),[1] the second of the name, occupies the summit of the pass in a craggy field on the very brow of the south-western slope of the hill, and about 750 feet above the sea. According to O'Curry the name is actually Cathair an aird rois, 'the fort of the high wood' (not door) in contrast to the wood of Feenagh in the valley behind it. A levelled fort near Mungret, in county Limerick, also bore the name of Caheranardrish. Of either 'door' or 'wood' no trace now remains. The caher is a nearly circular ring wall; the rampart coarsely built of large blocks. It is in parts, especially to the south-west, 9 feet high and 8 or 9 feet thick; it seems to have no batter or terrace; it measures 114 feet in external diameter, and is much injured to the north and east. A large gap gives access to it from the side next the roadway, and another to the south probably occupies the site of the original gateway. The garth is crowded with the ruins of modern houses, for it was inhabited down, at any rate, to the Famine years.

From it there is a fine view up the Caher valley to Caherbullog and Slieve Elva, brightened by the windings of the little river, while we look through the 'Khyber Pass' to the grey sea and the highlands of Connemara. A short distance farther and we reach the opposite brow looking down the Aghaglinny valley[2] and over the level ridges to the Telegraph Hill in eastern Clare. Below us, in a grassy nook surrounded by crags, lie two great cahers; while groves of trees, a rare and very pleasant sight in Burren, show

---

[1] The fifth, and most other sheets of the Survey, can be procured in 16 sheets, on the scale of 25 inches to the mile. Where possible I now give the subsidiary division as here.

[2] The Aghaglinny fort is noted in the *Journal, supra*, p. [66].

that the name Feenagh (Fiodnaigh in the O'Brien Rental, *circa* 1380) was not unwarranted in olden days.

CAHERFEENAGH[1] (O.S. 2). - The caher lies close to a ruined village, and on a sunny slope. It is a fine oval enclosure, the longest axis being north north-west and south south-east, and measuring 152 feet externally and from 95 feet to 105 feet internally, the latter measurement being obscured by fallen walls and bushes. The shorter axis east north-east and west south-west is 114 feet 6 inches externally, and 81 feet 4 inches internally.

The wall is built in three stages or terraces and in at least two sections; the lower terrace is 4 feet high and wide, the second 4 feet 5 inches high and 2 feet to 4 feet wide, the upper 5 feet high and 4 or 5 feet wide. The wall is 12 feet 8 inches to 14 feet 8 inches high to the north, east, and south, and has a batter of 1 in 12, being 17 feet 4 inches thick at the base. The masonry is curiously divergent in character; if we commence at the south and go round the eastern face we find it good and of fairly large flat stones, many 3 feet 6 inches long and 3 feet high, they are laid as stretchers in the base courses but as headers above.[2]

The filling is large, and is rather built than thrown in, the ivy has grown through the wall, and, on the day I planned the fort, a keen west wind sang and groaned through the interstices in a way which might easily have established the caher as a haunted fort, like the Lisananimas. We next meet a slight breach[3] and (facing the north-east) the gap of the gateway passing through the wall, but too defaced for measurement.[4] To the north of this the outer wall has fallen showing the clean built face of the inner section; the wall is here 8 feet 3 inches high and of large blocks.[5] In the next segment the masonry is very inferior, large and small stones being used indiscriminately in the facing, and spawls freely used to stop the crannies. In the northern segment large well laid blocks again appear of 'cyclopean' type.[6] The western segment is completely overthrown.

Internally there are considerable remains of three terraces, most of the lowest is intact, the second has suffered much, and was evidently once much higher as it has the remains of two flights of steps[7] to the north north-west and south south-west; these steps are 31 inches long, and 7 inches or 8 inches high, six remain above the debris in the northern flight, and only three or four in the southern; they run straight up the wall. The inner face of the upper terrace is too much defaced in many parts to enable us to decide as to the former existence of steps to the summit of the wall. The garth has been cleared, and modern walls have been built along the summit.

---

[1] Lismacshida and ffinagh were held by George Martin, of Gragans, in about 1675 (1675 Survey at Edenvale, p. 42). The same document states that Ed. Nugent held Cruogh, *alias* Clonmartin, Ballyvahane, Lisgogan, and Ballyallabon, in the same parish.
[2] 'a' on plan.
[3] 'b' on plan.
[4] 'c' on plan.
[5] 'd' on plan.
[6] 'e' on plan.
[7] 'f' on plan.

CAHERLISMACSHEEDY (O.S. 5, No. 2). - A massive and well preserved cliff fort remains about 700 feet to the south-east of Caherfeenagh, in the adjoining townland of Lismacsheedy. Its rampart is half moon-shaped in plan, abutting on a low cliff 30 feet to 60 feet high, and practically perpendicular, overhanging a fertile valley, pleasantly planted. The plan, like that of Cahercommane and some forts in Scotland and even Hungary, has an important bearing on the question of the age of the cahers as depriving of force the belief that Dun Aenghus necessarily consisted of three complete rings till the sea undercut the cliff below its walls. Above the caher rise craggy slopes and low terraces of grey and weather-shattered limestone up to the top of the hills in Aghaglinny.[1]

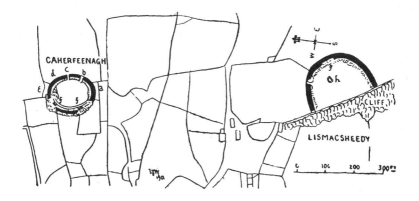

The Cahers of Feenagh and Lismacsheedy, Rathborney.

The rampart is very coarsely built of large slabs, numbers of which have been levered up in the adjoining fields; in some cases they have been propped with blocks underneath, like the slabs raised near the dolmens of Parknabinnia.[2] The wall is 18 feet thick at the ends and from 12 feet to 16 feet thick in other places; it is from 8 feet to 10 feet high, and seems to have been built in two sections, the inner 3 feet to 5 feet thick; it has large filling in some places. It is in fair preservation, save at the end of the southern horn, but has no trace of a gateway. The space enclosed is 170 feet along the cliff, where a modern wall has been built for the safety of the cattle, for the fort was formerly open between the horns; the garth is 147 feet deep. There is a recess in the wall to the north-east, perhaps for steps,[3] but now quite defaced, and it may have been formed by a collapse of the facing. The foundations of a hut D-shaped in plan, and 18 feet internally lie in the garth to the north-east.[4]

---

[1] See *Journal, supra*, vol. xxxi., p. [66].
[2] See *Journal*, vol. xxviii. (1898), p. 357 [39].
[3] 'g' on plan.
[4] 'h' on plan.

LISMACTIEGE (O.S. 5, No. 2). - At least seven ruined cahers lie on the slopes of the valley; the glen trends southward to Cahermacun, with grassy fields and the clear golden brook of the Rathborney River; to its left side barer crags arise. On the base of these lie two greatly defaced forts, one named Lismactiege, nearly levelled, though on a fine site, on a rocky shoulder at the bend of the valley. It is mentioned in the will of Gillananaeve O'Davoren, of Cahermacnaughten, in 1675, and was probably demolished as building material for a ruined village and modern farm between it and the road.

FAUNAROOSCA (O.S. 5). To the south of Lismactiege on the righthand side of the glen is a townland called, like that we have examined in Killonaghan, Faunaroosca. If this term (like the other Faunaroosca in Killonaghan) means 'slope of the quarrel,' the presence of the cahers in both makes it probable that it is no arbitrary name. The two lower cahers are much levelled and overgrown, and are confused by modern

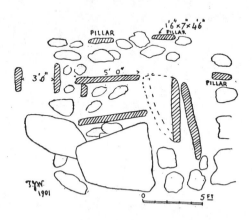

Faunaroosca Cromlech, Rathborney.

walls; half way between them lay a small cairn. Higher up the slope above the farm-house and on a shoulder of the hill 200 feet above the brook is the caher of Faunaroosca, a small ring fort built of large thin blocks in courses and laid as stretchers; the wall is 8 feet thick and barely 5 feet high, with small filling.

About forty yards above, and to the south of the caher, commanding a view over the abruptly rounded ridge of Croagh to the terraced hills across the valley is a very curious, but damaged, dolmen. It consisted of a small cist tapering eastward, the sides are 5 feet and 6 feet long, and 3 feet and 4 feet apart. The covering slab is from 3 feet 6 inches to 6 feet wide and 6 feet long. There are three end slabs suggestive of smaller chambers to the ends, and, perhaps, an outer fence of slabs as at Iskancullin and Ballyhogan. Three pillars less than 4 feet 6 inches high form with slabs a similar fence to the north about 3 feet from the cist.

CAHERMACUN TO RATHBORNEY. - South from the last, on an opposite shoulder of the same hill behind the farm-houses of Cahermacun, is a small irregular caher of the same name; it is greatly gapped, is about 120 feet in external diameter, and 900 feet above the sea. There are two small structures, possibly folds, and the cairn of Cairnbeg in a wall in Poulacappul near the top whence a plateau, which I am told is devoid of antiquities, extends to Lislarheen fort.

Near the road we find a nearly levelled caher opposite Faunaroosca, and a bramble-pestered circular caher nearly levelled to the field and about 80 feet in diameter near a bend of the stream in Croagh.

The earthen forts of Duntorpa and Rathborney and the caher of Cloomartin lie across the mouth of the valley. The first is planted with bushes, and the second forms part of the burial ground of Rathborney Church to which it gives its name, 'the Rath of Burren'; it is much defaced by interments, but is very well marked. Doontorpa possibly derives its name from a certain Torptha or Torpa, chief of the Corcomroes in about A.D. 750, or of his contemporary, a prince of Thomond.[1] The caher of Cloomartin is reduced to a ring of low and broken mounds.

GLENARRAGA OR BALLYVAUGHAN VALLEY (O.S. 2 and 5).

The antiquities of this valley[2] have suffered severely by the hand of man; even in 1839, as the Ordnance Survey letters state, Ooanknocknagroach fort had been 'just effaced,' and Caherwarraga destroyed and 'blotted off the face of the land.' The portion of the valley north of Ballyallaban lies in Drumcreehy parish, the remainder in Rathborney.

BALLYVAUGHAN.- Three raths and the remains of a third large fort of earth and stones, called a caher, lie near the pier of this little village. The 'caher' is a half-moon bank of earth and large blocks, with a few bushes growing upon it, resting on the drift without foundations; much was cut away by the sea before the present road and quay wall were made. The peel tower of Ballyvaughan adjoined it, but has entirely perished. The mounds extend for about 620 feet, and enclose a space about 430 feet long and 280 feet deep; they are 12 feet thick and 5 feet or 6 feet high.

The sea at this point has evidently made considerable inroads on the shore, whose foundations in the form of low reefs render all approach to the pier difficult and risky:-

> 'A dismal sound is that the shore surf makes upon the strand;
> A woful boom the wave makes breaking up the northern beach,
> Butting against the polished rock.'[3]

As we have pointed out before, the Irish disposition, with its keen sense of the beauty of nature (far in advance of the taste of other mediæval nations), and its melancholy undercurrent of romantic feeling, frequently selected sites for forts more noteworthy for the view than for either convenience or strength.

Ballyvaughan derives its name from the family of O'Beachain, and is named, with the neighbouring lands of Ballyconry, Dangan, and Feenagh, in the O'Brien's rental, *circa* 1380. It finally passed to the O'Briens in about

---

[1] Book of Ballymote. Torpa, son of Cermad, grandson of Dima, who, in A.D. 636, claimed the kingship of Munster from Failbe Flan.

[2] The name Glenarraga is in use among the peasantry for this valley, but only appears on the maps at 'Glenarra House.' It is possible that Caherwarraga may really be derived from the same source.

[3] Dirge of Cael - 'Colloquy of the Ancients.'

1540, in consequence of a disturbance which arose out of a small cattle robbery. This is recorded at full length in a deed published by Hardiman,[1] and gives an interesting picture of the lawlessness and the insecurity of life and property under the rule of Morogh the Thanist. The aggrieved persons set up crosses of interdiction, and got heavy fines of cattle, sheep and goats, eighteen litters of swine, a woman's gown, a shirt and a barread; but the place, after all, was adjudged to O'Brien in the end.

CAHERLOUGHLIN (O.S. 2), a large caher on the ridge near the sea, to the north of the venerable ivied church of Dromcreehy, has, since 1839, been divided into several fields, and in consequence is defaced and nearly levelled. It may, perhaps, have been named from Lochlain, chief of the Corcomroes, who died A.D. 983.

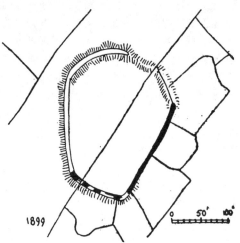

CAHERMORE-BALLY-CONRY[2] (O.S. 2). - To the west of Ballyvaughan, on a low elevation, with a

Cahermore-Ballyconry, Ballyvaughan.

beautiful view of the bay and valley and of the hills towards Finnevara, lies a large stone fort, bearing the common name of Cahermore; it is the Baile i chonradhi of the 1380 rental.[3] In plan, it is an irregular oval ring, 266 feet over all, north and south, and 212 feet, east and west. A modern wall divides its garth; the western part is laid in grass and the eastern in tillage, so no internal foundations remain. The western side is reduced to shapeless heaps of earth and stones, densely covered with hazel and brambles, and peopled with rats and birds; portions to the east are still 5 feet and 6 feet high, with good though small facing, and, where most perfect, 10 feet to 11 feet thick.

A cromlech lay in the fields to the south of Ballyvaughan; it is said to have been a small cist of four slabs and a cover; it has been removed since 1839. The adjoining seven forts are dilapidated and of no great size, except Lisanard rath, which is about 170 feet long; of the seventh caher only the souterrain and the foundations of the south-east segment remain.

KNOCKNAGROAGH (O.S. 5, No. 3) has, besides the foundations of the levelled Ooanknocknagroagh (which is called on the key-map, but not elsewhere, 'Boenknocknagroagh'), a better preserved, though defaced, caher near the same bohereen, a straight-walled moher to the north of the last, and

---

[1] *Trans. R.I.A.*, vol. xv., p. 28.
[2] In the Book of Distribution (1655), p. 474, Balleconree includes the 'wast rocks of Barrinononkio.'
[3] *Trans. R.I.A.*, vol. xv., pp. 39, 43 - *baile i chonradi.*

a small levelled fort with a souterrain on a slightly rising ground near Wood village. The foundation blocks of the destroyed Caherwarraga remain on a low knoll in a field adjoining the townland, but in Newtown or Ballynua. From its name it is probable that an eanagh or market was held near it, as at Eanty and Ballykinvarga, in this county, and Emania and other noted sites in other parts of our island. Dr. Macnamara suggests, however, that it contains the compound found in the local name of the valley of 'Glenarraga.'

DANGAN (O.S. 5, No. 4). - The eastern sides of the valley abounds in fort sites, though only two are of any great interest owing to the hand of the destroyer, whether road-maker, farmer, treasure seeker, or, the worst reputed of the foes of our ruins, the rabbit hunter. The townland of Dangan forms a grassy nook among steep, bare hills, with bold terraces and caves, and extends to their summit, over 1000 feet above the sea. No ancient structures are found up the crags; but there are three levelled cahers of small size, and a fourth, named Cahermoyle, is the largest and in better preservation.

CAHERMOYLE is probably the 'Cahernagree' in Dangan, named more than once in documents of the seventeenth century.[1] It rests on a low grassy knoll, and is hidden from view to the north by an abrupt craggy hill, ending in a ridge covered with coarse grass and bracken.

It is a ring wall, enclosing a garth 84 feet in internal diameter; the wall is 7 feet to 8 feet thick, and reduced to 7 feet high to the north and east, being levelled almost to the foundation at the west. It had a terrace paved with large thin slabs, 4 feet and 5 feet by 3 feet; this remains along the northern and southern segments, and in the former place is well preserved, being 3 feet high and 2 feet 6 inches to 3 feet wide. One recess, with a projecting block or step about 18 inches above the ground, still remains. The masonry to the north is coarse, of long, thin blocks, like the outer wall of Cahercommane; but there is much better though more irregular masonry to the east. Large field boulders, probably left *in situ*, are embodied on the wall. The filling is of small, round, field stones, and the base blocks, as usual, are the largest now apparent, often 4 feet long.

Cahermoyle – Dangan.

---

[1] As, for example, the Book of Distribution, p. 477, in 1641 and 1651, and a grant of 1668.

The gateway faces the east, where the wall is 7 feet 8 inches thick. Its inner passage through the terrace is 3 feet 6 inches wide, and its outer 2 feet 6 inches; it was flanked on each side by three posts, 4 feet high and 12 inches to 15 inches square. There are two large lintels – the inner, 8 feet 10 inches by 1 foot 6 inches by 10 inches; the outer, 8 feet 4 inches by 1 foot 6 inches by 12 inches; but they have been removed to admit cattle;[1] for it was peopled by sheep and bullocks on the day of my visit, and now (as probably two and a-half centuries since) deserves the name 'Cahernagree.' There are no hut foundations or 'traverses' (cross walls) in the garth.

The garth contains two 'caves' at right angles to each other, which I believe join into an L-shaped souterrain, though not fully accessible; the bones of sheep and other animals thrown into these in recent times warn us to caution in dealing with 'finds' in forts. One passage lies nearly north and south, and is at least 15 feet long, 4 feet wide, and at present is 3 feet high; the other lies at right angles, and it is the same size and (if it joins the first) about the same length as the other; the sides incline, and are of small stonework; both 'caves' are roofed with large slabs.

The fort, despite its secluded position, has a lovely view across Galway Bay, which is seen through a gap in the craggy ridge; it has an unimpeded outlook to the west to the Rath of Ballyallaban and into the Aghaglinny valley. There is a very massive, but evidently late, house near the fort, and a hut of doubtful age lies on the crags at some distance from its northern side.

BALLYCAHILL (O.S. 5, Nos. 3 and 7). – This townland[2] adjoins Dangan to the west. It once possessed a dolmen and seven cahers; one at the summit of the boldly-terraced bluff is shown on the map as partly levelled, and as 824 feet above the sea; another, on the slope, is an irregular moher; two, near the site of the cromlech and near the farmhouse, are small and levelled; two others, to the north of the bohereen, are quite overthrown and crowded with sloe and thorn bushes. It only remains to note briefly a less dilapidated fort.

CAHERNAHOOAN is a small ring wall, about 100 feet across, and lying on a grassy ridge. The wall had a facing of unusually rounded field blocks, with a filling of small, rounded stones, in consequence of which it has mostly collapsed. A short stretch to the east is about 5 feet high, and is from 5 feet to 6 feet thick; most of the wall in the northern half is defaced and overgrown. A late house-site and a deep hollow, with stone walls, probably a dug-out 'cave,' appear in the garth, and account for the defaced state of the caher. In a wall not far to the west is a hollowed block of limestone, resembling an ancient corn-crusher. I have seen similar ones since then at Moheramoylan and near Caheraneden. Further eastward, near the bohereen, is curious 'boat-shaped' enclosure, of doubtful age, with five large blocks to the east and four to the west.

BALLYALLABAN (O.S. 5, No. 7). – Few of our cahers are more beautiful in situation than those of Ballyallaban. When we leave the Gleninshen cromlechs we pass round the grey, bare brow of the hill, through crags and

---

[1] The view shows the structure before the removal of the inner lintel. The outer lintel lies to the right.

[2] The *baile i cathail* of the 1380 O'Brien rental.

streams, the wet rocks shining like silver network across the glen. Then the roads descends in loops above the Ballyvaughan valley, till we see on the slope below us a group of forts as shattered and outworn as the craggy shoulder on which they rest:-

'Forgotten, rusting on those iron hills,
Rotting on the wild shore, like ribs of wreck,
Or like some old-world mammoth bulked in ice.'

Beyond, lie two majestic ranges of terraced mountains, pearly grey with violet shadows. Through the open valley we see the distant city of Galway and the foam-brightened sea. Below us lie Ballyvaughan and the ruins of Newtown and Rathborney, while groves of trees, cultivated land, and green slopes, relieve the prevailing greys and blues of the landscape.

Cahermore-Ballyallaban.

CAHERMORE. - A fine stone fort, practically circular, measures 168 feet internally. The wall is from 6 feet to 9 feet high and 8 feet or 9 feet thick, with two faces of large well-fitted blocks (often 4 feet by 3 feet by 2 feet), with large filling. The batter (where apparent) is slight, and in some places the wall even hangs out. There is the unusual feature of a plinth or projecting base course (such as we see in our round towers and oldest oratories) along the north-western segment.[1] The inner face and filling have been removed from about 4 feet above the ground, leaving what Lord Dunraven considered a terrace, but which (like those at Balliny and elsewhere) is a mere makeshift. The light often shines through the interstices of the outer face with curious effect. Some trace of steps remained to the north-west, two blocks being once apparent; they have been, I think, removed or covered. The gateway (*a*) is a late mortar-built turret facing the south-east;[2] it has a recess for a porter's seat, on the north side. The gateway has an old-looking lintel, 6 feet 4 inches long, and is 4 feet 8 inches wide, and 6 feet high (no unusual dimensions for ancient dry-stone gate-ways), and, perhaps,

---

[1] A plinth also occurs at Kilcashel Fort in county Mayo.
[2] Part of it has fallen since this was written.

springing from the use of the materials of the original gateway in the reconstruction.

The garth contains some irregular enclosures; a long wall (*f*) crosses it from the south to the north north-east, probably forming a 'traverse'; this feature is found at Caherscrebeen and in some Irish and German forts. A circular hut foundation lies to the north, and an oblong building to the south (*b*). The latter measures 36 feet by 15 feet, and its sides and west end lean inward, which led Lord Dunraven and Miss Stokes to suppose that it had been a boat-shaped oratory; but its thin walls, 2½ feet to 3 feet thick, could never have borne the thrust of an arched vault or the weight of a corbelled one of 15 feet span. A rock cutting, with a wall and square platform, lie before the gateway (30 feet distant); another cutting approaches the fort on the north, and many blocks have been levered up and left unused on the crags. From the regular curve of part of the boundary wall of the field, about 100 feet to the west of the fort, and

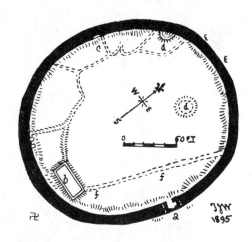

Cahermore - Ballyallaban

its evident following of the curve of the rampart, we might suppose that (as at Glenquin) there had been an outer, later, and inferior ring wall, measuring, perhaps, 400 feet across.

A 'moher,' or straight-walled enclosure, lay 90 feet south from Cahermore; it measures 117 feet across, with walls 6 feet thick, and has been nearly levelled since 1895.

A small ring wall, 70 feet from the last and to the east, occupies a slightly higher knoll. It had a wall built in two independent sections from the crag upward, as I had two opportunities of observing while it was in course of demolition in 1898. The wall was only 4 feet 6 inches high, and the sections were (the outer) 4 feet 3 inches thick, (the inner) 4 feet 1 inch. The foundations of the southern section still remain as the road contractors left it. A third foundation of an oval caher lies in a grassy field east of Cahermore.

It is a shameful fact that, in a country incumbered with stones, ancient buildings should be so wantonly swept away for the sordid gain of private persons; but educated public interest in and respect for ancient Irish remains are almost non-existent in the country.

RATH. - At the foot of the hill, 2000 feet to the north-east of Cahermore, is a very fine rath, nearly circular, thickly planted with trees and underwood, and girt by an earthwork, rising in parts 20 feet to 30 feet above the fosse, which is 6 feet deep, and usually full of water. The rath is over 100 feet in internal diameter, and about 200 feet over the fosse.

Three other stone forts, now defaced and almost levelled, lie along the edge of a 'turlough,' which the Rathborney stream in wet seasons converts into a lake.

The only other fort site at the southern end of the valley is (so far as I can find) one above Gragan Castle and near the road at the Corkscrew Hill, where it is plainly visible; it consists of two low concentric rings covered with bracken and quite defaced.

THE PLATEAUX OF CENTRAL BURREN.

ISKANCULLIN (O.S. 9, No. 11). - This townland lies to the west of the road and Carran Church, and to the south of Poulawack. It may be considered to be an upland of Noughaval ('Oughaval, as the people call it locally).[1] There are two little cahers not far from the road, circular in plan, built of thin but regular slabs, the walls seldom measure more than 5 feet in height. A crag track, running almost due westward from opposite the church, leads past the southern caher along the foot of a very low ridge. The holly trees, which gave the place part of its name, have perished, but a close-occurring series of outflows of springs from the seams of the ridge (not very usual in the uplands of Burren) fill several shallow pools, full of frogs and shadowed by hazels. Following this track nearly to the mearing of Noughaval we find in the fields adjoining the boundary-wall a group of antiquities of some interest.

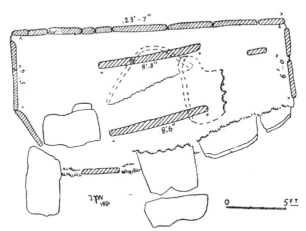

Iskancullin Cromlech.

---

[1] See for a similar elision *Irish Names of Places*, Dr. Joyce, 1st series (1871), p. 25.

A small caher,[1] little over 50 feet across (marked, but not distinguished from modern enclosures on the new maps), lies on the summit. It is built like the other cahers of long, thin flags, and consequently is of regular masonry. The wall varies from 5 feet to 6 feet in thickness and height, and can be located from the Carran road by two lofty shepherds 'outlooks' or pillars of dry stones. Within the mossy garth, among low tufts of wild roses, is a 'cave' 9 feet or 10 feet long, 3 feet 8 inches wide, and about 4 feet high, the sides are of dry masonry, and the top of thin slabs, rising over the present level of the garth.

Close to the caher to the south-west is an irregular 'moher,' rudely rectangular, about 130 feet by 100 feet, the wall seldom 5 feet high and 4 feet thick, of the same masonry as the cahers. Another 'moher,' about 150 feet each way, its walls gapped, but parts rising over 8 feet high, also of similar masonry, and without interior foundations, stands on the edge of Noughaval, a contemporaneous wall extending for 60 feet into Iskancullin.

In the field between and south of the mohers is a fine cromlech,[2] standing on nearly bare crag, with no sign of a cairn about it. It is, as usual, a cist tapering eastward, 8 feet 6 inches long, and 5 feet 2 inches to 4 feet 9 inches wide, made of thin slabs, 6 inches to 9 inches thick. The covering slabs have fallen. An enclosure of slabs surround it at a distance of from 15 inches to 30 inches at the sides, and 5 feet to 7 feet at the ends. Nine slabs stand to the north, at least five to the south and three to each end; the largest of these are 4 feet 8 inches by 4 feet, and 6 feet 3 inches by 2 feet 8 inches. The west end is slightly bent. There seems to have been a smaller cist within the enclosure near the east end of the main cist.

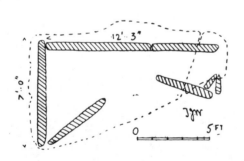

The Eastern Cromlech, Berneens.

BERNEENS (O.S. 5, No. 11). - We ascend once more to the high ground 'on the far hills, long, cold and grey,' behind Ballyallaban, and resume our survey near the cromlechs of Gleninshen, which we have already described.[3] The eastern cromlech of Berneens lies at no great distance from the

---

[1] Called locally 'Caherlochlannach,' a modern name not unfrequently applied to such forts, not known in the earlier days, but translated from the unhappy popular term 'Danish forts,' which we owe to Molyneux copying Giraldus Cambrensis.

[2] Mr. James Frost called my attention to this, as it is not marked on the maps. It is well known to all the men and women of the place as 'Labba yermudh' aus' granya.' As, in so many other cases, it was omitted from the Ordnance Survey, whose officials were (at least in Dublin) very unwilling to admit either ruins or names omitted in the less detailed Survey of 1839, while omitting the distinctive marks of forts shown clearly on the older maps.

[3] *Journal,* vol. xxix. (1899), p. 381 [59].

edge of Ballyallaban, in a field on the hillslope, to the north of the cromlechs of Gleninshen, already described. The cist is perfect, save for the
collapse of a block and the distortion of two others in the south side.[1] It
stands in a cairn which has been nearly removed, faces the east-north-east,
and tapers and slopes eastward from 7 feet to 22 inches. The top edges have
been hammered to a slope. The north side was a single slab 12 feet 3 inches
long, though now cracked; it slopes from 6 feet 2 inches high at the west to
1 foot 8 inches at the east, the west end slab 7 feet long by 6 feet 2 inches
high; the top is 13 feet long, and 7 feet 6 inches to 2 feet wide and 10 inches
thick.

BALLYGANNER

Journal xxvii. (1897), pp.119-120 [26-27]. – Since publishing the former
account I have again gone carefully over the southern portion of the ground,
and have been able to add a few more notes. To the south of the more
eastern of the 'two rude enclosures' (which has a spring flowing out of the
foot of the rocky knoll on which it stands), and due eastward from the fallen
cromlech near Caheraneden is a low grassy mound overgrown with low wild
roses. Set in the mound, lying north and south, is a block of limestone about
4 feet long; other slabs are seen nearly buried, and it seems very probable
that these are relics of small cist and tumulus. The same large field
possesses curious oblong mounds, rising a foot or 18 inches above the
general surface of the ground.

The three-chambered cromlech had an annexe of low blocks to the north,
like that in the cromlech on the hill top in Parknabinnia.[2] It is nearly buried
in earth and moss.[3] There are two fairly large cairns to the north-west of it,
near Cahernaspekee, they are 8 to 10 feet in height.

The 'ring wall, surrounding a sort of cairn,' is a very puzzling structure. It
is a well-built, irregular enclosure, 150 feet by 120 feet, made of blocks laid
as stretchers. It has a gateway to the south-east facing the eastern cromlech
in Ballyganner south. The outer lintel has fallen, but the inner face is
perfect; the outer lintel is 5 feet 6 inches by 1 foot 7 inches by 10 inches, the
inner 6 feet by 1 foot 6 inches by 10 inches. The gateway measures 4 feet 6
inches outside, and 4 feet 6 inches inside, being over 5 feet high, but partly
buried in rubbish, and was nearly hidden in hazels on the inner side. The
'cairn' is a ring wall of large blocks filled up to a height 6 feet over the level
of the garth with smaller blocks, the wall having a batter. It is nearly buried
in a great mass of fallen stones, evidently remains of some considerable
upper building. Occurring, as it does, close to the very noteworthy caher
which encloses the eastern cromlech of Ballyganner north, the question at
once arises whether it is another of a group of sepulchral enclosures of a
kind not yet described.

A circle of slabs set on end remains in the craggy field to the south of the
caher with the cromlech, and is either a hut circle or a burial place. There

[1] *Ibid..*
[2] *Journal,* xxviii. (1898), plan 3, p. 358 [40].
[3] This cromlech has also been figured in vol. xxx. (1900), p. 402.

are two slab huts, probably of late date, in the adjoining fields to the north of
the cromlech-caher, and another well-built caher with gapped walls a
quarter of a mile south-east from the smaller cromlech of Ballyganner South.
In Ballyganner South, to the west of the castle, and about half way between
it and Ballykinvarga, there is another caher on a rising ground. It consists
of a massive well-built ring wall, 11 feet 4 inches thick, and of unusually
large blocks, but now only 4 feet to 5 feet high. The gateway faced the east;
the outer opening was only 2 feet 9 inches wide (like Ballyelly and
Caherdooneerish); the passage through the wall splays inward to 6 feet 9
inches wide. In the southern side is a long souterrain 6 feet to 6 feet 8
inches wide, the sides slightly sloped. The top has fallen in for about 20 feet,

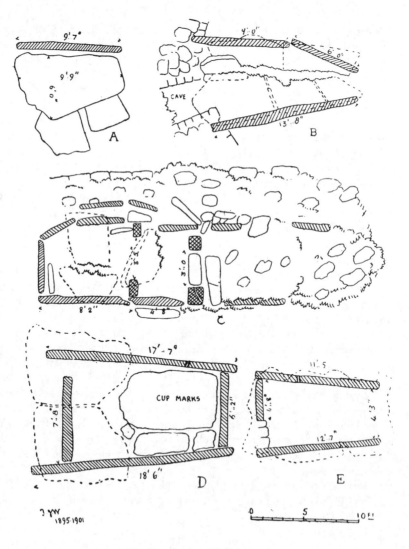

The Cromlechs of Ballyganner.

thence it curves near its western end, keeping concentric to the curve of the caher wall. It is 5 feet to 6½ feet high; the sides are of fair masonry, with a couple of ambrey-like recesses, possibly formed by the removal of certain facing blocks. Along the top of the wall on each side is laid a cornice of long slabs projecting 12 inches or 13 inches over the edge, and the whole is roofed by long, thin slabs. It is a conservatory of wall-rue and hartstongue ferns.

Before the gateway is a mound, with a low kerbing of nearly buried blocks, and in the next field to the east there is a heap of large slabs lying one on the other. The new Ordnance Survey maps mark the word 'cromlech' between these objects, but I am very doubtful whether this is correct, and the peasantry deny that there was ever a 'Lobba' standing there in human memory.

To the west of the fort, but between the bounds of Lisket, a conspicuous and fairly perfect cairn of earth and stones rises to a height of 7 feet or 8 feet, whence the ground slopes rapidly to the Noughaval road opposite Ballykinvarga.

Beside the bohereen from the Kilfenora road is another circle of slabs in the field, a few yards to the south-east of the larger caher on the hill top south of the great cromlech.

In giving here plans of all the more complete cromlechs of Ballyganner, we need only refer to the descriptions already published. The great cromlech of Ballyganner Hill, and the cromlech of Clooneen by the late William C. Borlase in *Dolmens of Ireland*, vol. i., p. 67, and p. 80. The eastern cromlech of Ballyganner South; the 'caher-cromlech,' the fallen cromlech, and the 'pillared cromlech,' near Caheraneden, in Ballyganner North, will be found described by me in the *Proceedings of the Royal Irish Academy*, vol. iv., Series III., page 542, but with only one illustration of the 'pillared cromlech.'

The cromlechs in Ballyganner North, of which one only has hitherto been illustrated, call for notice here. When the other papers were commenced, I had included the cromlechs along with the forts, but a wish to help Mr. Borlase in his work on *The Dolmens of Ireland*, altered my intention, although he was unable to use the material I sent him for the group north of Ballyganner Hill.

There are two doubtful specimens, one already mentioned as in a small tumulus, but only the west slab is *in situ*, and a second slab appears; it was possibly a small cist. The other is a small enclosure of slabs, set on end, but much defaced, lying in the centre of a ring wall of unusual rudeness, faced with waterworn slabs.

To the north-east of this, near Caheraneden, is the 'pillared cromlech' (C). I found traces nearly buried in moss and rubbish of a parallel kerbing of low stones, a few feet from the northern side. The main cromlech consisted of three compartments, 8 feet by 6 feet, with two pillars, 5 feet high, which rose about a foot over the roof slabs, the central chamber, 5½ feet by 6 feet, with pillars 6 feet high (2 feet above the roof); the third or 'eastern' compartment is defaced. A long lintel at the foot of the taller pillars probably rested on them, forming a trilithon, part of the top of the southern pillar having split off, as if from some superincumbent weight. The structure lies N.N.E. and S.S.W., and is of most unusual plan.

Another doubtful structure is the slab enclosure. It consists of an oblong enclosure of slabs, 4 feet high, the 'eastern' side and ends remaining; a small square chamber adjoins the 'northern' end; it lies N.N.E. and S.S.W.

South from the last are the blocks of a fallen cromlech of the usual type (A); the north side is standing; it and the top slab are each 9 feet 8 inches by 6 feet 8 inches. It lies east and west. A sort of road made by removing the top slabs of the crag (whose fissures lie nearly north and south), leads towards Caheraneden.

East from the last is the very remarkable 'cromlech caher' (B), a ring wall, within whose enclosure and partly embedded in the wall, is a large cromlech. It lies east and west, tapering eastward, from 7 feet to 4 feet, and consists of three side slabs, the southern 13 feet 8 inches long. The massive top slab is broken into five fragments, probably by fire. By the accident of using the interior as a 'dark room,' to change films in a camera, the curious fact became apparent that a small souterrain, 3 feet 8 inches wide, built of small masonry, roofed by slabs 4½ feet long, and nearly filled with small stones, ran through the rampart for about 3 feet into the cist itself. It in no place lay under the great side slabs.

In Ballyganner South, farther eastward, and beyond the group of forts in which the last cromlech stands, is a very perfect cist of five slabs (E) in the remains of a cairn. It lies W.N.W., and E.S.E. The north and south sides measure 11 feet 5 inches, and 12 feet 7 inches. It tapers eastward from 4 feet 8 inches to 4 feet 3 inches. The top slab has two curious channels, but manifestly water-worn, probably ages before the block was raised; it measures 13 feet long by 7 feet 8 inches wide.

The great cromlech (D) stands near the summit of the hill above the castle and caher of Ballyganner, and near two other ruined stone forts. It lies N.E. and S.W., the north and south sides being 17 feet 4 inches, and 18 feet 6 inches long,[1] and 7 feet 8 inches high at the western end. The edges of the side slabs, and the closing slab of the west end are hammer-dressed; the great top slab, once about 11 feet by 20 feet, and 12 inches to 16 inches thick, has broken into four parts; the eastern have fallen into the cist, and have little basins in the top as in Swedish dolmens. The interior narrows eastward, from 9 feet 7 inches to 6 feet 2 inches. It has been described and illustrated by Mr. Borlase, alone of the actual Ballyganner group.

In Clooneen is another nearly perfect dolmen towards the eastern end of the long ridge on which the last described monument stands, and on the southern slope. The south side is 15 feet 3 inches long, 4½ feet high, and about 1 foot thick. Three distorted slabs remain along the north side, and there are traces of an outer enclosure 3 feet outside the cist, the slabs over 4 feet high. It tapers eastwards, from 5 feet 6 inches to 3 feet 2 inches; the top is broken across the middle; it was about 15 feet long, and over 8 feet wide. It is described and illustrated by Mr. Borlase, who notes the resemblance of it and other cromlechs in Clare to those of Portugal.[2]

---

[1] Not 40 feet, as stated by Hely Dutton in the *Statistical Survey of County Clare.*
[2] *Dolmens of Ireland*, vol. i., p. 80.

'Thus the Ballyganner group of antiquities consists of Caherkyletaan, in Kyletaan; Cahercuttine, with two cromlechs, a cairn, a slab circle with a 'cave' and a small caher with an annexe; Caherwalsh, with a slab enclosure and two cairns; Lismoher; and the foundation of a caher in Noughaval; Cahernaspekee, with a cave, 'moher,' and cairn. Two ring walls, one with a slab hut; mound with a cist; earth mounds; the 'pillared cromlech'; Caheraneden, with slab enclosure and rock cutting; fallen cromlech. Three huts of doubtful age; ancient enclosure near the great boulder; ring-wall and 'walled cairn' and another caher, with a cromlech and 'cave' - all in Ballyganner North. Cromlech in a cairn, caher, slab circle; Ballyganner Castle and caher; great cromlech; two cahers and slab circle on Ballyganner Hill; caher, with 'cave' and supposed cromlech - all in Ballyganner South. Caher in Lisket. Three cahers, tumulus, and cromlech, in Clooneen. Caher in Ballyhomulta. The great caher, abattis, pillars, cromlech, wells, and three lesser cahers in Ballykinvarga. Kilcameen fort, graveyard, and cist; Caherminaun; fort with hut hollows; Caherlahertagh; and two other cahers in Caherminaun. Two cahers near Kilfenora road; levelled cahers in Maryville; caher with 'cave'; Ballyshanny Castle in a caher; caher in Ballyshanny. Knockacarn cairn and three forts on the bounds of Kiltennan and Ballyhomulta. While we must consider, as outliers of the group, the caher, two 'mohers,' and cromlech of Iskancullin, Cahermore, and Caheraclarig, in Sheshy; Caherscrebeen, and three other cahers, in Lemaneagh. In all - 52 cahers, 10 noteworthy cairns and mounds, 9, or perhaps 13, cromlechs, 5 'caves,' and 5 slab rings and enclosures.'

4

The Eastern Border
West Corcomroe
Glasha Group

The key to the study of the ring forts is held by Ireland. Her cahers,[1] from their excellent preservation, and because the features of the earth forts have perished, tell their story with unusual clearness. Outside of Ireland it is rare to find a fort retaining its walls, terraces, gateways, huts, and souterrains, or to find any literature contemporary with, and descriptive of, the forts. Indeed, even in Ireland the most instructive cahers are in Kerry, Clare, and Galway; here stand, bare to the light of day, what rarely - save in Cork and Mayo, and some few forts in Sligo, Donegal, and Cavan - can only be revealed by troublesome and costly excavation. The central group of these forts again lies in the Burren and its borders; and the fact that they have not been restored, gives them a value even above the magnificent duns in Arran, or some of the most interesting on the slopes of Mount Eagle round Fahan, as unaltered ancient buildings. But little apology need be made for offering to the Society, that published so much of my previous notes,[2] another instalment of a survey, which with many faults may at least claim to be the first systematic record of a unique group of buildings, of which the apathy of local authorities and the vandalism of those of all classes, on whose lands the forts and graves happen to lie, may soon leave but little of value.

---

[1] In this, as in the earlier Papers on the Clare forts, I use 'prehistoric' for any unrecorded early period, and 'fort' for a residential enclosure not necessarily for any military purpose.

[2] Forts near Killaloe, vol. xxi., p. 289; Moghane, &c., vol. xxiii., p. 384; Cahercommaun, &c., vol. xxvi., p. 142 [1]; Inchiquin, p. 363 [17]; Ballyganner, Kilfenora, &c., vol. xxvii., p. 116 [23]; vol. xxxi., p. 287 [89]; Carran, vol. xxviii., p. 357 [38]; Kilcorney, vol. xxix., p. 367 [47]; Caherdooneerish, &c., vol. xxxi., p. 273 [76]; Rathborney, &c.; Loop Head, vol. xxviii., p. 411; Bodyke, vol. xxxiv., p. 75; Burren, vol. xxx., pp. 294, 398. Also see *Proc. R.I.A.*, vol. vi., Ser. III; Cahers of County Clare, p. 415; vol. iv., Ser. III.; Magh Adhair and Cahercalla, p. 55; cromlechs, p. 542.

Such a survey grows on the writer. At first he sets out 'like a retrospective Columbus to explore the ocean of the prehistoric past'; then he gets hampered and discouraged; then his discoveries seem nearly complete, though an unknown continent lies beyond them. Then, at last, that deep saying asserts itself – 'If any man think that he knoweth anything, he knoweth nothing yet as he ought to know.' Groping onward (one's original design almost lost), many inconsistencies call for pardon. First I omitted and then included the dolmens; this was because I gave my notes on them to the late W. Copeland Borlase for his great work. Then the plan of describing the chief forts[1] forced me to include the crowds of lesser antiquities, and numbers of these were found on later examination, and call for notice; so I must crave merciful criticism where again I have to supplement my work in districts already described.

For the present paper, let us confine ourselves to the two edges of the Burren, that along the side of Inchiquin, and that detached spur of the limestone districts in Killilagh parish, now included in the Barony of Corcomroe. Hereafter, a portion from Cahermacnaughten to Finnavarra may better be treated separately; and then the series of papers will have covered, however imperfectly, the north-western plateaux, including Burren and the parishes of Killilagh and Kilfenora, in Corcomroe, with Rath, Killinaboy, and Ruan, in the Barony of Inchiquin, bounded to the south by Bealaghaline, Lisdoonvarna, Kilfenora, Lemaneagh, Inchiquin Hill, and the Fergus.

Whether a complete survey in the true sense will even then exist is, I fear, more than doubtful. Anyone who has worked over the uplands knows how hard it is to distinguish, whether in dull light or in the dazzling glare of unclouded sunshine (even at a short distance), forts and dolmens from natural ridges and boulders, and will forgive omissions. It is, however, less obvious that a feature in a fort may be excusably overlooked. After a long day, spent in climbing over rocks and dangerous walls, with ever growing weariness, pain, and lameness, one reaches a fort far from the road. The dull light, or the moss and bushes, conceal steps, or even a closed or half-buried gateway. Such omissions are, I believe, very few. The notes for these papers were taken on the spot, and rough descriptions (longer than those published) were written on the same day, or at latest on the following morning, as a precaution against slips of memory. The more important forts have been carefully planned, and many visited several times to check or supplement the descriptions – 'nobiliora, forsan, alii - ego quod possum.'

The names of the forts are not always satisfactory. It is often hard to get a good form, or even a phonetic one, of the names in use among the people; and sometimes these names are warped by some linguistic theory, or to conform them to information derived from some 'knowledgeable man' - clergyman, schoolmaster, agent, or 'sapper.' Sometimes I have had no little trouble in getting a real form, and then with the apology, 'The old people say so, but what do they know?' Many names have been rejected by the

---

[1] Cahercommaun, Cashlaun Gar, Roughan, Noughaval, Ballykinvarga, Caherconnell, Cahercashlaun, Cahermacnaughten, Balliny, Cahercloggaun, Ballyallaban, and Caherdooneerish were alone intened for description in 1895.

Ordnance Survey which are well known on the spot, and tally with old
records. Such names may be received with confidence, for such records are
hardly beginning to be known in these places. The 'educated classes' are of
little authority for local names, either taking no interest in them, or giving
them most inaccurately. We have found Ballykinvarga called after
neighbouring forts - Caheremon, Caherminaun, Caherflaherty, and Cahernaspekee - while in the Down Survey Books of Distribution it is called
Caherloghlin; 'Cahermakerrila' is locally (as in the records) Cahermacnole.
The nondescript names of Cahermore, Cahermoyle, and Caherlochlannach
are now superseding the true names.

Excellent as are the new Ordnance Survey maps, they sometimes fail to be
as helpful as those of 1839, by sometimes omitting to mark ancient
enclosures as such. When I note that the great inland promontory fort of
Doonaunmore, in Killilagh, with huge terraced rampart, 10 feet thick and
high, and over 300 feet long, the curious, though much levelled, hill-fort of
Croaghateeaun, and the interesting Moheramoylan, with souterrain, hut
sites, and a perfect gateway, are not even slightly indicated on the new
maps, comment is needless. I have no intention to originate theories in
these papers. Researches in Irish ethnology, lists of the actual distribution
of the forts, records of the implements and other objects found in them, must
first be made before satisfactory theories become possible. Meanwhile 'to be
a seeker is to be of the best sect next to being a finder'; and though theories
die, facts live, and remain current coin.

THE EASTERN BORDER

INCHIQUIN HILL (O.S. 16). - If we pass round the hill road to the south of
the lake of Inchiquin, we are surrounded with senses of no less beauty than
interest. Leaving the picturesque bridges and stream of the Fergus, with the
old ruined mill at Clifden, and the lofty tower of Tirmicbrain on the hill side,
above the terraced garden of Adelphi, we pass high above the lake,
overshaded with birch, larch, and other overarching trees. Vistas up steep
and wooded slopes, up runnels shaded with fern and tall foxglove, or down
to the lake, swan-haunted as in legendary days,[1] to the Castle of Inchiquin
and the great natural fortress of Doonauns, meet us at every turn. Then a
wild, rocky pass, between cliffs, opens to the left, and passing round a bluff,
we reach the high cross-roads at Crossard. We note the ruined chapel of the
short-lived Moravian colony, planted by the Burtons in 1795. There we get
pretty views on either side - one over lilac bushes, to the lake, the other
across the Fergus, the ivied court, the church and broken round tower of
Kilnaboy,[2] to the grey rampart of Burren.

---

[1] For the beautiful swan legend (so like that in the poem of Morris), see Dr.
Macnamara's Paper on 'Inchiquin' (*Journal*, vol. xxxi., p. 212).
[2] Mr. Robert Twigge has recently found a record identifying the hitherto
anonymous patron saint of this parish as Findclu, descendant of Aenghus Cinaitin,
and living in the seventh century.

CROSSARD CAHER lies down the slope: it is a late-looking and most rudely-built ring-wall, only 3 feet 6 inches thick, and 8 feet 6 inches high, the enclosure measuring 148 feet across the garth. All mark of the gateway has vanished, but an old road is traceable across the crags from the south-west side. The caher has no trace of terrace or house sites, and was probably a mere baun. We then pass the green woods and copper beeches of Elm Vale, noting that the well called 'Brian Boru well' on the map is locally 'Boru's well' (understood only as meaning 'red cow'), and we reach the townlands of Caherblonick.

CAHERBLONICK. - The name has existed at any rate from before 1540, when Henry VIII. confirmed to Morough O'Brien, King, and first Earl of Thomond, the lands of Caherblonghe. We need not trace the succession of its owners, but merely cite one late grant, rich in fort names, whereby in June, 1709, Andrew Hehir, of Cahermacunna, and his son, James, granted to John Stacpoole, of Ennis, the lands of Cahircomane, Cahirblunig, Cahir-nahally, Ballymacnavan, Lisnahow, and Fanamore.[1]

It is impossible to tell whether the name 'stone fort of the lard' is derived metaphorically from the richness of the land or from some tradition like that of 'the cellar full of deer's tallow' at Caherscrebeen, which lies just visible across the valley.[2] Where pigs abounded the name was usually 'Muckanagh,' and does not allude to lard. Caherblonick is on a limestone slope at the base of the ridge of Keentlae, falling in the shale hills of Boultiaghdine (locally understood as 'trodden into mire by cattle'), which, fluted by the runnels of several little streams, fall in steep slopes from the uplands of Keentlae. In one of these runnels was found a group of bronze celts, plain and socketed, and on the plateau above, a fine leaf-shaped bronze sword.[3]

Below the road, in craggy fields, ending in low cliffs above the broad valley, lie several forts. Beyond them we see the shattered tower of the late church of Kiltoraght, the strange, artificial-looking cleft on the hill of Ardnegowl, like an embanked road, the cairn of Clooneen, the brown old castle of Lemaneagh, with its gables and turrets, and the grey terraced hills of Leanna, Mullach, and Knockanes.[4]

The first fort is much levelled. As it is not far above Parcnahilly, it may be the Cahernahailly of the records. East from it, and above it on the slope, is a rectangular 'moher,' with thin walls of large, flat slabs, and, within, the foundations of an oblong hut and a small, circular annexe. It is not marked on the new map.

Caherblonick lies further to the north-east, about 100 yards away. It is a well-built ringwall of excellent masonry of regular blocks, usually about 2 feet 6 inches by 18 inches, in regular courses, with the unusual features of several pairs of upright joints, each divided by a line of single blocks about 2 feet long. We have noted a similar arrangement of joints carried to excess

---

[1] Dublin Reg. Deeds, Book IV., p. 465.

[2] *Journal,* vol. xxvi., p. 368 [21].

[3] Exhibited by Dr. G. U. Macnamara to the Society at Lisdoonvarna, 1900, and illustrated in the *Journal,* vol. xxxi., p. 358.

[4] These hills dominate all central Clare, and are visible even from Knockpatrick, Co. Limerick.

in the fort of Cahercloggaun, near Lisdoonvarna.[1] The rampart is 12 feet
thick, and from 6 feet to 8½ feet high, being best preserved to the north and
the west. It is more broken and of smaller masonry to the south-east. It has
a bold batter (often as much as 1 in 7), and has two faces, and a filling of
large blocks. One joint only runs for 5 feet up the wall, which suggests an
early rebuilding of the upper part. The garth is oval, being 125 feet east and
west, and 153 feet N.E. and S.W. Slight traces of the gateway are found to
the east. It had a threshold 3 feet 10 inches by 3 feet, so may have been
about the former width. Buried deeply in moss and cranesbills are two hut
foundations; one to the N.W. is oval, and 12 feet long, built against the wall;
the other is near the gate, and is 9 feet inside. There are only slight traces of
other enclosures, for the garth is filled up with 4 feet or 5 feet of debris.

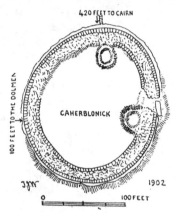

Caherblonick – Plan of Fort.

Like Cahercottine, near Noughaval,[2] Caherblonick has a dolmen and a
cairn near it. The cairn is a disfigured heap of earth and large blocks, 70 feet
in diameter, and 9 feet high. It lies about 140 yards to the north of the
caher, and is crossed by a boundary wall. It has, as usual, been explored by
treasure-seekers in several places.

The dolmen is about 100 feet to the west of the fort, and is called 'Labba'
or 'Lobba yermuth,' as usual. It tapers and slopes eastward. The south side
measures 10 feet 10 inches by 4 feet 3 inches by 6 inches to 8 inches, and has
a very regular hole (perhaps partly natural, but evidently partly ground)
through its side. The west end being 5 feet long, left, I think, an entrance
between it and the fallen north slab. The whole seems to have been 15 feet
over all, and 16 feet long, the axis lying E.S.E. and W.N.W.

The third caher lies 300 yards to the east of the cairn, Caherblonick being
almost equidistant from it and the western caher. It is on the edge of a low
ridge, round a deep 'bay' running into the slope. The wall is of beautiful
polygonal masonry, smooth white blocks very closely fitted together, and
only 6 feet high, with the unusual batter of 3½ inches to the foot. The fort is
oval, measuring over all 140 feet north-west and south-east, and 114 feet

---

[1] *Journal,* vol. xxxi., p. 12 [71].
[2] *Ibid,* vol. xxvii., pp. 117, 118 [24, 25].

north-east and south-west. The wall has two faces, and is from 9 feet to 12 feet thick, clinging to the edge of the crag to the north and north-east. The garth is filled up for 4 feet above the field, and has a hut site to the N.W

Another and smaller caher lies on the edge of the ridge on the eastern side of the 'bay,' just inside the edge of Drummoher. The mere foundations of three other cahers - two of small dimensions - lie in the valley at Caher-macon, and on the edge of Ballycasheen.

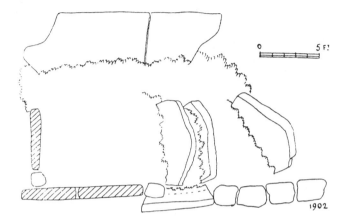

Caherblonick - Plan of Dolmen.

KEENTLEA. - The great wooded ridge of Keentlea, or Ceanntsleibhe, over the lake round which we have passed, is known in the older records as Ceann Nathrach, 'adder's' or 'serpent's head.' An ancestor of the O'Quins is called Aenghus Cennathrach, and may have either given to, or derived from, the hill his strange surname. Strange as is the name, it is not without an equivalent in a Celtic, but not snakeless, land. A 'serpent's hill' is named in Gaul in the fifth century as even then bearing an ancient name, 'Ad montem quem colubrarium . . . vocavit antiquitas.'[1] On the other slopes of this large ridge we may notice a couple of defaced cahers. I can hear of no trace of any fort on the top where stood the legendary 'House of Conan'; but Cahergal stood on a knoll in Maghera, and is levelled almost to the field.

Cahermackateer is called Caherwickyter in a 'Fiant' of 1601; Caher mac Teire in the Act of Settlement Confirmation to Murrough, Earl of Inchiquin, in 1676; and Cahermacdirigg in the Survey of 1675.[2] Only a low fragment of its wall, built with large, shapeless blocks, remains, embedded in a fence; the rest was cleared away for a cottage and garden. It lies behind the house to the south-west of the bench mark 316.5 on the O.S. map 16.

CAHERMORE KILLEEN (O.S. 17). - The old name of this fort was 'Caher-drumassan, or Cahragheeduva, in Killeen,' 1655.[3] It is a fairly preserved but featureless ring-wall, surrounded by thick groves of hazels. It is slightly oval, 135 feet to 136 feet internally. The wall is 11 feet thick for most of its

---

[1] Prof. Freeman (quoting Merobaudes), *Western Europe in the Fifth Century*, p. 280.
[2] Now at Edenvale.
[3] Book of Distribution and Survey, p. 515.

circuit, but widens to 12 feet 9 inches near the gateway, as is often the case. Only the north jamb of the gate remains; the outer opening cannot be measured; the inner passage is 6 feet 9 inches wide. The wall is of fairly large blocks - some 4 feet 6 inches by 2 feet; it consists of an outer section 8 feet thick, and a terrace 3 feet thick; the height varies from 6 feet to 8 feet or 9 feet; the batter is 1 in 4. It stands on a low crag with no outlook.

GORTLECKA (O.S. 10, 17). - Two dolmens remain near the foot of the strangely-terraced hill of Mullachmoyle, but in a delightfully retired grassy plain. Of the western dolmen, only the west stone is standing, and measures 8 feet long, 4 feet 6 inches high, and 9 inches thick. Some stones and broken slabs lie about among the hawthorns and brambles.

The eastern dolmen (O.S. 17)[1] was inhabited till recent times, like the dolmens of Parknabinnia, Commons, Slievenaglasha, and Cappaghkennedy. The theory that they were slab huts is, however, rendered very improbable by the fact that most show traces of mounds or cairns; and one was within human memory buried in a cairn. The Gortlecka dolmen formed the bedroom of a small cabin, and stood in a now nearly levelled cairn; it was of the usual type, tapering and sloping eastward. It was 12 feet long; the east end complete; the north 9 feet by 4 feet 2 inches to 5 feet high; the east 3 feet 6 inches long and the south 4 feet 3 inches. The irregular cover is over 7 feet wide, and 11 feet long, overhanging the end by 2 feet. The west end has fallen inwards, and leans against the north side; the dolmen being 5½ feet high. The top of each side is hammered, as is common in Clare; but in this case the inner faces of the sides have been picked to a smooth surface which I hardly ever noted elsewhere, even to a much lesser degree. The cover has curious 'footmarks' and other depressions.

TOORMORE (O.S. 25). - In the parish of Ruan, Dr. George U. Macnamara called my attention to a defaced dolmen,[2] unmarked even on the new maps. It lies to the south-west of Ruan, and not far from that village. It had been thrown down by a former tenant of the farm who met with some misfortunes which he attributed to his rash act. Strange to say, his successor, who broke up one of the blocks, hurt his hand soon afterwards, which may secure the preservation of the poor remains. It was a cist lying N.N.W. and S.S.E.; at the east 'end' is a stone 2 feet 5 inches wide, and 11 feet thick, and 4½ feet high; beside it is the base of a broken slab 34 feet long; the bases of other blocks to the west and north show that the chamber was 7 feet 3 inches long internally, and, perhaps, 4 feet 3 inches wide. A side slab 4 feet 6 inches by 6 feet lies in the enclosure.

TEMPLENARAHA (O.S. 25). - Westward, down the same road, is found the venerable little oratory of Templenaraha in Ballymacrogan West. It lies in Parcnakilla fort; the church is of fine 'cyclopean' masonry (like that in the Round Tower of Dysert O'Dea), and measures 24 feet by 16 feet 10 inches externally; the walls being 3 feet thick. The ring wall in which the church stands is nearly levelled; it measures 151 feet across the garth, or about 170 feet over all. The wall has two faces of large blocks with large filling; and

[1] Plan and elevations given, fig. 3a and 3b, p. [106].
[2] Plan given, fig. 4, p. [102].

was 8 or 10 feet thick. The history and dedication of the oratory would be of the greatest interest; but it is apparently nameless and unrecorded. The usage of 'rath' in the place-name for a stone fort coincides with several passages in our older literature.

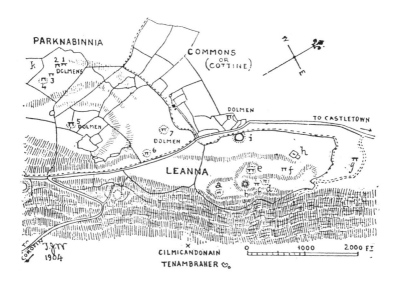

The Reabachan Group of Dolmens.
The references are explained in the text.

LEANNA (O.S. 10, 16). - Let us once more ascend that steep road among the hazel bushes on the flank of Leanna[1] where the hills are still green, and the great grey terraces have not yet commenced. We are again among the cairn-heaped upland with early remains on every side -

'Vastness and Age, and Memories of Eld,
Silence and Desolation, and dim Night;
These stones, alas! these grey stones - are they all
Left by corrosive hours to Fate and us?'

Had Borlase worked out this interesting group of dolmens and cists, I might have passed them by; but he has written rather confusedly, and passed over several of the remains. I described in a former Paper[2] part of this lying in Parknabinnia; but some ill-fate has attached to the townland, for the measurements in the Ordnance Survey Letters (14 B, 23, p. 66) are very inaccurate; Borlase overlooks the chief group; and despite my care three serious mistakes crept, while in press, into my description. I may here notice these errors the more emphatically. The north-west dolmen is there called 'the north-east'; the second cist is stated to be 17 feet 10 inches long, instead of 14 feet 10 inches; and the third dolmen is called 'a small cist 12 feet 8 inches'; the dimensions refer to its mound and circle of slabs. The cist, in

---

[1] *Journal*, vol. xxvi. (1896), p. 151 [10].

[2] *Ibid.*, vol. xxviii., p. 357 [39].

fact, is of three slabs, each only a little over 5 feet long; the east slab has either been removed or its place was taken by a block in the outer ring near the end of the side slabs. One other dolmen lies in the same field with the great eastern dolmen, marked 'carn' on the maps, and numbered VI. in my former Paper. The seventh cist[1] lies to the N.N.W. of the sixth dolmen, about 600 feet distant, and lying between it and the house there shown, and about 400 feet from the latter. It is in a low mound; the north and south blocks measure respectively 7 feet 10 inches and 6 feet 7 inches; the ends 31 inches and 28 inches; the cist tapering eastward; the axis, unlike the neighbouring cists, lying nearly due east and west. The cover rests beside it and measures 6 feet by 5 feet 3 inches; the slabs are thin (5 or 6 inches), and have the top edges hammered.

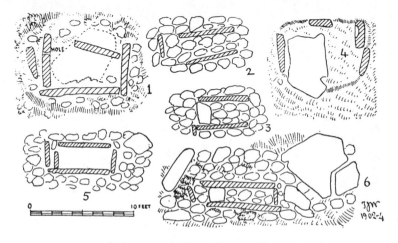

Dolmens and Cists, County Clare.
1, 2, 3. Leanna (e, d, a on plan p. 101)   4. Toormore.
5.Teeskagh.   6. Parknabinnia (7 on plan p. 101).

Entering Leanna, which lies east of the road from Kilnaboy to Castletown, and taking the remains in order as we go northward along the summit of the ridge, we find (*a* on plan) a cairn (not marked on O.S. 16) at the southern end of the top ridge. It is nearly levelled, and in its ruins I uncovered a little cist.[2] The north and south sides measure 4 feet 8 inches and 5 feet in length; the little chamber tapering from 27 inches to 26 inches; it must have been a mere 'bone box.' The principal cairn (*b*) on the highest point of the ridge, 528 feet above the sea, lies 516 feet to the N.N.E. of the last. It is much overturned, is 50 feet in diameter, little more than 8 feet high, and retains no certain traces of a cist unless some long, flat slabs in it are such.

The maps of 1839 and 1899 mark a 'cromlech' to the N.N.E. of it (*c*) where the trace of an old wall crosses the hill about 200 feet from the great cairn; but I never remember to have seen even slabs at the spot. A small cist (*d*) marked 'cromlech'[3] lies 200 feet farther to the N.N.E. of the last, and 200

---

[1] Plan given, fig. 6, above.
[2] Plan given, fig. 3, above.
[3] Plan given, fig. 2, above.

feet from the old wall. It lies in a cairn now nearly removed, and its sides are complete; the north measures 5 feet 3 inches, the south 4 feet 6 inches; the west lies 2 feet from the others, and is 18 inches long. The cist is therefore 6 feet 9 inches long, and tapers eastward from 32 inches to 22 inches; the axis lying E.N.E. and W.S.W.

It is a notable fact that, except the Ballycashen dolmen and the 'pillared dolmen' in Ballyganner, and No. 2 in Parknabinnia, all the Burren dolmens, from the great one on Ballyganner hill to the smallest cist at Leanna or Teeskagh, are made on the same plan so far as the chamber is concerned. As to the age of such structures, while some are almost certainly of the early Bronze Age, we must remember that (according to the Leabhar na hUidhre) Fothach Airgtheach, monarch of Erin, who was killed in A.D. 285 by Caeilte,[1] was buried under a cairn 'in a chest of stone.' This implies that cist burial was probably practised down at least to traditional memory, when our legends were first written, and teaches us caution, for no line can be drawn, at least in Clare, between the large dolmen and the cist. Such cists in other places have contained Bronze Age pottery, but up to this I know of none found in a cist in Clare.

The view from this high ridge all round is most extensive. The whole central plain of Clare lies open to the view - out to Slieve Aughty, the Keeper, and Slieve Bernagh. The ridge on which sits Moghane fort, the largest of Irish cahers, the spires of Ennis and Corofin, lake after lake to the beautiful wooded hills and broad sheet of water at Inchiquin, lie below us. The castles of Rockvale, Fiddown, and Derryowen on the edge of county Galway; Ballyportrea, the tall warden of the grey crags to the east, and ivied Inchiquin are visible to the east. Southward we see the low, green hills with flat-topped blue Callan rising over them. Northward the long slopes from Elva to the terraced edges at Glenquin; and westward the green hills, behind which fall the perpendicular rocks of Moher, and the lofty-seated hill-fort of Doon,[2] visible here, as we have also seen it far out to sea, one of the chief landmarks of the Atlantic coast of Clare.

The larger dolmens lie down the western slopes of Leanna hill. The first (*e*) is that described by Borlase.[3] It lies north-east and south-west, tapering eastward; the north side is 5 feet 4 inches; the south 8 feet long. It tapers from 5 feet to 2 feet 9 inches, and has a hole in the west end outside which is a second slab. The cover has fallen. The dolmen stands on a low earthen mound, and was covered by a cairn; it is the most conspicuous of the monuments, as seen from the road.

We may here note an almost inconceivable error in the great survey of Borlase (p. 69). 'Blocks of the size and symmetry of those used by the dolmen-builders would nowadays be far to seek.' This is an astonishing statement from one who had visited these hills. For acres, for miles, in these uplands, round almost every dolmen, are sheets of crag with large slabs detached from the under strata and broken along the lines of cleavage by

---

[1] Whom legend connects with the Glasgeivnagh hill, not far to the north of these cists. (See *Journal*, vol. xxv., p. 227.)

[2] *Journal*, vol. xxvii., p. 126 [32].

[3] *Dolmens*, vol. i., p. 75, fig. 78. See fig. 1, p. [102].

action of the weather, only requiring to be lifted and set in place to make dolmens as large and symmetrical as any now in Burren. As for large stones, the very field in Leanna which contains the monuments has almost rectangular slabs from 40 yards down to 3 or 4 yards long and wide. In Parknabinnia we find these slabs raised and propped at one side in sandstone erratic blocks, close to the main group of cists (*k*). While in Leanna large slabs, exactly of the size and appearance of dolmen sides and covers, have been set upright to make fences and apparently a large cattle pen.

Yet another dolmen (*f*) lies farther to the north in the same field down the slope. It has fallen northwards and consists of a south side still standing, or rather leaning, against the fallen cover, which rests partly over the prostrate north side. They measure: the south 9 feet 8 inches; the cover 9 feet 8 inches by 6 feet 4 inches wide; the north 10 feet by 6 feet 6 inches; they vary from 5 inches to 7 inches thick.

The 1899 map marks also a 'Dermot and Grania bed' in the north-western part of the field; it is, however, a large, oblong enclosure built of well-laid slabs, only one being set on end. Inside its enclosure is an oblong foundation, the ground inside being 4 feet lower than the garth, but with no remains of a cist. The 'Moher' (*h*) has a side enclosure to the north-east. Besides these remains, we find the walls of standing slabs, already noted; and a massive caher, with portions of its slab-built wall 6 feet and 8 feet high, lies near the road at the boundary wall at the foot of the slope (*i*).

To the north of the field on the unenclosed crag (the 'lake of stone,' before described[1]) in a slight mound remain the sides of yet another dolmen (*g*). It has been noticed and planned by Borlase.[2] The slabs are about 6 feet apart, and measure: the fallen northern side 8 feet by 5 feet 6 inches; the southern 10 feet long, and 3 feet 6 inches high, lying north-east and south-west, and having a hole aslant through it. It is not marked on the maps. Borlase supposes that there was 'a winding stone causeway leading across the moor to this structure,' but it is only a modernised (if not modern) macadamised bohereen leading from the main road past (not to) the dolmen, and to the top of the ridge, where a house stood in 1839. He falls into another error in identifying the Reabachan group as described in the Ordnance Survey Letters[3] with the cists of Leanna, instead of with those in Parknabinnia, standing, as they do, upon the actual Reabachan, now Roughan, Hill. Those noted in the 'Letters' are apparently Nos. 1, 2, 3 and 6, the latter one being then embedded in the cairn by the roadside, but is now open.

To complete the group, we must notice on the west side of the road the perfect dolmen of Cotteen or Commons. In 1839 it was inhabited by a certain Michael Coneen. Dr. Macnamara tells me that his father, in much later years, attended a patient in this dolmen. It has been very carefully described and planned by Borlase,[4] and consists of a cist of three large slabs, with a massive cover, 12 feet 8 inches by 8 feet 6 inches. The enclosure was from 5 feet 6 inches to 4 feet 6 inches wide; the sides 13 feet by 10 feet long,

---

[1] *Journal,* vol. xxvi., p. 151 [10].
[2] *Dolmens,* vol. i., p. 75, fig. 79.
[3] 14 B, 23, p. 66.
[4] *Dolmens,* vol. i., p. 76. See also p. [106].

and the slabs nearly a foot thick. There was a small side annexe to the south, once adapted as a habitation for the family pig. I found that (as so often) the tops of the sides had been clipped to a straight edge.

Thus the great 'Reabachan' group, so far as we have examined it, consists of three dolmens and two small cists in Leanna, one dolmen in Commons, seven in Parknabinnia, one in Ballycasheen, and one below Cahermore, in Roughan, *ie.*, fifteen monuments in all.

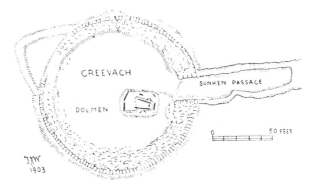

Creevagh – Ring Wall.

CREEVAGH[1] (O.S. 10). - When describing the remarkable dolmen in the ring-wall of Creevagh, I did not mention a noteworthy feature of its surroundings. There is a gap to the east of the ring, and from it (lying nort-east and south-west) is a sunken way like that leading from the fort to the dolmen at Caheraneden. The 'way' has been formed by removing the topmost layers of the crag. It is exactly 100 feet long from the inner face of the wall, which is 11 feet thick. The trench so formed is 12 feet wide at the wall, 16 feet at half distance, and 12 feet at the end; it nowhere exceeds 20 feet in width, or 5 feet in depth, and does not lie in the axis of the dolmen. The ring-wall is 83 feet in internal diameter east and west.

TEESKAGH (O.S. 10). - In the cairn, near the foot of the waterfall of the seven streams of Teeskagh, is a small cist[2] of thin slabs - the north, 5 feet 2 inches long; the south, 6 feet 6 inches, tapering eastward from 26 inches to 22 inches. The cairn is of large blocks, embodying a great boulder, evidently deposited there by older and mightier agencies than the cairn-builders. The heap is oval, measuring 28 feet north and south, and 25 feet east and west; it is on a low, bushy mound in that picturesque and delightfully secluded hollow.

TULLYCOMMAUN[3] (O.S. 10). - I propose adding to the slight account of the remains on the northern ridge in that townland some extra notes. The double-ringed caher, to the west of the road to Castletown, is now much defaced. The central wall has been levelled to within 4 feet of the ground at

---

[1] *Journal,* vol., xxviii., p. 359 [39].

[2] Plan given, fig. 5, p. [102].

[3] *Journal,* vol., xxvi., pp. 363, 364 [17].

the highest point; it was thin and of coarse masonry, both signs of late work. There is some slight trace of the passage inside the gateway facing the east. It is 5 feet 9 inches wide; near it lies a lintel 6 feet by 2 feet 3 inches by 7 inches for the narrower outer opening. The inner ring is 146 feet in diameter; the outer, on an average, 300 feet internally. Much of the outer wall remains to the N.W.; it is 8 feet high, and of the coarse, slab masonry seen in the outer ring of Cahercommaun; it has been much rebuilt in places.

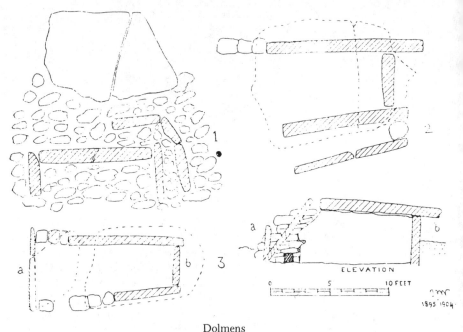

Dolmens

1. Tullycommaun. 2. Cotteen, or Common. 3. Plan and Elevation of Gortlecka.

CAHERSAVAUN,[1] the lake fort, measures 139 feet east and west across the garth, and 66 feet north and south. The wall forms a revetment to a rocky island, and is of good, large masonry 12 feet thick, and 10 to 13 feet high for most of the circuit to the west and south. It is more gapped and lower to the north. The garth is very rough, and there are no traces of huts or gateway. The latter probably stood at the end of the remains of the causeway; but it must be remembered that some lake forts had no gateway.

An old road leads up the ridge from near Cahersavaun to the low mound called 'Giant's Grave' on the maps. This is shown as a small cist-like oblong on the 1839 map; it is a long, low, pear-shaped earth-work, full of blocks of stone, and measuring 33 feet east and west, and 14 feet north and south, near the west end; it tapers to a point at the east end. A slab set north and south appears near the west side; but if this be the remains of a cist, there is no other trace of one.

On the summit of the green ridge, 48 paces to the east of the last, is a low, defaced mound of earth and stones. It is 35 ft. across, and has on the summit

---

[1] *Journal,* vol. xxvi., p. 364 [17].

a well-marked ring of stones round a circular hollow 15 ft. in diameter. It possibly represents that form of burial-mound mentioned in Irish literature from early times to the seventeenth century as belonging to pre-Christian and very early Christian days. The *Tripartite Life* records: 'Fecerunt fossam rotundam in similitudinem fertæ quia sic faciebant Scottici homines.'

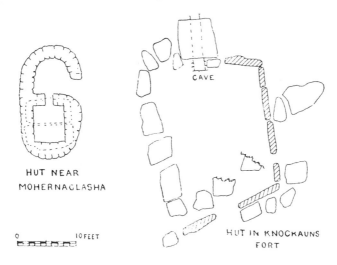

HUT NEAR
MOHERNAGLASHA

0   10 FEET

CAVE

HUT IN KNOCKAUNS
FORT

Tullycommaun - Huts.

The 'Third Life of St. Patrick' alludes to those ring-mounds and walls: 'Stat autem in loco ubi omnes steterunt quedam fossa rotunda et erat homo fossus.'[1] So does a poem of Cormacan Eigeas, which among the monuments of the great pagan cemetery of Brugh-na-Boinn notes that:[2] 'The three sons of Eochy Fedlech Finn are in their 'mur,' their lovely 'mur.'' Keating, in the 'Three Bitter Shafts of Death,' describes, among other early methods of burial, that in the small raths, or ring-mounds: first a grave, or fert, the size of the body was dug, and a small rath made, and a cairn or leacht was piled inside. Or else a small rath was dug, without any leacht or cairn, which had one opening for a man of science, two for a woman, and none for a boy. 'Ferta' seems to have been used even in the eleventh century for a residential rath, for, according to the *Tripartie Life*,[3] when St. Patrick measured a rath with the 'Bachall Isu,' the ferta was seven score feet in enclosure. In the 'Colloquy' in the Book of Lismore[4] Caoilte shows St. Patrick the tulach of Airnealach, son of the King of Leinster; 'the green-surfaced tulach closed over him, and his sepulchral stone was set up.' On a neighbouring tulach was the 'fert' of Saelbhuidhe (son of Feilachan, the King of Munster), who, with thirty comrades and thirty hounds, was slain with elf darts by the fairies, and was there buried with his weapons and jewels, 'and the tulach was walled up on them.' As might be expected, superstition gathered

---

[1] *Trans. R.I.A.*, vol. xxxii. (c), p. 249.
[2] *Revue Celtique*, vol. xvii. (1896), p. 281.
[3] *Tripartie Life of St. Patrick* (edited by W. Stokes), p. 237.
[4] *Silva Gadelica*, vol. ii., p. 128.

around the mounds. They were haunted by those 'elohim'[1] of the old Irish, the Tuatha De Dannan. Aenghus, son of the Dagda, haunts a tulach;[2] and the horrible banshee 'Bronach' said that her 'abode was in the green fairy mounts of Erin.'[3]

The Tullycommaun mound probably gave the townland its name, 'Tulach Chumann,' as in 1599.[4] It is a recognised 'sidh' or fairy mount, for I was told in 1895 that 'it had more fairies than all the forts on the hill.' An interesting allusion in the 'Wars of Torlough' (in 1311) may refer to this mound. Donchad, son of Torlough, and Prince of Thomond, fled to these hills, and camped in East Corcomroe, near Slieve Carne; his rival Dermot camped before him at Crichmaill, or Crughwell, in the valley beyond Cahersavaun; and De Clare behind Dermot on the great hill of Dloghan, possibly this very ridge. On the grey uplands that night Donchad's followers were beset by supernatural warnings, 'mysterious sounds, and phantasms of delusive dreams'; 'lights of all the fairy forts revealing themselves'; groans 'making deep reverberation of their plaint to fill fair Erin's woods and roll adown her stony rivers.' That night, moreover, the soldiers saw shades, and 'heard three feeble, long-drawn wails, lamentably low and sadly sweet.' Thus in 1311 the belief was in full vigour on these very uplands, and the Tullycommaun mound was in full sight of the camps of Dermot and Donchad across the swamp. The latter ill-fated prince marched the following morning past the end of the lake by the steep descent to our right down into Glencolumbcille and Glenquin, where he fell by the hand of a treacherous companion ere he reached the plain.[5]

Beyond the green ridge we once more meet with crags jutting from under the shale. Of these, at some distance to the east, lies a circular caher. The wall is very neatly built of slabs; it has a slight batter, and is 10 feet thick, being rarely 5 feet high, and sometimes levelled to within a couple of feet of the crag. The garth measures 75 feet east and west. There are in it a semicircular hut foundation adjoining the wall to the south, and another curved foundation near it. The gateway is hardly traceable; it faces the E.S.E. We finally reach Knockaun fort, close to whose western side, on a knoll, we find a very defaced dolmen.[6] It consists of a chamber 10 feet by 4 feet. The north side (its east end showing signs of hammer-dressing) and the east end,

---

[1] No other term combines the compound of god and ghost so well.
[2] Pursuit of Diarmaid and Grainne.
[3] Wars of Torlough.
[4] Comaun, or 'Chuman,' was a not uncommon personal name in the Corcomroes in early times, and is attatched to the great triple fort which is visible from the tulach across the glen.
[5] For the general subject of 'Tulachs,' see Paper, by J. O'Daly, in *Journal*, vol. iii (1854), p. 87; see also *Silva Gadelica*; the 'Pursuit of Diarmaid and Grainne' (S. H. O'Grady); the 'Battle of Gabhra' (N. O'Kearney); and the *Tripartite Life of St. Patrick* (W. Stokes). O'Daly is, I think, mistaken as to 'tulach' being very common in Clare place-names. We find Tullaghloghaun (Clooney), Tullycommaun (Kilnaboy), Tullyodea (Ruan), Tullyoghan (Kilraghtis), Tulla (nan apstol.), Tullachboy (Kilmaley), Tullaher (Killard), Tullabrack (Kilmacduan), Tullycreen (Kilmurry mac Mahon). Several, if not most, of these names refer only to natural mounds.
[6] See plan, fig. 1, p. 218 [106].

Moheramoylan Gateway

Poulnabrone Dolmen

Parknabinnia Dolmen

Caheranardurrish Gateway

with the cover and an outer row of slabs, remain. The side slabs are from 33 inches to 42 inches from the main cist. The cover is broken across, and lies beside the cist; it measures 7 feet 6 inches long, and from 7 feet 8 inches to 6 feet wide, and 10 inches or 11 inches thick. Borlase was told that the labba was called 'Carrikaglasha.'[1] I did hear the name locally, but the 'Glas' cow has left her name and reputed hoof-prints over the whole plateau.[2] On my first visit to the spot the dolmen seemed more perfect, and the cover-slab rested over the side. Knockaun fort has already been described[3] by me. I need only add that the wall is thin, and rarely 5 feet high, with straight sides, having the south-west corner perfect and rounded. The garth is 170 feet across east and west, and it contains the curious house foundation and souterrain of which I here give the plan (p. [107]).

Borlase has published the plan of some other cist as that of 'Carrickaglasha,' in Tullycommaun. This arises from some error, as the plan is of a different dolmen. It is of the typical kind, a box of three slabs tapering eastward; the north 8 feet long, the south 10 feet long, and from 48 inches to 30 inches apart, with two covering slabs. I am unable to identify it, but it is certainly not the dolmen there named. He found another one small and defaced to the south-east of Knockaun fort, between it and the dolmen of Slievenaglasha, but the description does not agree with the plan. Such little cists probably exist in numbers as yet undescribed; for even the most careful examination in this land of slabs and 'natural buildings' sometimes passes them by unrecognised, while others get disclosed on the removal of cairns and mounds, or even of modern walls, in which they have been embodied.

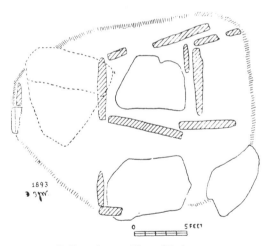

Ballycasheen – Plan of Dolmens.

---

[1] *Dolmens of Ireland*, vol. i., p. 73. Another dolmen is called 'Leaba-na-leagh,' or 'Leac-na-leagh.' See, however, Dr. Joyce's *Irish Names of Places*, Ser. II., chap. iv., p. 104, and note 'Leaba an laeich,' in County Cavan.
[2] For the legend, see my note in *Journal*, vol. xxv., p. 227.
[3] *Journal*, vol. xxvi., p. 363 [17].

BALLYCASHEEN AND CAPPAGHKENNEDY. - In re-examining these two dolmens I may note that the plans given by Borlase[1] are each defective. The first monument shows clear signs of being the remains of two structures. One was a small cist, to the south of the large dolmen, and 5 feet distant. There are other set slabs to the west, perhaps part of an outer ring or kerbing - a feature not unusual in Clare. The four sides of the chamber of the Cappaghkennedy dolmen are complete as here shown. We give a view of this fine monument; it was recently inhabited.

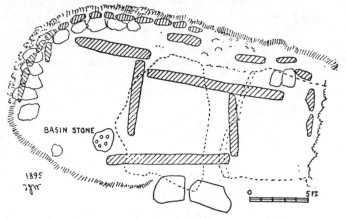

Cappaghkennedy – Plan of Dolmen.

RANNAGH EAST (O.S. 6). - I formerly noted a perfect dolmen lying (as I thought) in this townland,[2] but the new map shows that it lay a few feet over the bounds in the townland of Termon. With only the old map to guide me, and entangled in a maze of unmarked little fields and walls, I missed the actual dolmen of Rannagh, shown on the maps of 1839. It is embedded in loose stone walls, so as to form a sheep-pen, and lies not far from, in full sight of, and north-east from, the Termon cist.

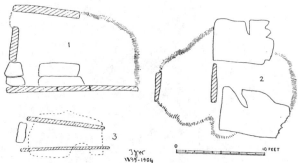

Rannagh East – Plan of Dolmens.

1. The Northern Dolmen.   3. Termon Dolmen, on bounds
   2. The Southern Dolmen.   of Rannagh.

---

[1] *Dolmens of Ireland.*
[2] *Journal,* vol. xxix., p. 382 [60]. The second (fallen) cist of Termon is there described at p. 381 [59].

The sides and west end are standing, but cracked as if by fire. The top edges are dressed to a regular slope. The south side is entire, 15 feet 7 inches long by 8 inches thick; and sloping from 4 feet 4 inches to 3 feet 10 inches high; it lies E.N.E. and W.S.W.; and the ground on which it stands has been so denuded that the lower edge is bare. The fragment of the north side is 7 feet 9 inches long; measuring at each end, the chamber is from 8 feet 5 inches to 7 feet 6 inches wide. The west slab does not close up the end, but leaves a doorway, as is not unusual. There is no trace of a mound or cairn; the dolmen, as we see, was of unusual size, but not even a fragment of the cover is recognisable.

TURLOUGH HILL (O.S. 3). - There is a high ridge between Oughtmama and the Gortaclare valley, lying within the edge of the former townland. There, only some 300 yards from the border of County Galway, is all that is left of one of the largest and most puzzling of the ring-walls of Ireland.[1] The ridge is well seen from Corcomroe Abbey, and there many years ago I first was told of this fort, which was not marked on the map. An elderly herdsman described it as 'a tumbled circle of stones on that hill'; the younger men then present did not know of its existence.[2] The ridge is steep, bare, and fenced with continuous high terraces of rock and enormous boundary walls. Even the Gortaclare people 'did not know of any caher upon the hills'; so I did not at the time try to visit so inaccessible and equivocal a ruin. Finding, however, that a fort was shown on the map of 1899, I was led to visit, and, with the aid of Dr. George U. Macnamara, examined, planned, and noted this great fort, though in stormy and bitter weather - hailstorms alternating with blazes of fierce sunshine.

The fort may have been known to Bishop Pococke in 1752. He writes[3]: 'I observed several large entrenchments on the mountains of Burren . . . one of them, they say, was the residence of O'Laughlin, King of Burren.' The bishop then describes Corcomroe Abbey, from which the fort is visible against the sky-line. The only other legend I could learn was from a local herdsman who passed over the ridge as I was making the plan. 'It might be as old,' he said, 'as the time of the Irish militia.' He, of course, meant the warriors of Finn, not their doughty successors. A cairn called Seefin, on Black Head, marks a legend of the great son of Cumhal, as existing in north Burren. We were fortunate, after a weary climb up a steep slope of earth and rocks, in finding a way from Gortaclare valley to the foot of the chief terrace, and thence found a pass up the rampart and got on to the plateau. The view was noble, and with the strong light and shade and the clear air, gave one an exceptional sense of its extent. The ridge, though the fort stands 800 feet above the sea, is higher to the west, where, fenced by a higher terrace, sits the fine cairn of Turlough, 925 feet above the sea. The

---

[1] I have very briefly noted this fort in *Proc. R.I.A.*, vol. xxiv. (c), p. 274 ; and the 'Handbook of the West Coast of Ireland,' *J. R. S. A. I.* (1904), p. 106.
[2] Accustomed to the endless remains of levelled enclosures on the hills, they, doubtless, from its great size, and no general view being possible, failed to recognise it as a congener of little ring-walls of 100 feet to 120 feet in diameter, so common in Clare.
[3] Dr. Pococke's *Tour in Ireland* (edited by G. Stokes), p. 107.

cobalt blue bay of Galway lay out to the bold peaks of Connemara, and
ended at our feet in the landlocked creek of Pouldoody, guarded by the dark
specks that were the two peal-towers of Muckinish and the Martello tower
of Finnavarra.[1] The huge terraced hills shut out the view of the sea
westward and to the north, where the hill of Behagh, over the clearly-seen
'Abbey of the fertile rock' and the abrupt steeps overhanging the Corker
pass shut out the end of Galway bay and its creeks, save the end of the bays
at Kinvarra[2] and Taman Point. But to the east of them lay open the
unbounded plains of Galway, and the lake studded central tract of Clare. To
the south, beyond the level-terraced sides of Gortaclare valley, rose Slieve
Carran with its conspicuous cairn; and to the north, seen almost from
overhead, lay the three little churches of Oughtmama.

> 'The footprints of an elder race are here,
> And memories of an old heroic time,
> And shadows of the old mysterious faith;
> So that the place seems haunted, and strange sounds
> Float on the wind.'

On a platform, if possible more bare and weather-blasted than the other
summits in the Burren, we find a low wall, with gaps at fairly regular
intervals. It proves to be a large enclosure measuring 675 feet north and
south, 735 feet east and west, or from 700 feet to nearly 760 feet over the
wall. It is of irregular plan, with a *re-entrant* 'angle' to the north-west. The
irregularity, as is usually the case, springs from the builders having selected
a ridge, 7 feet to 12 feet high to the north, 20 feet to 30 feet along the east.
A natural gully, 25 feet to 30 feet wide, makes a rising ascent up to the table
of the plateau.[3] It faces E.S.E., is 207 feet long, and was used for the main
entrance to the fort. Traces of the wall cling to the slopes at the mouth of
the cleft, which is there about 30 feet deep; but the gateway has been
destroyed to the foundation. Within the gate the sides are steep, and at one
point precipitous.

The wall is from 9 to 12 feet thick. The builders first laid small thin slabs
on the crag till a fairly level surface was obtained, and then built the entire
thickness of the wall with large slabs. It is rarely more than 4 feet or 5 feet
high, often barely 3 feet, and parts to the south are almost levelled. The
sides of the gateways are faced with slabs set on end.

Going round the wall 'sunward' from the gully, we find 145 feet from the
latter, at the abrupt south-east turn, two hut sites[4] adjoining, mere semicircular rings abutting on the wall. This is common in Clare and Kerry
forts, and the fact is even noted in the ancient Clare legend of the 'Voyage of

---

[1] Reputedly named from Bheara the Firbolg. There is a certain fairy king, Finvarra,
who dwelt in Knockma, in County Galway: see *Journal*, vol. xxxv., p. 34
[2] Kinvara creek is connected with the tenth-century legend of the voyage of the Hui
Corra in their atonment for their destruction of the churches of Connaught. They
went to the baile of Kinvara, watch the sun set from its haven, and then go out into
the deep 'to meet the Lord on the sea.'- *Revue Celtique*, xiv. (1893), p. 37.
[3] *a* on plan.
[4] *b*1 on plan.

Maelduin,'[1] written before 1100: 'Round the rampart were great snow-white houses.' Examples occur at Ballykinvarga and Mohernacartan in Clare, and not a few other forts in Ireland and Great Britain. Along the very slightly-curved south face are five gateways well marked by their great lining slabs. Between the second and third we find a hut site, and the third gate[2] faces Carnbower on the summit of Slieve Carran. The wall then curves in a semi-circle along the western face. At 82 feet from the fifth gate, which faces S.S.W., is a hut-ring (a garden-bed of close-growing, blue gentian when we saw it), and at the same distance from the ring is a similar hut-site, lined with set slabs like the gateways.

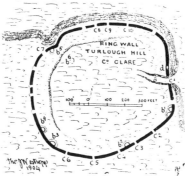

Turlough Hill – Plan of Ring Wall.

There are three gaps farther north, and a gap facing W.N.W., and looking straight at the castle, or, perhaps, rather the neck of Muckinish peninsula. There are no facing slabs to any of the western gaps; they may be accidental. The north-west gap is very probably a gateway,[3] as an evident path leads down from it along the slope at the 'dip'
already mentioned. East of it, at the bend, is a hut-site, and inside it, in the plateau, is an evidently artificial oblong cutting, or hut-hollow, some 5 feet deep, and full of heather, which only grows in sheltered spots, within the west segment of the wall. The *re-entrant* dip measures 77 feet over all.

When the wall resumes its regular curve along the north face, we find several gaps and gateways, one of which latter is illustrated. The three gateways marked by their largest slabs face almost due north. The second[4] faces the edge of a prominent precipice of the Corker Hill. A featureless gap is at the north-east turn of the wall, which is as abrupt as that to the south-west, and nothing save a trace of an oval chamber[5] is found in the reach of nearly 160 feet back to the gully. The wall is about 2,300 feet long. The garth platform is of bare, wasted, and often loose crag, like half-melted ice-sheets in snow; no traces of foundations are found upon it.

Clare is, as all know, exceptionally rich in huge forts. We have the triple Moghane, 1,500 feet by 1,100 feet, with walls 7,850 feet long; Langough,

---

[1] Leabar-na-hUidhre (*Revue Celtique*, vol. ix., p. 477).
[2] *c* 4 on plan.
[3] *c* 7 on plan.
[4] *c* 9 on plan.
[5] *d* on plan.

600 feet by 300 feet; Cahershaughnessy, 567 feet, and Cahercommaun, 320 feet by 245 feet; but this Turlough Hill fort not only is second in size in Clare, but stands high upon the list of the larger forts in Ireland. The structure, as we see, is most exceptional. The maximum number of gates in the actual cahers is rarely more than four. This fort had at least nine, probably a dozen. Inismurray cashel has five. Moghane, in its huge outer wall, has seven gaps; but few can even be provisionally taken as gates. Irish literature names four gateways in certain cases - for example, the murderers of St. Cellach[1] 'dwelt at Dunfidhne, where they have newly made a dun, with four doors in it,' which, by the way, they inaugurated by killing a swine.[2] The usual Clare fort has never more than one gateway.

The object of this enclosure is difficult to see. Who built so vast a wall on a ridge so storm-swept and difficult of access? If it was built to dominate all its surroundings, why was it not placed on the head of the hill at Turlough cairn? If for a meeting-place, whether religious or tribal, why was so inconvenient a spot selected? If a fortress, or walled village, why were there so many gates? If a temple, were there no inner buildings? It is improbable, to a degree hardly short of impossibility, that the monastic community of Oughtmama, who 'went aside into this desert place,' built such an enclosure on the brow, above their unwalled and clustered monastery, nestling in its sheltered green recess 500 feet below. Even where the monks used an early fort, it was rarely one more than 150 feet or 200 feet in diameter. This great stone problem lies, so massive, yet so indefensible - so inaccessible - yet overlooked by a greater height - so unsuited for pasturage or for gatherings, and, to modern ideas, scarcely fit for habitation. We turn to the few available legends and records. The former only tell us of early tribes - Irghus, Taman, Bera, and Cutra[3] in that part of Ireland. Even if we could accept the legend, none of these clans was of even legendary importance; they were soon expelled or exterminated, and are not even named in history. The great enclosure does not figure in the fort list (*ante* 900) in the Book of Rights, unless it be Tuam nheidin, with its brow to the land, for the Ui Eidhin, or O'Heynes, dwelt at its foot in the plains to the east. Moghane fort is marked on more than one Elizabethan map; Turlough Hill fort does not appear. In an elaborate inquisition of 1607[4] no such landmark is named as on the border of Clare. 'Up the mountain of Funchamore, and holding the very top of the mountain, butteth forward to Slieve Carne and to Tobberlyhe, thence to Curraghmore, and so it falleth into the bay of Galway,' says the Inquisition. It was probably defaced before 1839, or it could hardly have been passed over by the surveyors. Built for the most part on the bare rock, there is but little hope that excavation might help us. It only remains for me to describe and illustrate it, and to leave the solution (if any) to later antiquaries.

---

[1] The received account is evidently a mixture of two stories. In one, Cellach was of full age in 537; in the other, he was murdered between 650 and 660, at the instigation of King Guaire; but the allusion to the fort remains of value.
[2] *Silva Gadelica*, vol. ii., p. 65.
[3] 'Dindsenchas,' p. 78 ; *Revue Celtique* (1894), p. 478.
[4] Inquisition taken at Galway, August 11th, 1607 (P.R.O.I.).

TORLOUGH HILL FORT
the northern gate

CAHERBLONICK
the east fort

CAHERBLONICK and DOLMEN.

West Corcomroe.

Visitors to Lisdoonvarna are well acquainted with the Castle of Ballinalacken. As they drive round the flank of the opposite hill, a noble view opens before them. Below, from a deep valley, rises the old, brown, peel-tower of the O'Briens, with its lofty side-turret built at the angle of the precipice. It stands on a table-like rock, the faces richly ivied in many places. To the west the more gradual slope is thickly planted round the modern villa. Behind, however, there appears a wilder district, a wilderness of entangled green valleys, fenced in by sheer cliffs, and bushy hawthorns and hazels; above these, terrace behind terrace, lie the lavender-grey crags, then the towering precipices, capped with the grassy upland, where rests Caherdoon on 'the old rain-fretted mountains, in their robes of shadow-broken grey.' To the right is a wide expanse of the ever changing waves, 'the white-maned horses of Mannannan mac Lir,' out to the peaked highlands of Connemara and the long, low isles of Aran, the farthest topped with the fort of Dun Oghil, and beaded with the white houses of Kileany. It is the district behind Ballinalacken which we first purpose to explore in this Paper, then going southward along the coast.

KILLILAGH (O.S. 4). - The parishes of Killonaghan and Killilagh, in which these ring-walls lie, comprised, in 1302, two other parishes - Cromglaon or Crumlin, and Wafferig (? Ooafterig) or Oughtdarra. These probably covered the coast from the foot of Crumlin to the precipices at Cregg lodge, whence the people would naturally have gone to the churches of Killonaghan and Killilagh as to their most accessible spiritual centres. Other history, even of the most vague class, there is little down to the surveys of 1655.

As to the natural features, the high, brown upland of Knockauns Hill falls into spurs and plateaux. Ballinalacken Castle is on the southern spur. Oughtdarra comprises the deepest valleys to the first terrace, and is dominated by the great, mote-like hill and fort of Croghateeaun.[1] The second terrace from near Doonaunmore, with the plateau of Cahernagrian, abounds in forts, and lies in Ballynahown. In this townland, fenced to the south and west by lofty perpendicular or overhanging precipices, also lies the upland below Knockauns Hill where lie the forts of Caheradoon and Caherduff. The latter is on the brow of the steep, northern slope, just within the bounds of Crumlin, and forms the limit of our present explorations.

OUGHTDARRA (O.S. 4). - One of the most complete labyrinths of valleys, cliffs, and enclosures, even in the tangled glens of the Corcomroes, lies behind the little ruined oratory of Oughtdarra. We had the advantage of being guided by two of the local residents, Messrs. Hilary and Kelleher, both well acquainted with place-names and legends, and knowing every fort-site, cave, and old enclosure. So during a long day in late May (the very day the first news reached us of the great naval battle of the far East) I was barely able, with the aid of Dr. G. U. Macnamara, to examine and take notes and measurements of the sites. I had already worked over the uplands and down

---

[1] Croagh and Knock are very usually confused among the peasantry, but the shape of the hill favours the form 'Croagh' or 'Cruch' now in use.

to Cahernagrian; but will give my notes in order from south to north. The Ordnance Maps, both of 1839 and of the recent survey, are, I regret to say, most deficient in the marking of the natural features and antiquities of these townlands. The formal contour lines are most misleading; a dolmen and two of the most important forts (one with a wall 10 feet high and thick, and over 300 feet long) are unmarked, and one name is attached to a wrong fort. I give a diagram which, though rude and imperfect, may supplement the maps sufficiently to enable students to follow these notes.

Starting from the old road behind Ballinalacken we descend a steep hill, and find, in a pleasant recess behind the houses, a little ruined church. It is popularly attributed to Sionnach mac Dara; but little is locally known about him save that 'he built in Connemara and lived in Aran,' and that a curse in his name is so formidable as to be avoided even by angry persons. As the church is up to the present undescribed, we may note that the two western angles and a long fragment of the north wall are standing to their full height, and that the whole extent of the foundation is well marked. The church measures 21½ feet across the western face, and 18 feet 4 inches by 36 feet 5 inches internally; the walls are 8½ feet high; the masonry is of late type, and probably (like the cut stones) is of the fifteenth century. The south door has a bold chamfer; near it lies a block with a 'semi-octagonal' stoup, once projecting from the face of the wall. The jamb stones from the east light show that it was a narrow slit with a reveal and splay; an iron 'tang' of a glazed window frame is embedded in one block. All these features are torn down. Only children under seven years of age are buried in the little graveyard; and the dedication of the well is forgotten, the name being Toberaneenagh, translated 'wine well.'

Near the church are traces of an extensive orchard and large mortar-built enclosures, witnessing former cultivation; traditions relate to members of the Lysaght family, and to an eccentric hermit, a retired officer named MacNamara, who lived away from his family and friends in the wilderness. The whole place must, however, have been far more populous in early times, as seventeen forts, one of unusual size, and other traces of habitation exist in Ballynahown and Oughtdarra, and some seven or eight defaced forts at a place called Shanbally in Ballyryan, towards the sea.

To the west of the church is a long ridge with craggy knolls known as Cnockaun (to south), Cnockaun gall, near the houses,[1] Cnockaunatinnagh (from its fox earths), to the north. Foxes are not unknown at present; and we were told that at night 'one would tumble over more brocks than rocks' on the ridge.[2] Along the edge of the latter, towards the north-west, we found in large rows of blocks clear traces of an ancient wall and a bastion-like small enclosure the highest and sharpest bend of the ridge. Thence every field opens a finer view of the sea, and the great natural pyramid of Croghateeaun.

---

[1] Another knoll near these is 'Cnockaun ada cloich.'

[2] The Clare people believe that there are two kinds of badgers - the 'dog-badger,' which feeds on carrion, and cannot be eaten, and the 'hog-badger,' which is herbivorous, and excellent food. Badger-bacon was 'a dish to set before a king' in early times (Book of Leinster – 'Boroma': see *Revue Celtique*, vol. xiii. (1892), p. 47.)

CROGHATEEAUN is a mote-like, conspicuous hill, one of the best landmarks in the district, shapely and grassy, rising high above the plateau and even overtopping the lower row of cliffs. On reaching the top, where we were told to cross ourselves as a protection against the power of the 'Dannans' (whose chief stronghold it was), we found a flattened summit surrounded by the foundations of a strong ring-wall. The garth measures 54 feet north and south, and 60 feet east and west, and the wall is from 8 to nearly 11 feet thick of blocks 6 feet to 4 feet long. All the upper stone work has been thrown down the steep slope, but the foundations, even of the gateway, are well preserved. It faced the S.S.E., and (as can be seen by the plan) had two posts 2 feet apart, the passage widening inward from 3 feet 3 inches to 6 feet wide, and being faced with large blocks. There are traces of curved enclosures to the north-west and north-east. Below, on a rise to the south-east, were also traces of a wall of blocks larger and ruder than those used in the caher. A raised path wound down the hill from the fort towards the north-west, formed by a curved bank 18 inches to 2 feet high. The older people are firmly convinced that this is a most dangerous 'fairy fort,' and tell how some badger-hunters, after a convivial meeting on its summit, got overtaken by night. They soon afterwards returned home in sobered terror, declaring that they had seen 'the whole fleet' of its ghostly inhabitants.

We next passed a late circular enclosure with a much older-looking semicircular mound inside; near, and east of it, towards a cultivated field, is a small ring of tumbled stones, an ancient hut-site. Westward lies another but modern ring-wall, once a 'bull park,' called 'Moher a tarriff.' Then we ascend a range of cliffs 80 to 100 feet high by a grassy gully, and reach the projecting promontory of Doonaunmore with its strange 'farbreag' or detached pinnacle near the southern end.

DOONAUNMORE a fine example of the inland promontory fort of the type of Caherconree. It is about 500 feet long from N.N.E. to S.S.W., and is fenced across the neck by a great rampart 309 feet long, and curving outward in the middle. The rampart is 8 feet 3 inches to over 9 feet thick, with an internal terrace 5 feet high and 3 feet wide. Externally, it is from 8 feet to over 10 feet high in the middle, but is much broken towards the east end. It has reaches of good masonry (the blocks often 4 feet by 3 feet by 3 feet), with two well-built faces, a smaller filling of field stones, and at least one upright joint, and the trace of a second in the outward face. At one point, where it crosses a slight depression, there is a platform 4 feet to 5 feet deep outside the fort. The blocks present a most time-worn aspect; but as their inner surfaces are nearly equally channelled, the weathering must have taken place before the erection of the fort. Dr. MacNamara thinks that the slight traces of a thin wall to each side of the neck are ancient, but they did not seem very old to me, unless we suppose them rebuilt; and fencing was certainly needful to the east of the neck, where the side is sloping though steep. Inside the wall are traces of hut-enclosures nearly levelled. The only legend we heard was that the fort was the residence of a giant who was defeated, slain, and his 'druid's staff' lost. Certainly it might be said of the builders, as of the Kenites of old, 'Strong is thy dwelling-place, and thou puttest thy nest in a rock.' The cave called after the Lysaghts, 'Ooan a leeshagh,' lies to the east of the fort; neither it nor the numerous other small caves (so far as I could learn) show signs of habitation.

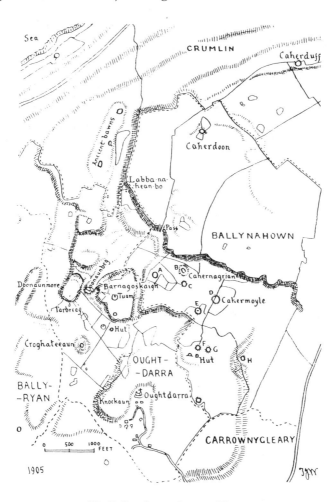

The Ballynahown Group of Forts.

Far up the valley, in the angle of the cliff where the three townlands of Crumlin, Oughtdarra, and Ballynahown meet, is a cranny and cave 'not belonging to any of them.' It is called 'Labba na hean bo'; and there, 'in the last great stroke for Ireland,' the decisive last battle – 'will be found the Ulsterman' who will play so great a part in the conflict. The personality of the 'one cow' is less clear; but it is certainly not the 'Glasgeivnagh' cow, although she, too, is said to have 'stayed' in the valleys of this place.

Across the pass, to the east of Doonannmore, the cliff is called Doonaunbeg, and is a reputed 'mote'; but I found no trace of walls to mark it as such. Farther eastward another gully ends in a long water cave; much of the roof has fallen in. Beside it, in a bold cliff facing westward, is the ope of Lysaght's cave, overhung by a regular 'mantel board' of rock, so regular as to appear artificial.

TUAM AN GASKAIGH. - From the end of the gully a slight depression bears the name of 'Barnagoskaigh,' the champion's gap. In the craggy field is a curious long fissure, partly natural, partly walled, and, for the most part, covered with slabs, so as to form a souterrain, 6 feet deep, and about 5 feet wide. It lies nearly east and west.

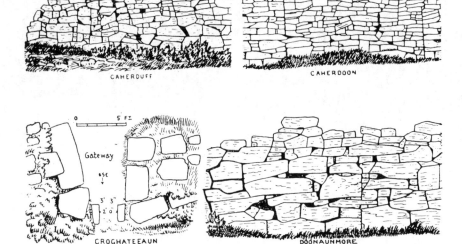

Details in Ballynahown Group of Forts.

The 'Tuam' is a monument of unusual character, under which some of the residents suppose that the souterrain passes. This monument lies in a little shallow amphitheatre of crag, and is called 'Tuam an Gaskaigh'; the edge of the depression is fenced at the top by an old wall, 4 feet 6 inches to 5 feet thick, of large, regularly-laid slabs. A slighter wall, nearly levelled, runs straight across the little depression from one end of the crescent wall to the other, forming a D-shaped enclosure, with the curve to the south. In the bottom of the hollow is the 'giant's grave.' It has to the north a slab enclosure, nearly square, two north slabs leaving a gap between them; a large block to each side, and four in a row to the south; the space measures 6 feet 8 inches north and south, but the sides are now disturbed. From near its south-east angle ran a line of five large stones lying north and south. Our guide remembered them side by side, and touching, but they are now dragged about. The 'champion,' said tradition, lay beside them with his great sword; so, in hope of finding it and 'some gold,' three or four young men overthrew the stones and got nothing. 'They had all to emigrate, and were not lucky'; but their act was not otherwise resented by the spirit of the mighty dead. No trace of a 'tuam' or mound remains.

Above the crescent wall, to the south-east, on a projecting crag, is the slight trace of a very small fort - or house-enclosure barely 50 feet across, and nearly levelled; it almost overhangs the hut-ring mentioned after Croghateeaun. At this point we descend into a narrow valley with good fields, hemmed in by parallel cliffs richly ivied, and a perfect prototype of embattled walls, bastions, and curtains. Up this valley we pass into

Ballynahown, for the eastern wall marks part of its bounds, and soon reach the Cahernagrian forts.

BALLYNAHOWN (O.S. 4). - It is usually called Ballynahooan, understood as named from the caves; others take the map-name, and derive it from the water-flows in the lower valleys. Ascending a steep pass, we reach the level of the upper terrace again. There we find an overthrown stone fort, wrongly called Cahernagrian on the map (A). It is nearly 100 feet across the garth, and the wall is too broken to measure the actual thickness (probably from 6 to 8 feet). It was of fairly large blocks and good masonry. It rarely rises 3 or 4 feet above the ground, and has traces of several hut-enclosures and other walls inside.

CAHERNAGRIAN. - The actual fort of the name, though small, was evidently the citadel of the settlement. It rests on a low, rounded knoll, sheeted with hazels, and strewn with huge boulders *in situ*, and well deserves its name from its sunny, sheltered position, near the foot of the giant wall of rock which rises directly to the north (B on plan).

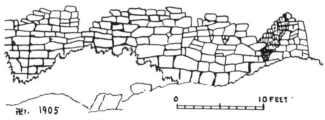

Cahernagrian – Rampart to North.

The fort is slightly oval in plan; the longer axis from north-west to south-east is 63 feet long inside, the cross measurement 57 feet. The wall is very well built with two faces of large, well-set blocks, each over a foot thick, but with small, rounded filling. It is altogether 6 feet 8 inches thick, is very neatly fitted, curved, and battered (the batter being 1 in 9). Where most perfect, to the north-west and north, it is still 9 feet high; but is only 5 feet high to the south-east. Inside are five well-marked but very irregular hut-enclosures, gardens of woodruff and orchis.

At the foot of the knoll, to the south-east, is another ring-wall (C), about 100 feet across and quite overthrown; it was probably a bawn. Further south, a fourth ring-wall (E), about 60 feet across, and much gapped, though still nearly 5 feet high; a ruined cottage stands in the garth. The largest of the forts is about 150 feet in diameter, and lies to the east of the last; it is crossed by a long boundary wall, and is so entirely overthrown as to be indescribable (D). It is remarkable that the smaller forts in north-western Clare should have been so systematically demolished. Balliny, Feenagh, Lismacsheedy, Caherdooneerish, Caherdoon, Cahercloggaun, Doonaunroe, and the Caherbullogs have escaped reasonably well, while nearly all the small forts, though often as massive and of as large blocks, are levelled almost to the ground.

Three hundred yards to the south of the 'house caher,' on a low knoll, are two (F, G) nearly-levelled cahers. They are closely similar. The walls of good, slab masonry, about 7 feet thick, and only rarely a few courses high;

the garths 99 feet to 102 feet across, and nearly circular. The gate of the
western fort faced the S.S.W. South from it, in the same field, is a curious
hut like that at Cahercuttine, near Noughaval. It consists of a circular wall
of large blocks, 3 feet 10 inches thick, with a gateway 3 feet 4 inches wide
facing the fort, northwards. The enclosure is 19 feet 3 inches across, and at
the wall, to the east, is the nearly-closed mouth of a souterrain. A defaced
and partly rebuilt cairn caps the corner of the knoll on which these forts and
hut stand.

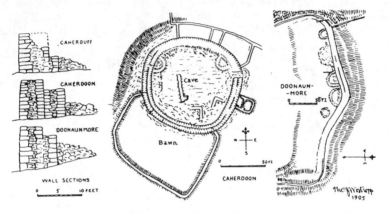

Ballynahown Group of Forts.

There is another caher, its walls only 3 or 4 feet high, on a bold crag 3000
yards to the east of the hut. Traces of other old walling lie round it in the
broken rocks. On the border, next Oughtdarra, a ring of small, mossed
filling marks another fort, and near it is an irregular bawn, with two low
'posts' of about 5 feet apart. I am told that another bold mass of crag is also
capped with a much-levelled fort, making, with Caherdoon, at least eleven
ring-walls in Ballinahown to the west of the hill road. To the east of it the
townland extends far up Knockaun's Mountain, and for nearly a mile and a
half to the Owen Callikeen brook on the borders of Kilmoon; but, so far as
the map and my informants could show, not a single fort exists in it, or the
great mass of some 3200 acres on Knockauns, Blake's Mountain, and Elva,
'for it was all woods,' added one. This was very probably true, as roots of
trees are found; so we see the forts were crowded together, on the crag
lands, on the slopes of the valleys near the sea, and on the high plateau.
Northern Clare appears to have scarcely altered since the Book of Survey
was compiled in 1655. Eastern Burren is still as it was written in the Wars
of Torlough, in 1311 and 1317, but various place-names and facts show that
trees once were found on its uplands.

Let us now return to Cahernagrian, whence a goat-path along the great
talus at the foot of the cliffs gives us a series of fine views of the forts and
pleasant green valleys, some stocked with cattle, and with pools, and even, at
times, streams; for Ballinahown means a place of 'rivers,' if the natives say
truly. The distant tower of Ballinalacken, dominating these townlands, the
grey sea and the rocks, level and shining like it, but fixed and lifeless, open
up to our view. Carpets of the mountain aven, creamy flowers on rich green
mats of foliage, cover the crags in parts; maidenhair and harstongue spring

up in the crevices, and the brilliant blue gentian, the primrose, violet, and woodruff, hide everywhere among the rocks, as we pass round the slope.

Round the angle we reach a most steep ascent, showing from the distance, as a conspicuous landmark, a brown smear, up the grey cliffs; it is a cattle pass to the upland. We scale it and cross the crags, losing sight of all else but the higher hills and the horizon seaward, till we note a wall rising over the crags and reach another fort, the loneliest of the group.

CAHERDOON is now getting named by the natives, 'Caherlochlannagh,' a mere late rendering of 'Danish fort' growing up in the decay of true tradition. It stands on a slightly raised sheet of rock, over 550 feet above the sea, and is an unusually fine and well-preserved ring-wall, beautifully built. As at Doonaunmore, the faces of the slabs are greatly channeled. I could not satisfy myself that the inner surfaces were equally worn. The plan and masonry are most regular, which favours its early date; for, as I have elsewhere shown,[1] the inferior masonry always rests above the better building. The caher measures 105 feet over all, and encloses a circular garth, 84 feet to 85 feet in diameter. The wall is built in two sections, each with good, separate faces, and each little over 5 feet in thickness, or from 10 to 11 feet thick in all. The inner section forms a terrace from 3 feet to 6 feet high; but I saw no traces of steps up to it. The outer wall has a batter of about 1 in 12 where not bulging out. The height varies, being 9 feet 6 inches to south-west, 6 feet 2 inches to south, 8 feet to east, and 6 feet to 7 feet high for much of the ring, save to the north-east, which is much demolished. It was probably kept for shelter on the sides next the sea. Several upright joints run up the whole height of the wall in the southern segment. The gateway faced the north-east; only the foundation of the northern pier is traceable. There are two nearly levelled loops of wall to the south and north, and the lower part of a small circular hut (joined by side walls to the rampart) on the south-east. In the south-west quarter of the garth are two modern huts, inhabited down to very recent times. There is also a souterrain, 27 feet from the western terrace, measuring 18 feet 8 inches, north-east and south-west, and 5 feet wide, lined with walls of small masonry, and roofed with great slabs, large and thin; one measures 7½ feet by 5 feet 4 inches, by 10 inches to 12 inches. Near the southern end, to the east, is a small side apartment, only 4 feet by 3 feet wide. It is interesting to contrast this fort with Caherdooneerish. The latter shows traces of rebuilding, patchwork, and, at least, two entire rings added to the wall, and showing differently spaced upright joints at various levels. At Caherduff all the work seems of one period; but the wall is much lower than at the other fort.

A defaced dolmen, called 'Labba' and 'Dermot's bed,' lies in the field to the east of the caher. It is quite overturned: a large prostrate slab and other stones remain, one leaning against the other; it is unmarked on the maps, and I could not find it on my last visit. An ancient enclosure lies in the next field to the east.

---

[1] *Journal*, vol. xxviii., p. 364 [46].

CAHERDUFF. - Crossing the ridge we find, a short way down its northern slope, on a knoll in front of a low ridge, an important fort named Caherduff, lying half a mile from Caherdoon. Nothing in its appearance suggests its gloomy name, unless, perhaps, that it occupies the shady slope opposite to Cahernagrian. It is built on a well-selected low knoll. The wall is 9 to 10 feet thick, and is of remarkably good masonry, more like Cahernagrian than like Doonaunmore and Caherdoon. It is over 10 feet high where best preserved, *i.e.* to the south and north-east, in parts 9 feet high; but great gaps occur, and the north and north-west parts are greatly defaced. The wall has two faces, and large filling, and has traces of a terrace, 28 inches wide. The batter is 1 in 12, and well carried out; much of the inner face has been destroyed. The garth is slightly hollow and very irregular, 96 feet across (north and south); the fort measuring about 116 feet over all. There are large rocks about the garth, and a slight, oblong hollow, as if the rock-surface was quarried out, and the space fenced with large blocks at intervals.

Caherduff Fort near Crumlin.

The outlook to the north is very fine, comprising all the Killonaghan Valley, and much of Galway Bay, Black Head, with Caherdooneerish, and the slopes, from the sandhills of Fanore (the site of one of the earliest settlements in Clare), Balliny (latest inhabited of the Clare cahers),[1] the Round Castle of Faunaroosca, and St. Onchu's Church. Every period of human history in Burren is represented in the scene. The other forts are of but little interest. The trace of a small ring-fort lies in the uppermost enclosed fields below Caherduff; and wandering over the plateau to the west

---

[1] *Journal*, vol. xxxi., p. 9 [68].

of the great cliffs, we found three rude old enclosures of slab masonry, partly rebuilt, but embodying ancient work, though neither regular nor massive. They were evidently cattle bauns. A low, grassy valley, and late house foundations, lay from them toward Cahernagrian, and the long pass from Oughtdarra.

INLAND FORTS. - These are of but little interest, but may be noted. Two earthen forts called 'mote' and 'Lislard' on the maps, and similar in character, lie on the ridge where the road descends to Ballinalacken. Each is a low earthen ring, with a rounded mound about 6 feet high in the garth, and may be sepulchral. The word 'mote' is even used for cahers in this parish.

KNOCKNASKEHEEN CAHER has been so completely demolished since 1839 that no trace can be found on the green knoll where it once stood, and which commands a beautiful view of the sea at Bealaghaline, with Doonagore Castle and the end of Moher to the south-west, and out to Callan and Slieve Bernagh to the south-east.

CAHERREAGH or CAHERKINALLIA is an ordinary ring-wall, much gapped and defaced, at the end of a long, craggy spur or knoll, projecting into a marshy hollow.

CAHERBARNAGH is levelled, barely marked by a few blocks and a slight ring, beside the road from Lisdoonvarna to Kilmoon.

BALLYREEN (O.S. 4). - The Ballyryan of the maps has a group of several decayed forts called Shanbally or Oldtown.

GLASHA GROUP (O.S. 8).

The only remaining group of any consequence lies along the seashore on the border of Corcomroe. The road from Ballinalacken to Roadford runs southward, and roughly marks the bounds of the shale and the limestone districts. As usual, stone forts are nearly absent from the former, and abound on the latter. They lie along a low ridge, rising northward to its highest point (about 300 feet above the sea) at the fort of Cahermaclancy, and falling thence northwards towards Shanvally in Ballyreen, and southward towards Bealaghaline Bay. The forts have suffered horribly by the hand of man. A few earth-forts lie near Killilagh Church and the hills at the end of the cliffs of Moher. Some (as Knocknastoolery) are of some size and interest. The only other antiquities are small cairns near the streams, and sometimes on actually marshy ground.

The place does not figure in early history, Glasha (Glaise) and 'the immunities of the MacFlannchada,' or Clanchies, being first named in the 1390 rental. The MacClanchies were hereditary brehons of Thomond, and often appear in local history both under the O'Briens, and even under English influence. So famed for their legal knowledge was this clan, that the unfortunate Gerald, Earl of Desmond, employed one 'O'Clankey, called Brehuff an Erle or the Earle's judge,' who was in possession of Shanegowle, near Askeaton, in County Limerick, in 1586, and is named that year in Christopher Peyton's important survey of the Earl's confiscated estates.[1] His contemporary, the merciless Boetius Clancy, was on the winning side, and left a dark tradition in Clare. He was sheriff of that county in 1588, and took active measures for the defence of Thomond from the Spaniards. Little defence was needed. The storm-tossed ships, with pestilence-weakened crews, came helplessly, seeking for shelter and water, along that dangerous coast, helped by pitiless men, and obtained no succour. Two ships are known to have perished at Tromra and Dunbeg. Tradition tells of a third at Doolin, and is borne out by the wreckage which drifted into Liscannor at the time the *Zuniga* lay off it in vain negotiations.[2] Those who escaped the breakers and the skeans of the maddened rabble of human wolves (who assembled to the plunder from all directions) fell into Clanchy's hands, and were duly hanged. The mound full of bones at Knockaunacroghera marks his work and in 1878, as a boy (and before the letters recording the wrecks in Clare had been published), I was shown it as 'the place where Boethius O'Clanshy hung the Spaniard grandee.' Clanchy accordingly stood well with Elizabeth's government, and was confirmed in the family 'immunities,' which were made into the manor of Knockfin, the name only surviving in the cross-road near the chapel.

In more peaceful times, says tradition, a princely house in Spain got leave to remove the bones of one of its sons; but they sought them in vain in that Golgotha of Corcomroe, 'in one red burial blent' with his brother officers and subordinates. It is wonderful how vivid tradition of the 'great Fleet' remains all along the Irish coast - so authentic that I have little hesitation in accepting even an unsupported statement, if older than 1880, when tradition began to get defiled. 'S.F.,' in *The Gentleman's Magazine*,[3] makes a curious mistake about Doolin and Killilagh Church; he regards them as the 'Dubh Glean' and 'the Abbey' named in the Cathreim Thoirdhealbhaigh, as the site of the fierce battle of Corcomroe in 1317. The real sites were at Deelin and Corcomroe Abbey, over fifteen miles away. After the civil war, in the disturbed times of 1655, the Clancies lost their heritage by confiscation. A later Boetius then held the Cahermaccrusheens, Cahermaclanchy, and Ballyroe, with Daniel oge O'Clanchy; Glasha, with Hugh Clanchy, and, as his own share, Cahergalleen, Tergoneen, and Toomullin. The confiscated lands were divided between John Sarsfield, Conor, son of Donough O'Brien, and Thomas Carr.

The destruction of the Down Survey maps of Clare, though most regrettable, is to some degree compensated for, the Book of Distribution and Survey for Clare being unusually detailed. There, under the parish of Killilagh, we find these lands (described as rocky pasture): Doonmacfelim, passed from Donough O'Brien to John FitzGerald; Doolin from Boetius Clancy to John Sarsfield; Tregownine, Corkeilty, Cahirgalline, West Glassie, Ballymaclancie, and Killeylagh glebe lands to the same. East Glassie, the property of Boetius and Hugh Clancie, went to John Gore; Caher Mc

---

[1] P.R.O.I., Peyton, p. 180.
[2] C.S.P.I., 1588: see *Journal*, vol. xix., p. 131.
[3] Volume xli., p. 89.

Crosseyne from Boetius and Donnell oge McClancie, to Conor, son of Donough O'Brien. It was arable, rough pasture, and pasturable mountain in 1655. Much of it passed to John Gore by 1675, the Edenvale Survey showing Ballyroe, Cragcurridane, Killeilagh, East Glassy, Ballymaclansy, and Cahermacreseine as his, while Tomolinny, Doolin, and Donegore, Tirgounine, Cahergaltine, and West Glassie belonged to Sarsfield. We need hardly say that Doonagore does not take its name from the Gores; for example, Terellagh O'Brean, of Innyshdyman, was granted 'Dounegoar' in 1582,[1] and the name occurs in other early records.

Lastly on March 30th, 1719, Brigadier-General Francis Gore, of Clonrone, granted in trust to John Vandelure, of Kilrush, and others, Cahircrusseen, Carhuegare, Tirgearnine, Dun mc Phelim, Cahirkeill, Cahirgunine, . . . Carhuenemanagh, West Glassy, Killylogh, . . . Timolin, Doneaghir . . . and Ballyvarry, *alias* Knockfinn, in the Barony of Corcom-roe.[2]

CAHERMACCRUSHEEN. - Beginning in this townland we find the remains of two cahers, nearly levelled; the more southern one, at the old bohereen, from Shanbally, gave its name to the place. At the boundary wall, next Cahermaclanchy, is a heap of blocks which marks a dolmen. It fell, or, as some say, was 'struck by a thunderbolt,' after 1890; and was a cist of the usual type of four slabs and a cover, embedded in a cairn. The sides are each about 10 feet by 4 feet, and lie side by side; over the north one lies the cover, 10 feet by 8 feet 2 inches wide to the west, and 6 feet to the east, being a slab from 7 inches to 9 inches thick. The west end is 5 feet, and the east 4 feet, which shows that there was the usual eastward taper. It is, as usual, named 'Labba 'iermuth,'[3] and probably fell when the supporting cairn was removed.

CAHERMACLANCY. - This fort stands on the highest point of the ridge, 302 feet above the sea. From it we look over a wild view, consisting of chasms and crags, to the cliffs of Oughtdarra and Ballynahown. Ballinalacken rises on its lofty crag to the north, amid clustering trees. Southward, we see the remains of several forts, the green hills of Killilagh, the round castle of Doonegore, and the cliffs of Moher, black precipices, the noblest, but only gloomy feature in that bright view; and to the west, the sea out to Aran. The caher is sadly dilapidated; much of the wall hardly rises a yard above the nettle-pestered heaps of debris. It was of fine masonry, the blocks 3 feet and 4 feet long; a few even 5 feet long. A gap in the south probably marks the gateway. An old herdman told me that there was a souterrain in the garth which ended in a deep pit, 'down into water'; the entrance is now visible, but filled up with stones. The fort is nearly circular; it measures 110 feet over all; the wall being from 9 feet to 10 feet thick. Some 300 yards away to the east is a nearly effaced square 'moher.' The maps show also two ring-walls northward towards the sea; these I did not visit, but the site is commanded from the chief caher.

---

[1] Report 14, D.K.R. – Fiants, 4263.

[2] Dublin Register of Deeds, B. 24, p. 320. Cahirgunine, probably in Tirgonine, and Carhuenemanagh, near Killilagh Church.

[3] First described by Borlase (*Dolmens of Ireland*, vol. i., p. 80).

GLASHAMORE. - Glasha fort, a circular mound, has been swept away since 1878. About 300 yards to the west of Cahirmaclancy fort, in a field on the border of Glashamore, are the foundations of a small ring-wall, 73 feet internally; the wall is 12 feet thick, of good blocks 2 feet 6 inches square, with small filling; it also has the entrance of a 'cave' in the garth. No gap for the gate is visible. The ribbed crags around it are full of the long crimped fronds of the hartstongue fern; and when I last saw it, the fort was like a saucer filled with wild thyme, magenta cranesbill, and golden bedstraw.

Another circular foundation lies in an adjoining field farther to the south-west. Near it is a remarkable cattle shelter, earlier than 1839, thick-walled, and so well built of good blocks as to suggest old work, especially at a semicircular portion with large foundation blocks. It is probably modern, but may have been built out of the material of some levelled forts.

GLASHABEG. - To the south of the 'cow-park' are the foundations of two more cahers. About two courses of good masonry and low green mounds mark their sites. They are nearly the same size, 86 feet over all. The more western is featureless, save for a very small cist or slab enclosure, 3 feet wide, and, apparently, once embedded in the wall. Its age is doubtful, but it suggests such cists or ambreys as occur in Kerry huts and (if the restorers were right) at Cloghanmore, in Donegal. Near this fort in the rock are very curious hollows, the shape and size of human footprints.

CAHERGLASHA, the more eastern of these forts, is interesting, though much levelled. It measures also 86 feet across the garth; the wall being 8 feet thick, and in places nearly straight. A gap to the north leads into a souterrain lying north and south for 15 feet; thence for 21 feet further it has fallen, forming a deep, grassy trench; then we meet a lintel 5 feet long, beyond which the passage is intact for 27 feet, and is said to have several small lateral chambers. At the end is a cross-wall 24 feet from the south segment of the wall. The souterrain is thus 63 feet long. The ruin of the northern end resulted from an attempt made many years ago to evict and exterminate a family of badgers which had established itself within the 'dark and covered way.'

Near these forts are some remains of a massive old straight wall of large blocks, some 4 feet long, and 3 feet high. It runs north-west and south-east.

BALLYVOE. - In the next field, to the south-west, lie the low foundations of a small ring, 40 feet over all. In another field, to the south, is an oval enclosure, 60 feet north and south, 76 feet east and west; near it is a large boulder, resting on several small stones, and the fort walls embody some rough rocks *in situ*, 4 feet to 6 feet long, and 3 feet high. There is a cross-wall 54 feet from the east across the garth; and to the north an arrangement of rocks, a few feet apart, with a space tapering eastward, suggests a dolmen, but may be natural. Between this and the sea is a huge tower-like rock, called Leagwee, looking like a castle from the lower slopes near Doolin.

Another fort of large blocks, but much broken, adjoins a ruined cottage; a fourth is square about 60 feet each way of large but late-looking masonry, and, probably, an old cattle-bawn. A cave or souterrain lies in the next field to the south-east.

BALLYCAHAN. - In this townland, which lies between Killilagh church and the sea, are the foundations of three circular cahers; they were only a few feet high even in 1878, when, at the suggestion of the late Dr. William H. Stacpoole Westropp, of Lisdoonvarna, I first went over the ground here.

Tooclae Group of Forts.

TEERGONEAN has also got the foundations of three cahers, nearly levelled before 1878; one may have been the Cahergunine of the records. Those and the forts I saw in Doolin are of small very regular masonry; the blocks 2 feet or 3 feet long, 18 inches to 20 inches high, and 2 feet thick, with two faces and small filling. The latter quality probably brought about their collapse, and facilitated their removal. The maps mark another site in Doolin, near the old silver mine. There is a defaced fort in Doonmacfelim; from its position evidently the chief fort of the place. It is named Caheradoon, and lies on rising ground. It is 108 feet across; the wall was removed fifty years ago to make the new road near the school. It may be the Cahergaline (suggesting Bealaghaline), as being near that townland, which boasts yet one more nearly levelled caher. Caheragaline or Cahergaltech, in Killylagh, was granted by Sarsfield to Mr. Foard.[1]

Caherkeily, Carhuekeily or Corkelly, is also named as near this place in the same deed and in the Book of Distribution. Between Caherdoon and the shore road we find two other cahers on a sheet of crag near the sea. The northern measures about 60 feet across, all its facing having been removed. The southern retains its wall, which is 7 feet thick, well built, with two faces, and 4 to 6 feet high, with a batter of 1 in 3. The large lintel of its gate is 7 feet 2 inches long, embodied in a ruined cottage in the garth. The garth is 65 feet across.

Farther to the east are numerous foundations in a field, called, as so frequently, Parc na Caheragh; a ring-wall, 50 feet across; a square moher, 30 feet by 36 feet at 28 feet from the last; and several other old-looking enclosures with large blocks. The sandhills near these have yielded flint implements, and traces of early settlement.[2]

To complete the lists of forts, between the road and the sea, we return past the wrecked peel-tower of Doonmacfelim to Killilagh church. This is a neat structure of the late fifteenth century, but with earlier records. I regret to say that since my brief description[3] was published in 1900, the east gable and window have fallen in the great gale of 1903, which also wrecked Clooney church in the Barony. Near the west end lies a flat-topped, circular mound, the resort, on all occasions on which I saw it, of a crowd of cattle enjoying the breeze on its summit. The top had been dug into deeply; it may be a burial-mound, and is only 90 feet in diameter. A low rath is on the rise to the east of the church.

The conspicuous earthen fort of Knockastoolery is on the hillside above Roadford, on a spur, and, I think, was partly carved out of the hill. It is over 12 feet high, girt by a deep fosse, with a high outer ring; and the narrow summit is crowned by two limestone pillars. The standing one is 6 feet 3 inches high, widening to the top; one edge has corrugations and flutings, to my thinking mere weather-marks, which some have supposed to be ogmic scores. I am satisfied that the other alleged ogams at Cloghanairgid, near Bohneil, and Lismulbreeda cave are mere idle and meaningless scores. The three scores on the slab at Temple Senan on Scattery may or may not be ogmic; and the Callan slab is probably a mediæval scholastic, though evidently far older than the late eighteenth century. The caher near the interesting round castle of Doonegore had been nearly entirely levelled by 1838; only a trace of its northern segment is now to be found.

The little stream which probably gave its name to Glasha, runs southward and sinks near Killilagh church, probably meeting a larger stream past Roadford, which runs over level sheets of rock, losing itself in the shingle and golden sands of the bay near Fisher-street. Above its mouth, on a high

---

[1] Dublin Register of Deeds, B. 1, p. 425.
[2] *Limerick Field Club Journal*, vol. ii., p. 50.
[3] *Journal*, vol. xxx., p. 287; *Proc. R.I.A.*, vol. vi., Ser. III., p. 135.

knoll, at Neadanea, an extensive and pleasing view is obtainable over the whole site, back to Cahermaclanchy and the cliffs at Ballynahown. On the main branch, called the Aille river, not far from St. Brecan's church, at Toomullin, are several large earthen forts - Knocknaraha, in Toomullin, Moanbeg, and an adjoining ring, and Aughavinna fort, near the stream. There are few other forts in the parish, only a small one in Gortaclob, near St. Catherine's; Knockalassa fort, near Lisdoonvarna; and some few sites and defaced earth-rings at Lurraga, Glasha House, and Tonwaun.

MOHER UI RUIS. On the Hag's Head (the ancient Kan Kalye of the sixteenth century topographers) stood a promontory fort named Moher which gives its name to the great cliffs at that place. It was unfortunately levelled as material for the telegraph tower, built in its ambit in 1808. It is probably commemorated on the modern name of Cahermoher Bridge, not far to the south - and is (so far as we know) the only promontory fort on the mainland coast between Donegal Head, near Beltard, and Dunnamoe, in Mayo. It was standing in 1780. John Lloyd, in quaintly inflated language, describes it in his *Impartial Tour in Clare.* 'On this western cape or headland lies the famous old fort Ruan, called Moher. . . the summit of a very stupendous cliff surrounded with a stone wall, a part of which is up. Inside of it is a green plain. . . This wonderful promontory, almost encompassed by devouring seas, and the opposite wild coast, really affords a horrible and tremendous aspect, vastly more to be dreaded than accounted.' If we consider the tower as made of the material of the fort, the masonry must have been very small. It commands a beautiful view of the coast from Connemara to Beltard. The forts of Dun Conor and Dun Oghil, and (unless we are mistaken) Dun Aenghus, in the Aran Isles, are visible from these cliffs; and beyond them, the furthest outpost of old Thomond towards America, the lofty lighthouse on the Brannock rock is clearly seen.

LEHINCH (O.S. 23). - This little watering-place deserves its name as being on a peninsula between the sandy, stormy bay and the creeks behind the shattered many-windowed tower of Dough. To the north of the castle and creek is a furze-covered knoll in a marsh, which may be a crannoge. Some distance along the Dael river is an excellent example of a rath, with deep fosse and outer ring, near New Bridge. In the townland of Dough, near the railway, are two neat, green raths called Parknareliga and Parknalassa forts; each has a raised centre, a fosse, and an outer ring. South from Lehinch is the dolmen of Calluragh described by Miss Parkinson in the *Journal* for 1901.[1]

DOONEEVE, or 'Doonmeeve,' as it is named on the maps, seems to have been a fort of considerable importance. It is called 'Doon Ivagh' and 'Doonmihil' by the country folk, and lies on the cliff near the Protestant church. Only two segments of fosse remain, cut deeply into the slope. The inner (western) is 10 feet deep, 9 feet broad at the bottom, and 30 feet at the top, cut into drift and shale rock. The second trench lies 46 feet away, and is from 6 feet at the bottom to 22 feet wide at the top, and 6 feet deep. The

---

[1] Volume xxxi., p. 437.

inner ditch is dry, but water runs down the outer. The greater part of these trenches has been so completely filled in as to leave hardly a trace. From the rapid inroads of the sea in our time[1] I find it hard to believe that they represent a promontory fort. The place has some interesting folk-lore attached to it, and is to some degree protected by its very repute. One man, at no distant date, attempted to till its garth, and was struck down as if dead. His wife, a 'wise woman' who 'had witchcraft,' on hearing the disaster, rushed to the nearest fairy spot and did charms. She then went to Dooneeva and ordered its unseen occupants to bring back her husband at once; the man, to the surprise of everyone, revived and recovered consciousness; while a stick was taken away as a substitute. Non-miraculous explanation seems very easy; but I believe all the ritual was done and said in perfect good faith. The traditions of this district are still to be harvested; I formerly attempted in these pages to give briefly those relating to the lost island of Kilstapheen or Kilstiffin,[2] still a reef (the sea breaking over it at low water) at the mouth of the bay, and, as such, marked on our charts. Near Moy is a battle legend, possibly an echo of that terrible frontal attack, up Bealanchip hill, in 1573, in a civil feud of the O'Briens. The legend, however, asserts that 'a Dunbeg man' took the cattle of 'Stapheen,' who set out in pursuit, and overtook the robber at Bohercrohaun. Both sides fought heroically, but in the excitement and struggle Stapheen lost the key of his island, and it at once sank under the sea. Once in seven years its golden domes rise over the green waves, but with ill omen to anyone who sees them, for the beholder must die before they reappear when seven more years have passed by.

CAHERS. – Besides the forts we have examined in this barony in Killilagh, at Doon, and at Ballykinvarga, a few Caher names must be collected. In Kilmacreehy parish was Caherycahill, now levelled, and Cahergrillaun in Loslorkan; Caherbarnagh, now levelled; Kahernafurresha, a defaced fort on a low cliff cut entirely by the sea, and so to the west of Liscannor. In Killaspuglonane were Caherlassaleehan; and Caheraderry, the Cathridarum granted by King Donaldmore O'Brien to Clare Abbey in 1189. The Cathair in Doire of the 1390 rental; evidently an oak forest then sheltered the almost treeless slopes. Liscannor fort is said to have been on the site of the harbour, and a few insignificant ring-forts remain in the parish. In Kilshanny parish were Caheraphreegaun, now gone, Caherycoosaun, Caherlooscaun, and Caherreagh, already noted as in Caherkinallia; also the fine cairn of Cairn Connaughtagh, 12 feet to 14 feet high, near the river Dael, and, possibly, the inauguration place of Cairn mic Tail. In Clooney were Cahersherkin (Cathair seircin in 1390), Caherballagh, and Lisdereenacaheragh in Knockagraigue. It is much to be regretted that no one seems to have collected any description of the forts of this most interesting county till 1839; and then the writers of the Ordnance Survey letters lost an unrivalled opportunity. That we came almost too late to save the folk-lore, and too late to record some most interesting structures and features, must be our excuse that our survey is not richer that it is. For the

---

[1] Bronze implements were found on the shore below the fort.
[2] Volume xxx., p. 289.

disturbance of its original system and the out-of-place additions, and possible omissions, in its pages, we can only trust to the forbearance of our readers, and their recognition of the inevitable limitations of one who worked almost single handed in one of the most difficult but richest fields of the 'prehistory' of ancient Ireland.[1]

[1] For this section of my Paper I have to thank not only (as so often) Dr. George U. Macnamara, but Miss Parkinson, and Miss G. C. Stacpoole, for fieldwork, and collecting legends for my Paper in the Lehinch district.

5

The two greatest needs of Irish archæology are certainly field surveys and excavations. When I commenced to publish my notes on the ring-forts of North-Western Clare, in 1895, my intention was only to give descriptions of the ten most important examples. I also gave my notes and plans of the dolmens to Mr. WilliamC. Borlase for his great work, and only included such in my paper after 1897. The first design I modified before the first part of that paper went to press, and (as recast) from time to time, from 1896 to 1905, the attempted survey appeared,[1] with many corrections and unavoidable repetitions, as materials grew or fuller descriptions seemed desirable.

At present it were too much to hope to print an absolutely exhaustive survey of so rich a district; the more modest design of giving accounts of all the more instructive remains is all that I attempt. With this object I may now be allowed to give a further part of the survey long laid aside for my study of the cliff forts. These papers, in a certain sense, 'complete' (if such a term be not too pretentious) the description of the great majority of the dry-stone forts in Burren, Northern Corcomore, and the parish of Kilnaboy, in Inchiquin. With the papers on the forts of the Irrus,[2] and those near Milltown-Malbay, in this *Journal*,[3] and those on the forts of Eastern Clare in the *Proceedings of the Royal Irish Academy*,[4] I believe that descriptions sufficient to enable students to realize the plans and features of the forts (whether of earth or stone, residential or otherwise) are given for all Co. Clare. The survey of such remains is not only necessary, but urgent. It is literally a race with Destruction. So little does the professed patriotism of the men of Clare bear fruit in the care for or preservation of their country's past, that since 1895, and much more since I began my work on the county

---

[1] *Journal,* vol. xxvi, pp. 142 [1], 362 [17]; vol. xxvii, p. 116 [23]; vol. xxviii, p. 352 [35]; vol. xxix, p. 367 [47]; vol. xxxi, pp. 1 [62], 273 [76]; vol. xxxv, pp. 205 [94], 342 [116].

[2] *Ibid.,* vol. xxxviii, pp. 28, 221, 344; vol. xxxix, p. 115.

[3] Vol. xli, p. 117.

[4] Vol. xxvi (c), pp. 217, 371; vol. xxix (c), p. 186.

in 1878, the ruin of its remains is alarming. What may be left to Irishmen of the next century in what is probably the district of Europe richest in these early remains (that from St. Finan's Bay to Galway Bay), I fear even to conjecture. The deadly triad (the road-maker, rabbit-catcher, and treasure-seeker) is at its malign work, tearing down and defacing gateways, terraces, and steps, as well as lofty ramparts, huts, and sepulchres, for selfish or foolish ends. No wholesome public spirit exists in this matter, so that the County Councils, which have the power, do not use it, excepting in the honourable cases of the councillors of counties Cork and Galway. The latter first conserved the remains near Tuam. This good example has had no effect on their less enlightened neighbours. It is impossible to speak of the outrages against ancient remains occurring constantly over this large tract of country, with the severity for which they call; all that can be done is to secure views, plans, and descriptions of the fast-vanishing antiquities.

As 'the study of the forts is the study of the homes of the early Irish,' it might be expected to excite sympathy and win workers; but how many (even among Irish antiquaries) do more that give an occasional paper on the remains? How many more encourage or help the few workers? Some who are interested in the medieval history, genealogies, and architecture of Ireland oppose studies in 'prehistory' as 'heaping up prehistoric rubbish.' Others, glorying in their country's early legends, resent the results of more critical workers; like the poet's hapless knight, they awake on 'the cold hill-side' of fact, after gorgeous visions of 'kings and death-pale warriors,' and they are offended. By hard work, not by 'exaggerating things that never happened' (as a cynic said of us), may 'the ancient glories of Ireland' be secured. Our ideal must be that of the ancient miner - 'he setteth an end to the darkness and searches out the furthest bound, the stones of darkness and the gloom.' A brilliant example of what energy can do is set to Ireland by the antiquaries of France.[1] Virtually, since the last section of this paper was read to our Society in 1905, a great work has been done in that country. Not (as in Ireland) a mere half-dozen workers with no State support or public sympathy, but a large band of well-equipped antiquaries have done that work. Yet we may get courage, for our neighbours have won European attention, and their study of Irish work has spread it farther than was ever the case before. When we add to this the value attached by foreign antiquaries to the collection of the Royal Irish Academy - largely resulting from the writings, the unsparing study, and deep insight of Mr. George Coffey - we may hope that Irish Archaeology in giving to the continent of Europe may have much given to it from those working in a wide field under

---

[1] I especially refer to the fine reports of each individual Congress of the Prehistoric Congress (espically the Compte-rendu de la 3me Session, Autun, 1907, p. 997, for a comparative study of the early forts of Europe, by Dr. A. Guébhard), the Bulletins of the Prehistoric Society of France, and the Reports of the Commission for the study of early enclosures under the last-named Society. Of individual papers, I also refer to *Les enceintes préhistoriques des Pré-Alpes maritimes*, by Dr. Guébhard (printed at Nice, 1907); Bullenins 25-26 du Club alpin français: and his *Le vrai problème des enceintes prèhistoriques* (Congrès II). I purposely refrain from citing (save in one case too apposite to omit) papers in other French societies.

brighter auspices than ourselves. So little accessible is their survey to most Irish workers that a brief outline of some of its results should interest and help our antiquaries.

The conclusions so far derived by the French 'Commission d'étude des enceintes préhistoriques' are not very dissimilar from our own, save that we Irish have a richer literature, and evidently adhered to the primitive types to a far later period than was the case in France. It is no exaggeration to say that the plan, the features, the structure, and the masonry of the walls are indistinguishable from those of Ireland. Taking the 'Castellaras' (ring-walls) of the Alpes Maritimes, we see the curious 'running together' of the layers of stones, seen so well at Caherminaun, and the careful fitting and small packing pieces in the unavoidable interstices; the wall, with two faces of large stones, and with filling sometimes thrown in, at other times more carefully packed while the faces were being raised; the almost needless clinging of the walls to the lesser projections of cliffs and rock-edges, their structure, in two or more sections, sometimes forming a terrace; and the beautifully laid, almost rectangular, natural blocks. All these might occur in Ireland or the Irish equivalents in France, without exciting any surprise or any feeling that the features were rare or exceptional. This is equally the case with the plans; a series of well-defined types both of earthen and stone forts occur, identical with those of Ireland. The fortified spur, whether a sea-headland (as most frequently in Ireland) or, more commonly in France, an inland spur; the crescent fort, abutting on a cliff or steep slope; the ring-fort, oval, circular, or D-shaped in plan, with (at times) two or three concentric walls, or a side annexe; its square equivalent; the high and low flat-topped motes, round or square, in some of which excavations have disclosed not a few Gaulish and Roman remains, while others proved to be of the later Middle Ages - all are represented in France, as in Ireland. Identical, too, with those in Ireland, are the basin-stones found in French forts and the gateways, having jambs formed by the coursed wall-facing and strong lintels. That several of the French stone forts go back to pre-Roman times is well established. There are, of course, exceptional features, like dry-stone walls embodying frameworks of beams (noted by Cæsar),[1] the round bastions of the dry-stone fortress of Constantine (B-de-Rh.), or the towers flanking the outworks of such forts as Mount Milan (C. d'or) or Neiron (Var.), which have no Irish equivalent; for our early countrymen (and even the builders of the late peel towers and courts) rarely concerned themselves to provide for flank defence. Anyone anxious to compare definite examples should study the pre-Roman Camp du Bois at Rouret (Pré-Alpes Marit.) with Dun Aengusa or Cahercommaun. The former is called a 'Roman camp' as loosely as some here use the term 'Danish fort.' It rests on a hill 1547 feet high, and is fenced by two half-rings; the inner garth is about 283 feet by 113 feet deep, the outer 16 feet to 65 feet distant from the inner wall, which has fallen in part to the south and is 7 to 8 feet thick. The inner wall is fairly perfect, some of its blocks 4 feet long and over 3 feet high, of good masonry, with small stones filling the crannies. Compare Dun Conor in Aran with the Castellaras de Mauvans. The French fort differs but little in

---

[1] This, of course, is not unknown in Great Britain.

design, save in the curious entrance of its annexe, where the ends overlap, making a short passage. It has a fine oval central ring and a nearly defaced outer one; judging from the fine photographs, upright joints (a very 'Irish' feature) occur. The equally fine Castellaras de La Malle (Alpes M.) has typical lintelled gates or posterns. The D-shaped plan, found at Caherdooneerish, in Clare, has a representative in another Camp du Bois, at Cœlan (C. du Nord), but it has a fosse and a slight outer ring.

The straight-fenced promontory fort, like Doonegall, county Clare, may be compared with one at Bois l'Evêque at Villey le Sec (the mound 20 feet to 26 feet thick at the base, with a fosse outside, and over 300 feet long), or with the finer Camp de Voeuil, a great earthwork with a slight curve and a sharp turn at the right (E.) end, across a bold spur like Doonaunmore in Clare. Unlike the Irish forts, the core of the earth consists of a mass of calcined (apparently not vitrified) rocks.[1] The variety so common in Ireland, having a fosse with a mound of dry-stone wall convex to the land, finds an excellent French example at Dramelay in Jura. A good example of the double wall is the 'pear-shaped' enclosure of Casteou-Vassou or Collet-Assout (Alpes M.). These are only a few of the examples illustrating Irish types.[2]

I emphasize the similarity not to assert a common origin for these forts (as I inclined to do in the first of the present series of papers in 1895-6), but rather the reverse, to show how the human race in Europe (and indeed in S. Africa and N. America) possessed an instinct, or rather a 'hereditary accomplishment,' which led them to build such 'forts.' So children, playing on the sands, dig miniature replicas of the rath, with concentric circles, or an annexe, and the mote, with its bailey; or the country labourers dig a fosse and a ring-mound round a plantation, or build a dry-stone ring-wall for that or some other object. On the other hand, there was evidently abundant communication in very primitive times between Ireland and the Continent, and building suggestions may have been imported from the latter, like the early forms of ornament, from the Bronze Age down. The old idea, not yet extinct, of Ireland's complete originality and isolation from Europe, has little to commend it to scientific workers. That such structures occur in France, from possibly Neolithic to post-Roman times, and, with all such types, all across Europe, from the Ural mountains to the cliffs of western Ireland, and that the types reappear in such isolated regions as Mashonaland and the valleys of the Mississippi and Ohio, gives too weighty a caution to be overlooked, and precludes the idea of any type of entrenchment belonging exclusively to any one period or race.

The types do not spring merely from the sites. We have not only crescent forts on high cliffs, but also on the low field, at Ballycar Lake, where Cahernacalla was dug.[3] Irregularities in the curves of the wall occur equally

---

[1] *Bulletin Soc. Arch. de la Charente*, 1899, described and figured by M.A. Cognot.

[2] It is only in the publications of the *Soc. préhist. de France* that I find any descriptions of buildings comparable to Turlough Hill Fort or the Cathair of Ballydonohan: see *Journal*, vol. xxxv, p. 224 [111] and *Proc. R. I. Acad.*, vol. xxvii, p. 395. Cf. *Rapports soc. préhist. de France*, 1907, p. 4, and 1909-10, p. 421.

[3] *Proc. R. I. A. Acad.*, vol. xxvii, p. 227.

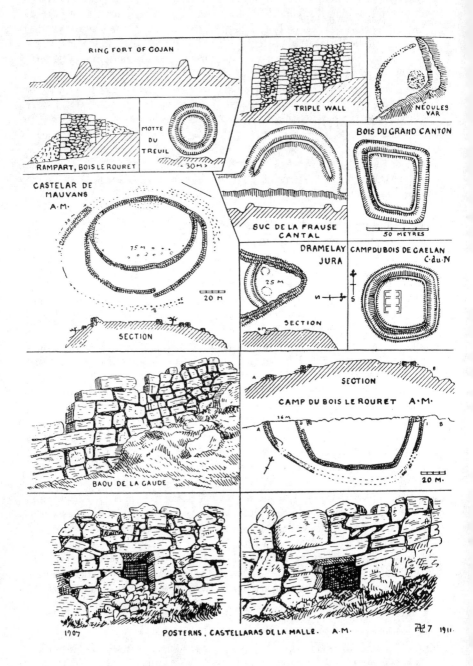

Examples of French Forts.

in the fortified rock platform and on open plains like certain Corcaguiny forts and Innishmurray Cashel. The ring occurs indifferently in level fields, spurs, and steep slopes. Like the whole subject, this question is at present far too unstudied and fresh for anything but diffident study and suggestion.

Another problem which is slowly coming forward I press on the attention of other workers (especially those labouring in the fields of early Irish literature); being little qualified (though compelled) to face it myself. The question is whether certain existing forts are neither residential nor sepulchral, but ceremonial.[1] The fact of either of the former uses does not, of course, prevent the last, but it is not improbable, and seems implied by several early elements in Irish literature, that some of these ring-forts were temples. Whether such were the case or not, in the vast majority of the Clare forts, other questions of like nature might be asked such as whether the human skeletons found in the ramparts of some forts (such as Dun Conor, Tara, &c.) were victims offered to the 'dedication' of the fort. Human victims were offered at the foundation of Emania Fort[2] in the fourth century before our era (if Cormac's Glossary be correct), while when Dun fidhne was made by four chiefs, Cuchongeilt (Eoghan Bél's son) asks a swine-herd for pigs 'for this their fort's inauguration . . . as many of the swine as shall seem sufficient.'[3] The usage has a close equivalent in the horse-skulls placed in the walls, or under the floors, of certain old houses (like Edenvale and Moyreisk, in Clare, and Attyflin, in Limerick), to my knowledge, and in other cases even living cats were immured in holes in the newly built walls.[4]

Of the forts described in this section, however, none seem to be of this character, though it is possible (if not probable) that Turlough Hill,[5] Creevagh, Cahernabihoonach,[6] and Magh Adhair may be such. The second (with its rock-cut avenue and enclosed dolmen), and the third (also surrounding a dolmen) recall a French side-light on these and the slab fences and 'peristyles' at other dolmens and cists, such as Iscancullin and the pillared dolmen of Ballyganner and Leanna. Such enclosures in France

---

[1] *Supra*, vol. xl, p. 291.

[2] *Three Irish Glossaries* (ed. Whitley Stokes, 1862); Cormac's Glossary (c 800), p. xli. The horrible legend of the burial alive of Odran (a companion of St. Columba), with his own consent, may be found in The Book of Lismore, p. 7. See also *Proc. R.I.A.* (1870), p. 267.

[3] Life of St. Cellach, in *Silva Gadelica* (S. H. O'Grady, translated), vol. ii, p. 65.

[4] *See Folk Lore*, vol. xxii, p. 54.

[5] For this group see *supra*, vol. xxviii, pp. 357 [39], 359 [41]; vol. xxxv, pp. 217, 218 [105] ; vol. xxvi, p. 119 [26]. If the antiquaries of Co. Cork had not since the time of John Windele absolutely ignored their fine series of forts, we might find very apposite cases; at least one is found in Cahermoygilliar.

[6] Such, I find from Mr. O'Dea, the owner of Ballyganner Castle, is the local name of the 'Dolmen Caher,' of Ballyganner, it having been a haunt of thieves: *Journal*, vol. xxvi, p. 119 [26]. It may be identified on Map No. 9 of the recent Ordnance Survey (division 11), by being close to the S.E. mearing of Ballyganner North, at the word 'cromlech,' and due north from the B of the townland name of Ballyganner South. The small fort to the N.E. is in the 'Cairn Caher.'

range from the Neolithic period down to at least Roman times[1]; in Clare they may go back (as the dolmens probably do) to the Bronze Age; but some of these slab fences may be of the later Middle Ages. The Irish certainly had little scruple in combining burial-places, residences, and temples, or at least ceremonial forts, as is shown clearly at Tara, Usnach, and Rathcroghan.

Last year yielded to the collection of the Royal Irish Academy six urns and numerous flint implements from a cairn in Drumruagh Fort, Co. Tyrone; and the bronze ring-pin, leaf-shaped chert implement, and worked flint implement from Dun Aengusa, found by Dr. Colley March, which, with the remarkable collection from the Dunbel raths, Co. Kilkenny, belonging to this Society, show what a work has yet to be done for Irish forts.

None of the forts here studied seem in any sense 'military.' Caherlisaniska and Poulacarran are overlooked, and to our mind commanded by closely adjoining high crags. Only the weak little fort of Garracloon occupies a really strong position.[2] Probably except Caheridoola (in the forts other than the Lisdoonvarna group) all are late and evidently decadent structures. The latest and most decadent of all are probably the bawns or cattle-pens in Gleninshen, and the south end of Poulacarran Valley. The bawns of Gleninshen, for aught I can see to the contrary, may belong, like the park walls of Lemaneagh, to the latest seventeenth century.

THE FORTS. - Need I again commence by stating that I use the term 'prehistoric' for any unrecorded early period,[3] and 'forts' for residential, sepulchral, or ceremonial enclosures? Of over 2400 forts in county Clare, there are in Burren some 310, in Inchiquin some 320, and in Corcomroe 190, but in the richest district recorded in this paper and its predecessors lie some 500 forts only. Of these I have given notes on about 350; the others are in (so far as I have seen them) mere defaced rings of debris, or rude, late, featureless cattle pens. In no case has one of these forts (even such important ones as Ballykinvarga, Cahercommaun, Caherdooneerish, Lismacsheedy, or Turlough Hill Caher) been conserved or vested as an ancient monument. Of the rare features - perfect gateways (which hardly exist outside Mayo, Galway, Clare and Kerry) are found at Ballykinvarga, Poulcaragharush, Caheranardurrish in Glensleade, Moheramoylan, Lisananima, and the 'Cairn-Caher' of Ballyganner. Others standing in my recollection, at Dangan, near Ballyvaughan and Cahercuttine, not to speak of others evidently entire in very recent days (such as Rannagh, Moheraroon, Lismoher, Caherlisaniska and Caherminaun), are now defaced and the lintels

---

[1] See a very helpful paper, by M. Ulysse Dumas, *Bulletin Soc. préhist. de France*, 1908, pp. 156, 183. I cleared as far as I was able the annexe of the pillared dolmen of Ballyganner, and made a plan of the entire structure, my previous ones only giving the actual dolmen.

[2] This does not imply 'strong position, weak fort,' for Cashlaun Gar and others on strong, naturally defended sites are very massive, and others on level fields or in hollows, thin-walled and poorly built.

[3] It is interesting to note that in the French studies, so closely akin to those of our Irish forts, the same difficulty is felt. 'L'épithète *de préhistorique* . . . mais qui doit s'efforcer d'inventorier le plus grand nombre possible de monuments sans histoire.' (Rapport 3, Commission for the study of enclosures).

thrown down. Outside of Clare, I only know of the three at Dun Aengusa, in Aran, one at Ballynasean, in the same island, four at Innismurray in Sligo; others at Coolcashel (Kilcashel) and Cashelbarna, in Mayo; Dunbeg (Fahan) and Staigue in Kerry and Cahermoygilliar, county Cork, but others very possibly remain and should be recorded and photographed; that at Grianan Aileach is (of course) rebuilt. Antiquaries in 1893 laid down that there were no terraces or steps in Clare *cathracha*,[1] but there are terraces (and walls in two or more sections) at Ballykinvarga, Caheridoula, Caher-Mullach, Caherahoagh, the upper fort of Ballyallaban, Glenquin, Caherbullog Lower, Cahernaspekee, Caherschrebeen, Cahercommaun, two at Moheraroon, Caheradoon in Ballynahown, Doonaunmore, Poulacarran crescent fort, and probably Poulgorm; steps remain in Caherminaun, Ballyshanny, Caherahoagh, Cahercommaun and perhaps Caherdooneerish. Plinths remain outside part of the wall of Ballyallaban Caher, and inside that of Cahercuttine and Caherduff; Creevagh and Cahernabihoonach enclose dolmens. Of unusual or complex plans – Cahercommaun is triple, the outer walls being of crescent plan, Glenquin, Cahergurraun, and Tullycommaun cahers are double: Doonaunmore and Anneville (Inchiquin Lake) are inland promontory forts, and Caherlisaniska an unusual type of cliff fort; Cahercashlaun, Cashlaun Gar, Tirmicbrain, Croaghateeaun, and the east caher of Moheraroon are fortified knolls; Turlough Hill fort has numerous gateways; Doon near Kilfenora has a rock-cut fosse, steps and piers, and Ballykinvarga, is one of the four Irish forts possessing an abattis, while Creevagh and Cahernabihoonach (*bitheamnach*, a robber) enclose dolmens, and a cairn and small cist existed in Caheranadurrish (Glensleade) in 1895. These notes show how remarkable a group still exists, though in great jeopardy, in north-western Clare, and I hope may justify this attempt to continue if not to complete the survey of that district, even should it lead to no effort to preserve even a few of these important remains.

In Clare, at the very least, the forts of Bealboru, Magh Adhair, Cahercalla, Cahershaughnessy and Moghane in the eastern half; Cahercommaun, Glenquin, Cahermacnaughten, Lismacsheedy, Doonaunmore, Cahercottine, and, above all, Ballykinvarga in the north-western, and Doonegal, Lisnaleagaun, Liscroneen, and Dundahlin in the south-western part should be vested. It is not a question of spending money, for any 'restoration' is greatly to be deprecated, but only to secure each structure from further injury. Were the above bare list, by any good fortune, accepted, and others ordered to be preserved, it could be easily extended. Ballydonohan Caher, Lugalassa, Lisnagree, Langough, the double forts of Drumbawn and Creevagh near Quin, and the square fort of Culleen in the east, Caherdoonerish, Turlough Hill, Cahercloggaun, Caheranardurrish near Glensleade, Cahercashlaun, Cashlaungar, Caherconnell, Lisnastoolery with Cahernabihoonach and Creevagh near Glencurraun, with their enclosed dolmens, Cahergrillaun and Doon in Burren and its borders, Mullach in Inchiquin, Cahermurphy Castle earthworks, Dundoillroe, Doonaghbwee, Lisduff near Moveens, and others, in any country save Ireland, would be

---

[1] I have been contradicted in the early days of this survey for stating the contrary, for the subject of forts was then regarded as 'closed.'

held worthy of conservation. If this is not soon undertaken, the vandalism of country gentry, farmers, rabbit-hunters, road-menders, and treasure-seekers must soon reduce the well-preserved and remarkable remains of Clare to the condition in which antiquities are found in county Limerick.

BELL HARBOUR GROUP (O.S. 3).

The extreme north-eastern corner of Burren ends in two valleys, the more southern, in which the 'Abbey of the Fertile Rock,' Corcomroe, and the three very early churches of Oughtmama stand, between Turlough Hill and Behagh Hill; the northern, between Behagh and Finnevara hills, opening from the well-known oyster creek of Pouldoody to the creek of Finnavarra running back to Corranroo, just over the border, in county Galway. Two of the forts were very accurately described in these pages (vol. i, p. 294) by Mr. Thomas Cooke, in 1851, but one has since then been entirely defaced. They are chiefly remarkable for their souterrains, which are, in plan and complexity, far more like those of Galway,[1] Meath, and elsewhere than those of the rest of Clare, which are as a rule extremely simple, straight at Kilmaley, Ruan, Cahermacnole and elsewhere, or curved, as at Ballyganner (S.W. Cathair), the hut site, near Horse Island, Rinbaun, and Cahercashlaun; L-shaped, as at Cahernagree and Ruan Hill fort. They have very rarely got side cells, as at Lisnaleagaun near Kilkee, Caherdoon above Crumlin and Caherglasha; still more rarely have they got traps in the passage, to hinder and imperil an intruder, as at Mortyclough.

BALLYVELAGHAN or 'PARKMORE' is on the shore below Pouldoody creek, and passing the low mound with a pillar of cut-stone blocks, 'the Monument of Donoughmore O'Daly,' as it is called, we ascend the gently sloping fields by a lane, and reach the low *liss* of Parkmore. It consists of an unusually thick, flat outer ring, 30 feet wide, with a fosse 12 feet to 15 feet wide and 3 to 4 feet deep; over this the main earthwork only rises 7 to 8 feet and a few feet over the garth. The inner fort is 111 feet to 116 feet over all (Cooke differs but little, giving it 120 feet), and the whole earthwork is 204 feet over all, or, as Cooke gives it, 220 feet. This plain low rath is of little interest but for its souterrain. Like most, if not all, of the Clare earthworks, it was once probably faced with dry stonework, but all trace had vanished by 1851, probably (as usual in grass land) for road-metal or lime.

The 'cave' opens in a bramble brake in the outer face of the main mound and was evidently closed by a slab of stone 4 feet square lying just below the ope in the fosse. The axis lies E.N.E. and W.S.W. The eastern chamber is 26 feet long, and 4 feet to 6 feet 4 inches high; the sides are as usual of very small stonework, with a slightly concave curve, so that the upper space may be as narrow as possible under the lintels: these roof slabs are of limestone, 5 to 9 inches thick, and about 6 feet wide. At the west end of the outer chamber is a low lintelled 'creep,' in the roof of which a manhole leads to a

---

[1] A closely similar souterrain in Ballinderry Fort, near Tuam, is described by Dr. T. B. Costello and Mr. R. J. Kirwin in the *Journal of the Galway Archæological and Historical Society*, vol.ii, p. 105, and especially p. 115.

small cell overhead; from it another ope leads down to the western chamber. The first cell is 26 feet long by 5 feet 8 inches wide, the inner 14 feet by 9 feet 6 inches wide and 6 feet high, the latter opening into the fosse.

The situation, on a low green ridge partly in tillage, overlooks the long tidal creek called Bell Harbour and Pouldoody famed for its oysters; to the east it commands the hamlet of Burren or Mortyclough standing on the edge of its Turlough, a swamp or shallow pool, according to the weather, full of bog-bean and golden iris, with a causeway through the middle. The violet and grey terraced hills half encircle in to the south and the wooded upland of Finnavarra to the north.

FINNAVARRA. - If this is not a 'sea name' like Kinvarra,[1] we may take mac Liac's legend 900 years ago deriving its name from Bir, or Beara, the Firbolg, brother of the builder of Dun Aengusa in Aran. About a mile west from New Quay lies a souterrain, probably a rath cave, but its fort is levelled; I did not find it, so give briefly Cooke's account. It has three cells, the outer 21 feet by 5 feet wide and about 5 feet high; thence a passage 5 feet long 3 feet high and 2 feet wide leads through a trap-door on to an elevated platform at the end of the middle chamber; the latter 25 feet long by 7 feet wide and 6 feet high, and is at right angles to the outer cell. Thence an ope 2 feet wide and 3 feet high leads to a sloping passage down to the inner cell parallel to the middle one, but 5 feet lower. At its inmost end stood a small slab cist, the cover resting on four uprights; bones were found under it, but no full account could be recovered by Cooke. It will be remembered that some such arrangement was found by Thomas Molyneux at Warington, county Down, in 1684; and similar small bone boxes are recorded in Sweden.

MORTYCLOUGH. - The *cathair* of Mortyclough closely resembles Ooan-knocknagroagh, partly reduced to the very foundations and standing on a low rise near the road, south-west from the village, to which it has given its name, *Mothair tighe cloice*, the enclosure of the stone house. Some have derived the name from a supposed monument of Mortough garbh O'Brien, who fell in the battle of Corcomroe, in 1317. Having settled that, they localize the battle here, and even call it the battle of Mortyclough. The Cathreim Thoirdhealbhaigh leaves us in no doubt as to the army in which Mortough fought coming by Bealaclugga to attack its rival at the Abbey of Corcomroe, and as to Mortough's burial in the chancel of the Abbey. The 'Stone House' is probably the house foundation in the ring-wall. The fort was of the usual type, about 160 feet over all, of good limestone masonry. Little of the facing remains, enough to show that the wall varied from 15 to 18 feet thick to the east, and 21 feet to the south, apparently of one section with two faces with small filling. It is rarely 4 feet high, save to the south-east, where a short reach is about 6 feet high.

The souterrain lies in the southern part of the garth. I found it filled up to less than a foot from the roof slabs; one could barely see under them in the

---

[1] The pretty sea name 'Rossalia' occurs on the creek near New Quay. It was an old property of Lord Inchiquin (Murrogh the Burner) in 1641-55. Ballyvelaghan was then held by Turlough More O'Loughlin, Owen son of Lissagh O'Loughlin and William Neylan.

south-east chamber. It is so thoroughly defaced and choked that I could not check Cooke's account. The entrance was to the south-east, but another ope had been broken in at the north-east side of the caher. The south-east cell was oval, 32 feet by 6 feet, and 6 feet high. A low passage opened to the left at the inner end for 9 feet, being 2 feet 4 inches wide, and under 3 feet high. In its roof was a manhole over 2 feet square to an inner cell opening on to a raised platform 3 feet high, as at Finnavarra. The inner chamber was at right angles to the first, 27 feet long and 6 feet high and wide. The upper inner chamber had the farther end rounded. The house foundation in the middle of the fort is 54 feet long by 30 feet wide.

MORTYCLOUGH LISS. - This earthwork lies south-west from the caher beyond the Killeen graveyard, and near the creek. It has no outer ring, only a fosse 9 feet wide and 3 feet deep, over which the inner ring of gravelly earth rises 7 feet, or 5 feet over the garth; it is 18 feet thick at the base, and 3 feet thick on top, with an entrance-gap to the south. There are no foundations in the garth, which is 189 feet to 190 feet across, and nearly circular - the fort is 244 feet over all. The ope of the souterrain lies to the north-west of the garth, at 30 feet from the mound, under which it runs, being 34 feet 6 inches long, 4 feet 10 inches to 6 feet 5 inches wide inside, and 2 feet 10 inches at the entrance, and 6 feet inside. It has (like the south-west *cathair* of Ballyganner) a projection cornice and 12 lintels from 8 inches to 1 foot thick, and from 21 to 39 inches wide. At the left of the inner end it has a shallow side recess 1 foot 4 inches deep and 4 feet 6 inches long; a space 2 feet 6 inches deep opens at that end under the roof, but does not seem to be a passage.

There are dilapidated ring-walls, one at Behagh, and one cut through by the old road to the Abbey; a much-levelled fort on Scanlan's Island; another called Gortagreenaun in Rine near Finnavarra point (O.S. 2), and an earth fort, Lissavorneen, at Finnavarra.[1] The first is possibly the 'Caher-idon' (Caheradoon) in that position on a map of 1580, unless the latter represents Mortyclough Caher. The only other fort in that neighbourhood is the very remarkable one with its ten gateways (possibly more) on the ridge of Turlough Hill above Oughtmama.

GLENINSHEN (O.S. 5).

A dilapidated dolmen lies about half-way between the Corkscrew Hill schoolhouse and the dolmens of Berneens and Gleninshen, already described,[2] about a mile and a half to the north-east of Caheridoola, in Rathborney parish, near the trigonometrical mark '635' feet. It is on so dangerous a crag, full of deep fissures, hidden by moss and mountain avens, that, when attempting to reach it from the west, I was completely baffled by a series of dangerous falls, while from the east I was more successful, but got two bad falls, one accompanied by a considerable reach of a lofty dry-stone

---

[1] There is a Lissavaun Hill in Behagh, but I believe no trace of a fort remains there.

[2] *Journal*, vol. xxix, p. 380 [58]; vol. xxxi, p. 286 [88]; *Proc. R.I.A.*, vol. xxvi (c.), Plate xxiii.

wall. The monument did not repay the pain and risk; the north slab is 12 feet 3 inches long, sloping eastward from 4 feet to 2 feet 6 inches high, and only 3 to 4 inches thick. At 14 inches from its east end is a cross slab 4 feet 2 inches long, reaching a fragment of the broken south side. It is in a heathery hollow with no outlook.[1] Nearer to Gleninshen are two slabs set north and south in a low cairn, evidently once a small cist. They command a fine view down Glenarraga to Ballyvaughan and across the bay to Galway.

I find I have not yet described in these pages the eastern dolmen of this townland. It is only conventionally separated from the two in Gleninshen, with which it lies in line to the north. It is a fine structure; a simple cist, perfect but for the collapse of one of its southern slabs. The north slab is 12 feet 3 inches long, and from 3 to 6 inches thick; the western is 7 feet long; the cover, like the north slab, has split from its large size and unusual thinness; the cell so covered tapers eastward from 6 feet 6 inches to 1 foot 10 inches, and from 6 feet 2 inches to 1 foot 8 inches high, the north side lying E.N.E. and W.S.W. The dolmen was once covered by a cairn of which little trace remained in 1895.

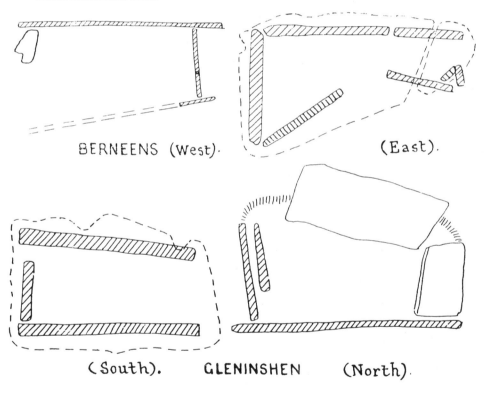

BERNEENS (West).   (East).

(South).   GLENINSHEN   (North).

Dolmens at Berneens and Gleninshen

CAHER-GLENINSHEN. - East from the last-named dolmen (beyond a grassy depression, with a streamlet pouring with quick current from under a rock)

---

[1] I give along with its plan those of the other Berneens and Gleninshen dolmens.

lies a late, rude enclosure called 'the caher.' It is evidently a cattle bawn, roughly square, of badly built slab walls, with small filling, and 5 feet 4 inches to 6 feet thick. Only near the south-east angle are they even 5 feet high; it measures 120 feet square, and has no foundations in the garth; it closely resembles the dry-stone walls built about Lemeneagh by Sir Donat O'Brien at the end of the seventeenth century.

GARRACLOON CAHER. - South-east from the last, on a bold rock knoll, across a winding valley, is an apparently large fort. On climbing the 'shoulders of sharp crags and windy shelves,' we find only slight remains, the apparent wall being a low rock-ledge. The fort stands at the upper end of a long, narrow pass from Gleninshen up to the plateau, on the southern platform of the knoll. Its wall is 7 feet thick, of large blocks, evidently largely replaced at a later date by a wall of coarse, flat stones. The garth is oval, 105 feet E.N.E. and W.S.W. by 71 across; it had a side annexed to the south extending down to the pass. It is, I believe, the most silent and lonely place I have been in, even in the 'silent places of the Burren'; no living thing, not even a bird, was to be seen or heard on either of my visits. It overlooks Poulgorm and Glensleade, already described, out to Elva, Callan, and Inchiquin Hill. Below it, on a rock-shelf to the south-west, is a low ring-wall; two similar ones, also featureless, 100 feet across, with walls 6 feet thick, lie to the west of the main valley. A third, better built ring, lies near the east dolmen of Gleninshen; its wall is only 4 to 5 feet high, and is levelled to the east. All four are evidently cattle bawns, but earlier than the Caher of Gleninshen. The fine ring-wall of Caheranardurrish, and its perfect gateway, lies not far from the southern.

BALLYMIHIL. - Going south from Garracloon Caher we pass a fifth bawn of fine slab masonry; this is marked (but not as ancient) on the new survey. I re-examined the remains from it to Cragballyconoal,[1] but little need be added to the former notes, save that the great square *cathair* near the Mackee's house proves to have had a slab set in the middle of the side wall of the entrance, with its edge out like those in Moheraroon caher, Dunbeg, near Fahan in Kerry, and the Scottish brochs. The cover of the north dolmen had, since my first visit, been pushed out of place, and was ready to fall, so usually is wanton mischief at work in Clare. The slabs set in the rock-crevices near Ballymihil dolmen are very curious, resembling crosses, animals, birds and dragons; they were probably set up to fill the endless leisure of herdsmen, and are usually formed by nature alone. The apparently modern cattle-pen to the north of the 'White Labba' of Cragballyconoal is on the foundations of another well-built ring-wall.

EANTY AND POULGORM (O.S. 9).

In Kilcorney parish, two of the forts passed over with bare mention in a former paper[2] deserve full description. On either side of a picturesque gorge is a fort, Caherlisananima and Caherlisaniska; the first is an extremely

---

[1] See *Journal*, xxix, p. 371 [51], for previous notes.
[2] See *Journal*, vol. xxix, p. 373 [52].

dilapidated ring-wall on a slight knoll on the hillside; the second is an interesting link between the ring-fort and promontory fort.

CAHERLISANISKA. – 'The fortified fort[1] of the water' - the name occurs as Drumliseenysiyach in 1655.[2] This fort, called from the little pool at the foot of its cliff, affords a very good example of how well the ancient builders accommodated their plans to the sites chosen for forts. The spur had only cliffs to one side, so could not be defended like a promontory fort; its platform was too narrow to make it a simple crescent fort, while the knoll at the end of the spur lent itself to a ring-fort, and the builders adopted the characteristics of the three designs.

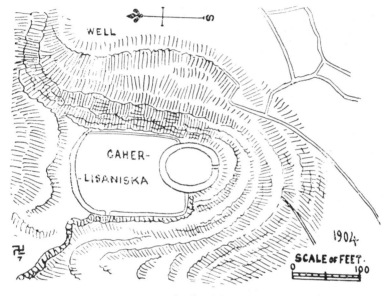

Caherlisaniska

An oval cathair occupies the rounded south end of the spur, being 74 feet north and south, and 50 feet east and west. The inner facing is much dilapidated; the outer is of good, coarse work, 6 to 8 feet thick and high, save to the south-east, where it is over 9 feet high, of large blocks without filling, and only laid in courses at the south entrance. The gate was apparently only 30 inches wide, and 6 feet high and deep. The east pier is intact; the lintel lies at the entrance 6 feet 8 inches long by 3 feet wide, and 5 to 6 inches thick, and, perhaps, covered the passage length way. A gap, with no trace of piers, opens to the north into the outer court. This is formed by a loop of wall joining the ring, running straight along the edge of a low crag, and turning sharply across the spur to meet the edge of the cliff. Its northern end is overlooked by a bold, higher bluff, suggesting that missile attack was not foreseen, or at least not feared, by the designers. The wall of the outwork is far better than that of the ring-fort, which is very unusual, as

---

[1] I duplicate the English words in imitation of the 'Caher-lis.'
[2] Book of Distribution and Survey, Clare (P.R.O.I.), vol. ii, p. 468.

the annexe is usually an afterthought; it is 4 to 5 feet thick, and 6 to 8 feet high, on a ledge of the same height.

CAVES. - Several small caves, including the 'robbers' cave' of Sturgaddy (evidently Sturagaddre, 1665), lie along the base of the cliffs to the west of the gorge, and Poulawillen Cave in the gorge itself. It probably is at the denomination called Powlewollen in 1655, the divisions of 'Enogh' (Eanty) being then Moher O'Laghlin, Kerragh, Anaghbeg, Drumliseenysiyach, Kraganalossaf, Powlewollen, Lisananamagh, Enoghbane, ffanaghleane, Stunagaddre (Sturagaddre), Lisneglayragh, Moylan, ffodree, Boolemore, and Cloghbooly.[1]

Excavations in these caverns should be profitable both to science and archaeology, to judge from the results of Mr. Richard Ussher's work in the caves at Edenvale and Newhall in the same part of the county.[2] His slight examination of the caves in Glencurraun yielded evidence of very early human occupation, but his methodical work disclosed relics of a very cold period, the bones of elk, reindeer, lemming, wolves, and huge bears, with primitive human settlements, yielding charcoal layers, flint implements, bone pins, and pierced shells, with possible traces of cannibalism. Of early civilization, bronze and golden bracelets, an inlaid silver belt-clasp, amber and medieval skeans were discovered.

Going up the hillside to the north-west of the caher we find a narrow, trench-like cutting in the rock adapted as a dwelling by roof-slabs and dry-stone partition walls. Crossing the old road which leads along the ridge from the great stone fort of Caherconnell up to the dolmen of Poulaphuca and down into the Turlough valley towards Corcomroe Abbey, we reach a small, low fort named Lishagaun. A few blocks projecting from its northern segment show that it was partly of stone. On top of the ridge above the valley of Poulgorm are two other forts.[3]

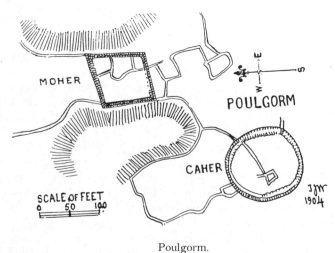

Poulgorm.

---

[1] Book of Distribution and Survey, Clare (P.R.O.I.), vol. ii, p. 468.
[2] *Trans. R.I.A.*, vol. xxxiii (B), p.1.
[3] See *Journal*, vol. xxix, p. 374 [54].

CAHER-POULGORM. - It is nearly circular, and measures 105 feet across the garth. The wall is 9 feet thick, nearly levelled at the south and east, but opposite where it is well preserved it is 3 feet less, from which and from the smallest of the facing and other traces, it was evidently built in two sections, the outer 6 feet thick, with two faces; the inner (perhaps a terrace) 3 feet wide. The outer facing is of large, coarse masonry, with no apparent batter, and 7 feet high. There are some foundations of late houses, and it was evidently inhabited down to the eighteenth or even the nineteenth century.

MOHER. - Close to it to the north-east is a remarkable straight-sided 'moher' of far better masonry than the last. It occupies a narrow ridge between two deep hollows (with steep sides), and is built of long slabs. The south wall is 9 to 10 feet thick; the side walls are nearly 10 feet high, forming a revetment with very large foundation blocks; the northern is now barely 5 feet high and 8 feet thick. The north-west angle is perfect; it is finely built, and as square as the angle of a modern house. This is probably a late feature, for in the straight sided 'mohers' near Cashlaun-Gar, and Knockaun Fort, the 'corners' are rounded, and the same is true of the great dry-stone bawn on the bounds of Knappoge and Ballymarkahan near Quin in eastern Clare.[1] Still the masonry at Poulgorm is of a much older type than several of such angular enclosures, and may be seven or eight centuries old, or even more. The garth is 70 feet across, and has three irregular enclosures along its eastern wall.

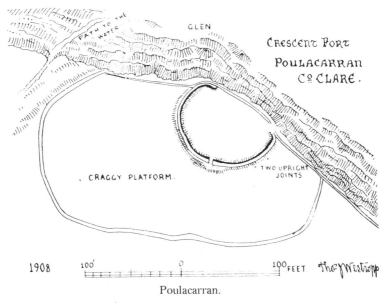

CRescent Port

PouLACARRAN
C? CLARE.

GLEN

CRAGGY PLATFORM.

TWO UPRIGHT JOINTS

1908   100'   0   100 FEET   The Westropp

Poulacarran.

POULACARRAN (O.S. 9). - The two ring-walls shown in the extreme south of this picturesque valley are late, rude structures, with thin, coarse walls, 4½ to 5 feet high and thick, on rough crags, and with no hut foundations. I take this opportunity to substitute a more accurate plan for the incorrect

---

[1] *Proc. R.I.A.*, vol. xxvii (c), p. 375.

one in the 25-inch Ordnance Survey Map (given in my former notes)[1] on the cliff-fort near Fanygalvan, in which it is shown as a ring-wall with a 'half-moon' outwork.

It is really of two crescent walls abutting on the cliff of the lower 'Faugher' or rock-terrace below Fanygalvan. It encloses a garth 92 feet across and 67 feet deep in the middle, with traces of house enclosures to the north. The fort has an unusual feature, for instead of the horns of the crescent abutting on the cliff they turn inward along its edge for about 10 feet and 12 feet, which possibly misled the surveyors into the belief that it was once a complete ring. The inner wall is of good, coarse slab-masonry 6 feet thick, and 5 to over 6 feet high, being most perfect to the north. Two upright joints remain to that side. It has two faces, with but little filling, and at one part to the south-east remains an outer facing only 31 inches thick. This is unique in my experience, for, though the outer sections, thinner than the inner ones, are found (e.g., at Caheridoula, described below, at Dunbeg fort, near Fahan in Kerry, and Ballylin Caher in western County Limerick), nothing so flimsy as this facing seems to occur elsewhere. It extends for over 30 feet, with further traces of foundation, but does not seem to have existed to the north of the gate. The gateway faced to the south-east, and was 4 feet wide, with a long lintel 6 feet 3 inches by 10 inches, and over it a relieving slab 4 feet 6 inches by 2 feet 9 inches, as is very usual. It has been recently thrown down to admit cattle. The side piers are built in courses with large blocks. The wall along the precipice is modern, to keep cattle from falling over. The outer enclosure is a slight, defaced structure, 4 feet thick, either very late or rudely rebuilt. The path leads down the cliff to a deep, wet little hazel glen, beyond which is the ridge on which lies the double Caher of Poulacarran, already described[2]; the water-supply of the fort probably lay in the glen.

MOHERAROON (O.S. 9).

Going south from Poulacarran, round the ridge of Fanygalvan, with its conspicuous dolmen,[3] we find, close by the road to Castletown, a group of stone forts. The western, beside the road and in Sheshymore, is a mere ring of filling, thanks to road-menders.

The second caher lies not far to the north-east, in Moheraroon,[4] and is a conspicuous little ring-wall on a crag covered with low hazels. The wall is very coarse and badly built, of shapeless large masonry, to the north-east. It has a terrace 18 inches wide and 1 foot 8 inches high, the wall 1 foot 8 inches higher, or 4 feet 4 inches over the garth, which is 3 feet higher than the outer crag. The wall is 7 feet 8 inches high and 6 feet 6 inches thick at that point, and 4 feet 8 inches wide on top. The fort is 94 feet over all, and 81 feet across the garth. The gateway is defaced, but its lintel measures 4 feet 8 inches by 1 foot 6 inches by 8 inches; so it must have been narrow.

---

[1] *Journal,* xxviii, p. 363 [45].
[2] *Journal,* vol. xxviii, p. 362 [44], Plan No. 3, p. 363 [45].
[3] *Ibid.,* vol. xxviii, p. 360 [41].
[4] Locally 'Moherroon' or 'Moor-roon.'

CAHER-MOHERAROON. - This fort lies to the north of the last. It is of better but coarse masonry. Much of the wall to the south and east is thrown down, probably by rabbit-hunters. The rampart is circular, 6 feet 6 inches thick, 7 feet 6 inches high to the south, and 7 feet high to the north and north-east. There are remains of a terrace 3 feet wide, from which is a flight of steps of unusual arrangement, rising from the platform of the terrace in a recess and running up the wall. The more usual types are the sidelong steps in a recess, and the simple steep flight, which in the apparently very primitive steps in the 'modernized' (if not late) fort of Caherahoagh[1] becomes an actual ladder, with spaces under the stone rungs. In Dangan (Cahermoyle), near Ballyvaughan, we have a recess with one shelf-like step in the terrace itself; and in Dun Eoghanachta, in Aran, a flight begins some feet above the ground in the terrace. The gateway faced the east, and was recently overthrown before 1896; but one pier is entire, with a lintel resting on it, and a plan and elevation are recoverable. It had another opening, with very slightly inclined jambs, and unusually high (7 feet). The jamb was of fourteen courses of thin slabs, averaging 5 to 8 inches thick.

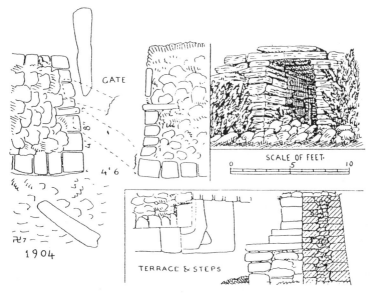

Moheraroon.

The passage is 4 feet wide, increasing inward to 6 feet at a point 4 feet 6 inches from the outside, again very unusual. Here two slabs are set in the wall, their edges projecting into the passage, doubtless at a wooden door, the north being 10 inches higher than the south slab. Inside these, the passage is 4 feet 3 inches long (making it 9 feet long in all). The lintels measure respectively, from the outside inwards, 5 feet 4 inches by 13 inches by 3 inches, 6 feet 2 inches by 20 inches by 11 inches, and 4 feet 9 inches by

[1] *Journal*, vol. xxvi, p. 366 [20]; *Ancient Forts of Ireland*, fig. 13, No. 6; *Proc. R.I.A.*, p. 192.

14 inches by 17 inches. The first lies outside the gateway; the others rest
on the pier. Another lintel lies in the garth, and is 6 feet 10 inches by 25
inches by 6 inches, and near it one 4 feet 8 inches by 19 inches by 5 inches,
either belonging to the inner passage or a relieving slab. The upper course
of the gate (as at Cashlaun Gar and the souterrains of Mortyclough caher
and the south-west cahers of Ballyganner) projects like a cornice, the better
to support the lintels. The sum of the breadths of the lintels, 8 feet 9 inches,
so closely corresponds with the length of the passage and the three outer (4
feet) to the outer section, that it very probably was roofed for its whole
length (like Cahermoygilliar, county Cork). In this, as in its height, its
splay, and its cornice, it is most exceptional, and it is a loss to archaeology
that it was not examined before its destruction.[1] The unfortunate haste and
lack of interest in prehistoric remains when the 1839 Ordnance Survey
hurried O'Donovan and O'Curry through this rich but difficult district, and
the difficulty of the country and the shortness of the time at my disposal
from 1892 down, left it undescribed till, like an older fortress, 'the gate is
smitten with destruction, the fort and towers dens for ever.' A hut circle lies
145 feet east from the gate, but not in line with it. The structure was
probably of wood, fenced (as at Ballyganner Hill near Cahernabihoonach)
with a ring of slabs, 3 feet to 3 feet 6 inches high and long, round its base.
Most of the slab rings known to me in Clare are close to forts, but strange
to say, outside their ambit.

FANYGALVAN. - The fourth cathair lies to the north-east, about 500 feet
away from its neighbour, just over the edge of Fanygalvan. It is by far the
best built fort of the group, though its wall is thin, only 4½ feet to 6½ feet
thick, and rarely 6 feet high, with eight courses and a batter of 1 in 12. The
masonry is large and carefully fitted, some of the blocks being 4 feet to 4 feet
9 inches long, and 14 inches to 16 inches thick. It measures exactly 100 feet
across the garth, and about 112 feet over all. Inside, two loops of late-
looking wall adjoin the rampart. The gateway faced south. Its eastern pier
rests on a foundation block 4 feet 6 inches long. The place whence the
corresponding block was recently removed is visible, but the actual width is
not clear. It will be noted that as we go northward each cathair is better
built than its predecessor, and is probably older, as bad masonry is a late,
decadent feature in the cathairs of Ireland. The Moheraroon forts lie along a
craggy ridge, beside a low green valley, hemmed with steep bluffs and low
cliffs, the dolmens, pillars, and mound on Fanygalvan Hill being visible up
its gap to the north, and the curious rock called Farbreaga, or 'sham man.'
At the southern end of the valley in Fanygalvan, and not far from the road, a
low knoll, with steep sides 6 feet to 9 feet high, with a flat top, tempted the
early fort-makers to enclose it with a wall, of which some three or four
courses of large blocks only remain. There are no house sites inside. The
garth is 84 feet across, and is 2 or 3 feet higher than the outer ledge on
which the wall rests. It is all turfed with the hay-scented woodruff and
rosettes of the saw-fern.

---

[1] I give an illustration to scale, only part of the right jamb is restored.

CAHERIDOOLA (O.S. 9). - From this section onward I hope to begin a series of notes completing the description of several more of the interesting forts round Lisdoonvarna. The first of these is Caheridoola, which I may claim to have first identified in 1896. There is great difficulty in getting a satisfactory phonetic form of the name, and its Irish original is absolutely uncertain. Dr. George U. Macnamara at first inclined to believe that it meant fort of the O'Dooloughtys, but, finding that there was a tribe named 'O'Doolan' connected with the Corcomroe district, he modified the former view. The Cathreim Thoirdhealbhaigh describes one of them in 1313 as 'Donal O'Dulin, he being of the seed of Mogh Ruith, forbear of the noble Fergus' (Mac Roich, the tribal ancestor of the Corcamodruadh), who in the frontal attack on the steep ridge near Tulach (O'Dea most probably) 'first hurled his javelin to the opposing line' of Clan Brian. 'He then handed a spear' to Prince Murchad O'Brien 'to throw when the battle opened,' which ended in the latter's complete victory. In the song of his chief bard (still preserved), sung when the king 'stood over that bent-sworded, broken-speared carnage of noble bodies,' we find mention of 'O'Dulin of the able horses.' They do not seem to make any mark in the later history of Thomond. There is no evidence, however, to show that they held the townland; so, accordingly I prefer to leave the name an open question as regards the original form, and give the best attested later phonetic form here, with a record of its variants.

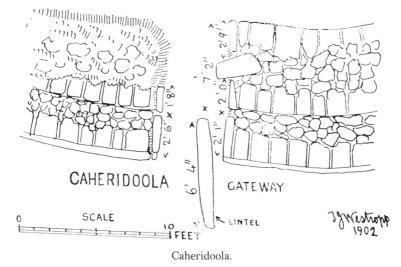

Caheridoola.

It was once a separate townland, like Kilbract, but, like the latter, has been now merged into Cahermacnaughten. I do not find any earlier record of the name than its occurrence in 1624 in the Inquisition *post mortem* of Donough, Earl of Thomond. It is there called Caher Idula. It appears as Caherwooly in 1641, held by John O'Davoren, Caherahoula or Caheridoula in the Book of

Distribution, 1655; and Caherigoola in the Edenvale Survey of 1675.[1] In a deed of 20 December, 1712, John Walcott, of Croagh, county Limerick, conveyed to John Kennedy the lands of Lisaliseen, Cahermacnaughty, Keillibruck, Caheridoula or Caheradoula, Lismactiegue, Ballyganner, Mohernacloughbristy, Deelin, and Slieve Carran (all in Burren), for certain trusts - a valuable light on the fort names in the barony.[2]

I was ignorant of the latter deed, and was not searching for the lost fort, when I got casually from some people in Cahermacnaughten, in 1896, a name which I copied as Caherywoola, Caheryhoolan, Caheryhoolagh, Caheryhoolagha, and Caherywhoolaha from my various informants. I soon after, on going over the Surveys, recognized its identity with Caheridoola or Caherwooly, and adopt the first as probably the least misleading form.[3]

The cathair occupies a low knoll of limestone crag about 800 yards to the north-east of Cahermacnaughten.[4] It is marked, but nameless, on the 1839 maps and the recent survey of 1899. The knoll is at the end of a long ridge, and is about 10 feet high to the west. The fort is well built, with large regular slabs of limestone in even courses. The wall is of two sections. The inner varies from 7 feet 2 inches to 8 feet thick, the outer from 3 feet 3 inches to 4 feet. It seems to be an afterthought, as it conforms to the rock faces, whence its irregularities, for the inner runs in a fairly regular curve. Each has two faces and filling, and their united breadth usually approximates to 11 feet. The wall has been levelled to the garth, and therefore rarely exceeds 4 feet or 5 feet high. The fort is 92 feet overall, and about 70 feet inside. It has no definite hut sites or foundations in the garth. The gateway faces S.S.W., and had side slabs set on end through both sections, the outer being 5 feet, the inner about 6 feet, at the passage, which is 3 feet 10 inches wide and 11 feet deep. It had two lintels, now fallen, measuring - the outer, 5 feet 8 inches by 16 inches by 9 inches; the inner, 6 feet 2 inches by 9 inches by 12 inches; so that it was of the normal type, with coursed jambs.

In the field below is a confused mass of old-looking enclosures and hut-sites. The cathair, therefore, was evidently the centre of a hamlet. Only one hut was rectangular. Despite its inconspicuous position, it has a wide outlook to the south and east over the ridges of Baur and the valley of Kilcorney to the cairn of Poulawack and the castle mound of Lissylisheen, while the faint blue hills of Slieve Bernagh in the far east of the county rise over the hills along the borders of Burren to the south-east.

Between it and Cahermacnaughten is an ancient dwelling, a 'horse-shoe wall,' the enclosure divided into two compartments, evidently a house and forecourt, with an outer yard.

---

[1] Copy in Public Record Office, Dublin. It gives the following fort names, Cahermacnaghtin (held by Walcott) in Noughaval parish; Lismacshida, ffinagh, Lislarhy, Lismacteige, Lislogherne, Lisduan, Lissilisine, Caherigoola, Lisgogane and Ballyallaban, in Rathborney.

[2] Dublin Registry of Deeds Book, vol. ix, p. 285. Mohernacloughbristy is probably one of the enclosures at Cahernabihoonach at the great 'Broken Rock,' Cloch Briste.

[3] Dr. MacNamara recently records the form Caherghoolin (? Cathair Ui Dhulain).

[4] See *Journal,* vol. xxvii, p. 120 [27].

The Distribution mentions two stone forts near Caheridoola, named Kaheriskebohell and Kahirballyungane. They may have been the defaced ring-walls of Doonyvardan to the north, or two others in equal decay to the south.

In connexion with the district I must add a few notes to those on the interesting partition deed relating to Cahermacnaughten.[1] The deed used by me in my previous work was found by O'Donovan in 1839, in possession of Michael Reilly, of Ennistymon. It was dated 3 April 1675, signed by Gilla-na-naev oge O'Davoren, and witnessed by James FitzGerald and Francis Sarsfield. 'Be it known' (it ran) 'that the sons of Gilla-na-naev oge O'Davoren of Cahermacnaughten, in the parish of Rathbourney, viz., Hugh and Cosny, partitioned as follows'; it then recited the division of the lands of Cahermacnaghten, Lissmacteige, Lisduane, Lisnaloughran, and (Kil)Colman Baire in Kilcorney parish, giving the mears of Cahermacnaughten, viz., the stream of Sruhaunduff flowing from the mountain, the western ditch of Buaile Liaganach to Urlingmore and to the west side of the caher. The village of Cahermacnaghten included the sites 'of the big house of the caher within,' the 'Kitchen House belonging to it,' the 'house of the churchyard on the west side of the caher' and all the gardens extending westward from the road of the garden of Teige Roe, son of Giolla Feichin; 'the house between the front of the big house and the door of the caher,' the site of 'another house within the caher at the north-west side, and the 'large house, which is outside the door of the caher,' from Bearnan Fanain-an-Tayaill, at the east, westward to the above road; also 'the Fahy or green of the Booley,' and the road from the green westward to Moher Turtanagh; the water of the village and of Shruhanduff and the well of the village are common and free to all.

There were two copies; one signed and sealed by Cosny was given to Hugh, and the other by Hugh to Cosny. This is not a puzzling document at first glance, save that our copy is signed neither by Hugh nor Cosny, but apparently by their father. However, Dr. George U. Macnamara has found (and I hope ere this paper is published may have given it to the antiquarian world[2]) another copy almost identical with this, but dated in the reign of James I, about 1606. Evidently then for some family reason it was recopied and signed, in 1675, by the later Gilla-na-naev oge O'Davoren, whom we find holding lands in the district at the time of the Down Survey. Dr. MacNamara adds that the garden-plots near the cathair, which even appear in the 1839 and 1899 maps, have disappeared, and that the students' houses, mentioned by Frost, are only heaps of stones cleared off the land. There is a well 23 yards west from the cathair, and about 90 from the road wall. The field in which it lies is the 'Parc na leacht,' and the term 'Park' has an interest, for, in the note in O'Davoren's Glossary, we read of one thus - 'the *park* is my residence, Magnus for Donall (Ua Dubdáboirinn or Davoren), and he himself is travelling through Ireland, 1569. Finished at the Céissóic,[3] by Cormac son of the Cosnaidhe for Donall hua Dubdáboirinn.'

---

[1] Published by the late Mr. Frost, *History and Topography of the County Clare*, p. 18.

[2] In the *Journal of the North Munster Archaeological Society*.

[3] Some unknown place called the 'Shallow Basket,' from its shape, or some wicker structure.

Cahermacnaughten was of course the chief seat of this learned clan of literary men and law teachers. In hopes of identifying the places in the deed, Dr. MacNamara and I went round the townland in 1902. The *dark little brook*, welling out of the bogs at the foot of the shale ridge, near Binroe, is unmistakably the 'Sruhaunduff.' Buaile liaganach is forgotten, but is probably some of the craggy pasture land at the west end of the townland full of the flat slabs, or *liags*. Urlingmore may be the rough long grassed *urlan* or lawn west of the cathair. The mearing, between the townlands of Cahermacnaughten and 'Caherwooly,' is very probably the well-marked line of old walls beginning 400 yards east of the road from Noughaval, continuing the line of the bounds of the former division and Lissylisheen, touching the ancient hut garth, and passing 500 feet west of Caheridoola northward. 'Bernan Fanain an Tayail' may be the gap or depression running north-eastward from Cahermacnaughten to the ridge of Caheridoola. 'Moher Turtanagh' lay westward from the green of Cahermacnaughten fort, and is probably some forgotten enclosure towards the so-called church or north from it. The main local difficulty is the reputed 'church'; there was a townland of Kilbract, or Kilbrack, or Keillibruck at, and probably (like Caheridoola) merged in, Cahermacnaughten. If Kil implies a church, the ruin may represent it, but there is also a 'house of the church-yard' in the partition deed 'on the west side of the caher.' The 'church' ruin is unlike every other church known to me in Clare, save the burial chapel at Kilmoon Church. Both seem to date somewhere about 1600, so the 'church' may have stood when the partition deed was first made. It is true that it is named among several buildings certainly 'within the cathair' which led me to locate it as the large foundation in the south-west section of the garth. I now think it is much more probable that the two western foundations represent the great house and kitchen-house, and that the north-east site is the house in front of the latter, between it and the door of the cathair and the building west of it in the north-west sections, 'another house within the caher at the north-west side.'

May I briefly describe the 'church' as an appurtenance of a ring-wall and early settlement, though very late in origin? The building is called a church since before 1839, but no burials have been made in it, though this is also true, or apparently true, of some undoubted church ruins in Clare. It is at latest of the early seventeenth century, and is externally oblong, 30 feet 7 inches by 61 feet 6 inches over all. The end walls are 4 feet 6 inches thick at the ends, but hardly 4 feet to the sides. In each of the ends is a row of corbels, but the gables above the height of the sides have vanished. There are three windows and a plain pointed door to each side; the former are defaced, save the most western of the south lights, an oblong chamfered ope with a plain hood with stepped ends. At 17 feet from the east wall is a cross wall with a recess in the middle, facing the western or main room. To the north, but in the east room, is a recess with a slab. There were slit lights in the gables; one door had a roll moulding; the ope of the southern is destroyed, but the flat inner lintel remained in 1902. Whatever the real nature of the building may be, I am more than doubtful that it ever was a church. If so, it must have been carefully designed to conceal its character from the outer world.

THE COROFIN DISTRICT.

The extreme richness of the north-west angle of the County Clare in prehistoric[1] remains rendered an attempted survey far longer and more difficult than one could have foreseen when, in 1895, I laid the first of this series of papers before the Society. We have now reached the eleventh of the series; with one more paper I hope to close it, completed, at least as regards all structures of any importance. Begun in May 1878, and continued (at first at long intervals, 1883, 1885, and 1887), I have, from 1892, striven to work over the district as methodically as possible; but no worker can have been so many years as even from 1892 without modifying and widening his views. Structures, only briefly noticed in the earlier sections, seemed to be of greater importance as the value of their lessons was better appreciated. Trying to revisit in later times the chief remains, new facts stood revealed. So perilous and difficult were the fissured and often overgrown crags, that I had at first turned aside from sections of the county which later experience led me at all risks to examine. From these causes I soon found that a perfectly methodical design was sacrificed. Completeness of description, however, is of far greater importance, and the table giving the forts and dolmens under each parish in their natural sequence (with which I purpose to conclude the work) should compensate for the broken design, and bring together all references in the series of papers.

It became plain, even before the first part was published, that, instead of merely describing some eight or ten of the chief forts, a survey was needed.[2] Though this detailed task called for far longer and more severe work, and for more patience in students of its results, no one can question (however my personal work may have fallen short of my ideal) that this, and not merely records of exceptional remains, could alone be valuable to scientific workers. After Mr. Borlase's book, *The Dolmens of Ireland*, appeared, the notes (which I had previously sent to him as soon as I examined any such monument) were included along with the forts. No one realizing the swift destruction falling on Irish field antiquities will grudge the publication of such notes; but the subject is neither popular nor fame-winning, and, to those who are interested only in history or elaborate architecture, must always be distasteful. Scholars both of our islands and the Continent, however, have already formed a different judgement.[3] To those who wish to follow it on

---

[1] I (as usual) apply the term 'prehistoric' to any early but unrecorded period, even if within the limits of history in general.

[2] The earlier notes relate to Eastern Clare. Magh Adhair, vol. xxi, pp. 462-3; Killaloe, xxiii, p. 191; Moghane, Langough, &c., xxiii, p. 281; and Cahercalla, xxvi, p. 150 [9]. The survey of the forts of the other parts of the county may be found - the eastern half in *Proc. R. I. Acad.*, Sec. C, vol. xxvi, p. 217 (Newmarket and Tradree), p. 376; (Quin, Tulla, Bodyke), vol. xxix, p. 186; (Killaloe) South-west Clare, vol. xxxii, p. 58; (Broadford to Clooney), *Journal*, xxxviii, pp. 28, 221, 344; xxxix, p. 113; xli, p. 117. Many are briefly described, with plans, in 'The Cahers of Co. Clare,' *Proc. R. I. Acad.*, vi, Ser. III, p. 415.

[3] It is satisfactory to note the valuable work done by Mr. H. T. Knox in the *Journal*, vol. xli, pp. 93, 205, 302, and by Dr. Costello and Mr E. Holt in the *Galway Archæological and Historical Society* (vols. ii, p. 105, and vii, p. 205) on the forts of Connacht.

the field, great are the fascination and interest; for the wildernesses blossom
with flowers and ferns; and the dainty colouring of the rock-ledges and their
shadows, the lovely outlooks to distant hills and out on the sea, the ivied
cliffs, the spray of the waterfalls, the loneliness, and the strange weird
sounds on the uplands, have a vast and lasting charm. No one fully realizes
how he loves the strange hills, glens, and plateaux till, after absence, he feels
the joy of returning to them again, no matter how often this may recur.

The types of remains may be briefly enumerated as: - (1) promontory forts
on inland spurs; (2) simple ring-walls or ring-mounds; (3) ring-mounds of
more complex character, with more than one girding wall; two, as at
Glenquin and Tullycommaun, or three, as at Cahercommaun; (4) the more
or less rectangular 'mothair'; (5) the hitherto inexplicable parallel
earthworks, as at Ardnagowell; (6) ring-walls for worship or sepulture, like
that around the dolmen of Creevagh and those at Ballyganner. Of other
remains: (7) pillars, which are few; (8) simple tapering cists, usually in a
mound, or cairn, the mound rarely higher than to the bottom of the cover;
(9) anomalous monuments, like the pillared dolmen of Ballyganner or the
enclosure of slabs round the cist of Iskancullin; (10) carns and tumuli, often
with cists and kerb blocks, sometimes mere memorial carns; (11) tumuli
within an earth-ring (like Lislard and the Mote), or carns within a stone
ring-wall; (12) avenues, formed by removing the surface layer of the crags;
(13) huts, which are usually badly preserved, but which were beehive
structures, sometimes of several cells; (14) souterrains, usually simple,
straight, curved, or L or T-shaped, in plan. Rarely do side cells occur. The
nearest approach to a fort with a raised platform is the rock-cut fort of
Doon. One fort, Ballykinvarga, has a remarkable abattis. Alignments and
large circles of stones are unknown in the district. None of the complex
(and therefore possibly later) gateways with side cells and loopholes exist;
all are simple passages, with a lintelled outer gate, and, as a rule, coursed
jambs, far more rarely with stone posts. The steps are equally simple, in
Clare, usually running straight up to the terrace, or from it to the wall; a few
examples of sidelong steps occur, as at Cahergrillaun and Cahernahoagh.
There is rarely a second terrace. The wall is sometimes built in sections,
like the Aran forts. The masonry of the stronger and probably older forts is
very perfect, with beautiful curve and batter; cells never occur in the walls.

The district originally intended to be worked (as may be seen in the
second section of this survey) covered the Barony of Burren, or East Corca
Modruadh, along with the craglands adjoining it in the parishes of Killilagh
and Kilfenora, the parishes of Kilnaboy and Ruan in Inchiquin, and a portion
of Dysert and Rath. The present section completes the Inchiquin portion,
and I hope to complete the Corcomroes in the closing paper. There are,
roughly speaking, 280 forts in these parishes - in Kilnaboy about 90, in Ruan
over 100, in Rath 30, in Dysert O'Dea over 40, in Kilnamona 20.

RUAN PARISH (O.S. 17).

Twice in the Cathreim Thoirdhealbhaigh we read of 'Ruan of the grass-grown hollow *uamhadha*'; the latter word, locally pronounced *Ooan,* is used indiscriminately for a *cathair* or a souterrain. The first notice creates a difficulty, and may be a headless slip of memory; but the last, in May, 1318, undoubtedly refers to this district. Here Sir Richard de Clare camped for the night before the fatal Battle of the Ford before Dysert O'Dea. The epithet is most appropriate, for Ruan abounds in ring-forts; to attempt a complete survey might add rather to the length than to the value of my survey, so I will only select a couple of important groups, and a few other examples. The Liss names are numerous: Lisnabulloge, Lisbeg, Lisduff, Lisheen-vicknaheeha; the fort to the north of the last is locally Lisheenahuckera;[1] Lisnavooaun, Lisronalta, Lismuinga, Lissyline, and Liscarhuanaglasha (Carhuanalashee *alias* Cahernamart in 1666). To complete the Liss names known to me in the adjoining parishes I give Lisduff, Lisvetty, and Lisheenaboughil in Kilnaboy, and Lissyogan and Liscullaan in Rath. No such names occur in the parishes of Kilkeedy, Kilnamona, and Dysert so far as I am aware.

DROMORE and RUAN (O.S. 25). - Three low earthen forts of no great size, and planted with hawthorns, lie to the east of the road from Teernea to Ruan.

LISHEENVICKNAHEEHA, 'the little fort of the son of the night,' is the most southern of these. This weird name may after all be simply derived from some former occupant, for the name, *Mac na haidche,* appears in our Annals from 1104 to 1281. I have not found it in later records, a fact which favours some age for the *liss.* The form (if correct) seems akin to the name Cahervicknea in this district about 1650. It is a very low little earthen fort studded with hawthorn bushes.

CAHERMACREA (O.S. 17). - This once fine *cathair*[2] is most probably the Cahervicknea of the Down Survey and other documents of the mid-seventeenth century: *r* and *n* are interchangeable in local phonetics, as Croch and Knock, Cahermacrole and Cahermacnole.[3] The maps affix the modern name to a large oval ring of tumbled mossy stones in a thicket; the ring measures roughly 300 feet east and west, by 250 feet north and south, and (from the small amount of material anywhere remaining, the absence of facing and the lack of internal foundations) was probably an unusually large bawn, or cattle pen, against wolves. So far as I can find, no one attaches the name to it at present.

The ring-wall, now called Cahermacrea, is I believe entitled to the name. It was an important, massive cathair of excellent masonry, carefully fitted, and of large blocks. The wall is 7 feet high for a long reach, the batter is

---

[1] I believe my informant referred to the northern fort and not to 'Lisheenvick-naheeha.' It is Lisín an chróchaire (little fort of the hangman), telling a grim story of some forgotten execution.

[2] Noted in the *Journal,* vol. xxvi, p. 368 [22].

[3] The Cahermacirrila of the O.S. maps.

usually from 1 in 7 to 1 in 12; its facing is inferior to the east, but gets better
at the north-east, at which point are several upright joints, as at
Cahercloggaun and 'Caherbeg' on Knockauns mountain. Some of the facing
blocks are 19 inches by 11 inches by 16 inches up to 36 inches by 12 inches
by 16 inches. The wall is about 9 feet thick with large filling, but the inner
facing was of small blocks and, as so usually, has collapsed. The garth is 110
feet across; the fort being about 130 feet over all, and, being thickly planted,
all traces of house-sites are gone. Parts of the outer wall have been rebuilt
to protect the trees, and all trace of the gateway seems removed.

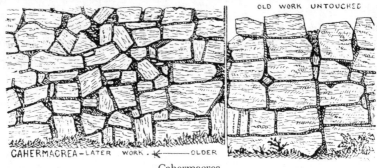

Cahermacrea

LISAVOOAN or CAHERMORE, beside the road leading southward leading to
Addroon (the site of a very curious dolmen formed of high pillar slabs),[1] is a
thickly overgrown and nearly levelled stone-faced earthwork. It has a fosse
12 feet wide and only a few feet deep, and slight rings almost obliterated to
the north. There is a straight souterrain in the garth in a thicket of hazels;
it lies north-west and south-east, the walls being of small masonry roofed
with shapeless surface slabs. It is nearly filled up. The road has cut into the
rings along the south segment. A small defaced fort, Lisbeg, lies west from
it, and to the north at the cross-road is Kilranaghan, a large levelled ring
200 feet across.

LISSYLINE, north from Ruan, is a very low earthwork, somewhat oval, 250
feet north-west and south-east by 230 feet, with a shallow fosse, the mounds
regularly set with hawthorns. To the south-west is a defaced normal *liss*
called Lisheenamuddagh, a low fort with a bank and fosse; its diameter is
about 110 feet over the bank.

PORTLECKA (O.S. 25). – On the grassy ridge south from the village and
ruined church of Ruan is a *cathair* commanding an extensive view to the
Glasgeivnagh Hill round by Callan to Aughty and Slieve Bernagh, the
ramparts of the eastern plain of County Clare. The ring was stone-faced,
and is now rarely over 4 feet high, consisting chiefly of heaps of field stones
with foundations of the outer facing of large blocks and more rarely traces of
the inner face. This wall was from 15 to 18 feet thick, and enclosed a garth
183 feet east and west, 177 feet north and south, and 217 feet over all. It is
strange that this evidently very important fort is nameless. The garth is
levelled inside, being raised like a terrace 5 feet over the field to the south-

[1] *Proc. R. I. Acad.*, vol. iv, Ser. III, Plate IX, No. 4, and p. 545.

east and lowered a couple of feet to the north. There was an inner house-circle, the wall 9 feet thick, and still over 3 feet high, extending for about 114 feet in the south-west segment. Another defaced enclosure lies beyond it to the north-west of the garth. In the centre of the fort is a souterrain of some interest. It is L-shaped in plan, the longer limb lying north-west to south-east. The southern entrance is 2 feet by 3 feet wide; the passage 17 feet 8 inches long and 4 feet 6 inches wide; at 8 feet it narrows to 15 feet 3 inches from the ope: this narrow passage being 2 feet 3 inches to 2 feet 10 inches wide. In the right (north-east) side is a recess 18 inches square, which, like a shallower recess opposite, was evidently for a doorpost.

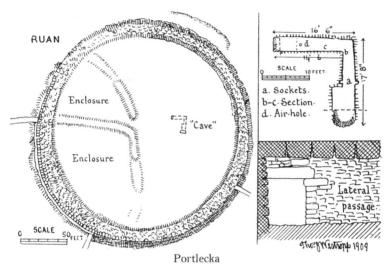

Portlecka

This is, I think, the only case I have found in this barony, though there are set stones perhaps for beam sockets in other souterrains. The passage turns at right angles to the south-west, being 5 feet 5 inches high at the turn. The next wing is 16 feet 6 inches long: the side walls are as usual of small masonry, with no cornice ledge such as we find at Mortyclough and Ballyganner. The souterrain is roofed with large slabs of limestone. There are two large slabs and four lintels over the outer passage, and seven over the inner, at two places are carefully arranged little openings, evidently shafts for air and light.[1]

Three entirely defaced ring-walls lie between this fort and Dromore Lake in the townland of Portlecka, and another lies in Nooan. This townland is interesting both as recalling the 'grass-grown *uamhadha*' of history by its name, and as having been once rich in early remains, now miserably defaced. Of three other forts, one has the stone facing of good masonry intact to the south-west, the rest nearly all removed by road-makers. The souterrain lies in the open field between the two eastern forts, and is nearly stopped up; its

---

[1] For ventilating shafts see Lubbock's *Prehistoric Times* (5th ed.), p. 121. They occur in several Irish forts, e.g. Ardfinnan Rath.

entrance has a large lintel 8 feet 10 inches long, 3 feet wide, and 1 foot 7 inches thick. There is no trace of any enclosure round it.

CAHERNANOORANE. - This is a much-injured little ring-wall on a rising ground on the border of Ballymacrogan West. It is said to derive its name from the fairy songs heard in it.

TEMPLENARAHA. - Below the last (in 1897) I found a very interesting though defaced ruin; a little oratory in a large ring-wall. The latter was 151 feet across the garth, the wall of large blocks was overturned, and only in a few places was the well-laid facing visible, rarely 3 to 4 feet high. At 87 feet from the eastern curve lay the remains of a little oratory, the 'Temple of the Rath': it was of fine 'cyclopean' masonry, beautifully fitted together, and was 24 feet long by 16 feet 10 inches wide over all, the walls being 3 feet thick. The west door had inclined jambs formed of large slabs running through the wall; no part was much over 4 feet high, nor did any other feature remain. A neighbouring farmer had so little regard for antiquity or respect for church remains that he removed the ruin altogether in February 1906; poetic justice overtook him, as the calf-shed he built of the material collapsed, killing the animals in it not long afterwards. Strange to say, in Tooreen, not very far away, another outrage on our antiquities was avenged on the perpetrator. A man blew up a dolmen to clear his land, and in the explosion he was struck on his right hand by a splinter of stone, and was long crippled. A hope is left that such incidents may get known and may discourage such sordid, unpatriotic destruction of our early remains, a blot on the present inhabitants of Clare and elsewhere. I have noted and given a plan of the wrecked dolmen in the *Proceedings of the Royal Irish Academy.*[1] Four small stones (one to the west and three to the east) remain, and part of the cover, one of the eastern stones being rather a low pillar, 4 feet 6 inches high.

CAHERLOUGH GROUP (O.S. 17). - This portion of the district lies between Ruan, Monanagh Lake (the Lough Cullaun of the maps), and Lough George. I can find no ancient name for these lakes. Near Kells (Cealla) on a low green ridge opposite Ballyportrea Castle, lies a large and, as usual, very low liss with a fosse, measuring about 250 feet over all, with two low rings; in its ambit lies the bossed stone cross described by Dr. G. U. Macnamara in these pages.[2] It is between Lough Cullaun and the lesser lakes of Knockaundoo and Toole's Lough, and commands the approach from the ancient ford of Corravickburrin (*Cora mhic Dhaboirean*) at Kells Bridge.[3] The fort is about 200 feet across; inside the fosse is a souterrain, to the east side an oblong foundation and the venerated hawthorn called *Sceach an bheannuighthe.* The early church of Templemore or 'Moor' probably stood in a fort, as there is a souterrain near the graveyard, but I did not see any ring on either of my visits. It and a legendary church site at St. Catherine's gave the name Cealla 'churches,' now 'Kells.' The St. Catherine's site is now an orchard, and, strange to say, O'Daly's biting satire in the early seventeenth century (A.D.

[1] *Proc. R. I. Acad.,* vol. xxvi, p. 465, plate xxv. See also *Journal* xxxv, p. 212 [100].
[2] *Journal,* vol. xxx, p. 32.
[3] See Cathreim Thoirdhealbhaigh, 1317. Near it were 'Bescnate's streaming banks.'

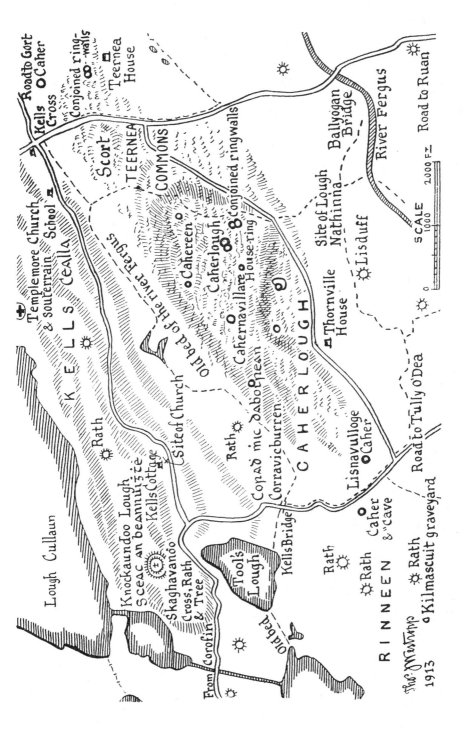

Plan of Caherlough Group

1617) lampoons the people of Cealla for 'digging in the churchyard in the snow.' Burials have been found deep below the surface.

The old bed of the Fergus is now dry, but is still crossed by Kells Bridge over water-fretted sheets of rock, the fissures of which perhaps contain valuable antiquities. Dr. Macnamara found from a very old woman (who did not survive very long afterwards) that this old ford was named Corravickburren. This identifies it with an important ford of the Fergus, crossed by the army of Prince Dermot O'Brien, in 1317, on his way to the battle at Corcomroe Abbey; it was then called *Cora mhic Dhaboirean* or MacDavoren's weir. South of the river bed and of Kells rises a long rough ridge of crag sheeted with dense hazels and thorns largely in the townland of Caherlough. It lies about a mile from the townland of Tullyodea and the fort of Liscarhoonaglasha or Cahernamart.

I think it probable that here and not at Tully the fierce little battle of *Tulach* (? Ui Deadhaid) was fought in 1313, when Prince Murchad O'Brien led his first attack on his opponents of the house of Brian Ruadh. He was aided by the O'Kellys of Aidhne, some of the Burkes, O'Maddens, Comyns, O'Loughlins, and Macraith O'Dea, with the men of Cineal Fermaic. O'Shanny brought them news that their opponents had mustered on Tulach's slopes to the southward with the clan Mahon O'Brien, the O'Gradys, and the Ui Bloid of eastern Clare. The foe saw Murchad's banners on the mountain moor, and soon he was leading his forces under a shower of missiles up a 'steep-cut, rough, and seamy' hill 'steep hillside,' 'a projecting bluff,'[1] and with difficulty he got foothold on the table-land on top, and after a fierce, bloody fight, drove the enemy down into the wooded country; few could have escaped but that night fell, and Murchad's force could not pursue through 'the close and rugged country.' With the morning the Prince proceeded to take pledges from Corcavaskin in the south-west of the County Clare, and soon had driven out the sons of Prince Domnall and Mahon O'Brien, who fled to Richard de Clare at Bunratty Castle.

The battle certainly did not take place on the ridge of Tully, a grassy, gently rising, broad-topped hillock. It was fought up a 'steep, rough, and seamed ridge,' on top of which there was hardly room to fight for the short space during which the issue hung doubtful. It commanded the approach from the important pass of Bealach Fhiodhail or Rockforest. All of these facts suit the Caherlough ridge; the only difficulty lies in the name, *Tulach*, and, the titles of battlefields are notoriously artificial. The ridge is most difficult to examine between the often impenetrable thickets and the dangerous fissures of the rock beneath, which is practically earthless. It has a curious group of late-looking forts which I purpose examining.

The first of the group lies just within the townland of Rinneen, divided by the side road from the end of Caherlough on its eastern edge. Caher-Rinneen is a nearly levelled but interesting ruin. The wall is from 10 feet to

---

[1] No similar feature is found at or near the other Tulachs, Tulach na nEaspog in East Clare or Tulach ui Chuirc near Kilfenora; while Tullycommaun seems off the track, and has no narrow ridge on top, though, as Mahon fled to Inchiquin, and the Kinel Fermaic came in to Murchad and went with him to Corcavaskin, the site is not impossible. But the question is at present uncertain.

11 feet 4 inches thick, the garth 73 feet across north-east and south-west along the axis of the souterrain. The 'Ooan' (*uamha*) is 6 feet 4 inches from the wall at the south-west, and is T-shaped on plan; the longer limb is 20 feet long and 4 feet 3 inches wide, its southern end is roofed with large limestone slabs for 12 feet. The cross-wing at the northern end is 13 feet 6 inches long and 4 feet 2 inches wide; only three of its lintels remain. It is 42 feet from the wall. North from the end is a trace of a hut-enclosure adjoining the rampart.

LISNAVULLOGE. - This lies due east from the last in Caherlough, a stone fort planted with hawthorns, and quite overthrown. Going up the lane as far as Thornville we pass two nearly levelled rings, and climb up the difficult crags to the north-east of the house. Cahernavillare lies on the summit; it is 63 feet over all, the stones so spread that its thickness cannot be measured. At 300 yards to its north-east lies Cahereen in a nearly impassable thicket; when I found it the fort was buried in bracken 6 feet high; the garth is 57 feet across the wall, as usual a tumbled ring of mossy stones. At 800 feet to the south-east lies Caherlough, almost exactly 1000 feet due east from Cahernavillare, and about 200 feet from Caherlough. Between the last two, but close to the last, is another small house ring of mossed blocks, barely 60 feet over all. The modern wall (apparently so unnecessary in this wilderness) curves round upon the old wall.

CAHERLOUGH. - The chief fort is about 95 feet across, thickly overgrown, on a most dangerous fissured crag. The wall has large facing, well set, with a slight batter of about 1 in 10 and about 9 feet thick. The fort has a large, but evidently later, annexe to the east; it is 114 feet across inside. The wall is built of large, coarse blocks, and is only 6 feet thick and 5 feet high, without filling (a late indication), on the bare ribbed crags. Inside, near the south, is a house-enclosure of large, rough blocks.

To the south-east is another far smaller *cathair*, also with a side enclosure. The former has a wall of coarse, large blocks, with no batter, 5 feet high, and 7 feet 6 inches thick. There are two hut-sites in the garth, which is 93 feet to 95 feet across, also a rock-cutting (probably once roofed to form a souterrain). It has a lining wall, and lies east-south-east, and west-north-west, being partly buried in debris. The fort-wall embodies several large blocks, which evidently lay on the crag before it was built. The annexe (unlike that at Caherlough) is carefully bonded into the fort; it is 6 feet thick with a little filling, and it is evidently contemporary with the fort. The rough garth is 60 feet across north and south, and 75 feet east and west.

Another slight ring-wall, nearly levelled, lies some 700 feet northward from the last. Over the north edge of the townland, beyond the road from Teernea Cross to Ruan, and in Teernea, was a curious fort, 8-shaped in plan, of two equal rings, and excellent masonry with two faces and filling. It seems to have been built in one piece: the wall is usually 4 feet to 4 feet 6 inches high; so thick are the sloes and hazels everywhere (inside and outside) up to the wall, that I could not get any cross-measurements.

North from it, in an open field, is the last *cathair* of the group, also in Teernea. It is 102 feet wide inside, the wall 6 feet thick to the west, where it is only 3 feet high and 10 feet thick, and over 4 feet high to the east. The north and north-west parts are levelled to the foundations, which are of large blocks.[1] Of the other fort-names in Ruan, I note Rathcahaun, Rathvergin, Lisronalta, Lisbeg, Lisnavooan, Lisduff, Lismuinga, Lissyline, Doonanoge, and Ooankeagh.

DYSERT, RATH AND KILNAMONA PARISHES.

CAHERCLANCY. - I examined three stone forts in this townland. The actual Caherclancy is greatly defaced, a laneway runs through it, and the road to Ballygriffy Castle has encroached upon its base. Much of the wall of large blocks, with a slight batter, and about 5 feet to 5 feet 6 inches high, remains, but calls for no remark.

The other forts lie south of the road; passing across the thyme-tufted crags, we see on a low knoll, half-way between the road and the eastern fort, a large slab with a cave dug under it. The fort is greatly injured; only part of its walls is standing, 5 to 6 feet high, coarsely built with bad stones, and probably late. There are no foundations in the garth, which is about 100 feet north and south, by 80 feet east and west; it may be a bawn or cattle-pen of its neighbour fort.

The western *cathair*, on the contrary, is one of the finest pieces of masonry in this district of nobly built forts. It stands 68 feet to the west of the last, on a low grassy knoll, above a depression. It is from 6 to 7 feet high, and 10 to 12 feet thick, the last of the western side, with two faces of beautiful polygonal masonry of large blocks, but rather wide joints, and is fairly perfect all round. The batter is regular, 1 to 1 ½ in 4. The garth is level, and is raised 5 feet above the field; it is 90 feet across, and large, old hawthorns grow round the edge. The fort measures 110 ft. to 120 feet over all.

There are over thirty forts of earth and stone round Ballygriffy, and nearly sixty from Ruan to Dysert; none call for any special notice, being commonplace and featureless; a few deserve slight mention.

LISNANOWLE in Rath is nearly levelled to build the wall and back gate of Cragmoher House beside it. The records[2] give Cahernemoher and Cahergreenane in Cragmoher, alias Dromfinglas, 1655. It may be the 'stone fort of Dromfinglas' (if the castle is not intended) in the Inquisition on the death of Donald O'Brien of Inistymon in 1588.[3] It is named in the will of Matthew Sweeney of Lisnanoule, yeoman, Feb. 3rd, 1695; the testator orders his burial in 'the church of Coude (Coad).' There are curious outspoken directions about the mares and cattle; and two cows were named 'Dufheane' and 'Cronedovagha.' The fort seems to have had two ring; considerable foundations of the inner one remain.[4]

CAHERCORCANE in Rath is a nearly levelled ring-wall. A coin of King John was recently found in its gateway. Conor (son of Mortagh) O'Brien

---

[1] One of the Teernea cathairs is called, in 1655, Caher Tirnavoghter in the Book of Distribution.
[2] Book of Distribution, p. 526.
[3] Public Record Office, Dublin.
[4] Will, Killaloe Registry.

owned Cahircorkeane, and was pardoned in 1591.[1] I could hear of no stone fort in the adjoining Cahernamona. There are three typical earthern ring-forts between it and Corofin railway station. Liscullaun has a rath with a conjoined larger annexe to the north-west, about 150 feet over both rings. Of other forts I may name - Rath Blamaic (an ordinary low earthen fort, and near it the base of a tumulus or cairn of earth and large blocks). Cahervickaun and Caher Macgorman (utterly defaced when the adjoining houses were built); they lie in a detatched part of Kilnamona on a hillside.[2] Thence a steep road crosses the low part of Cappanakilla Ridge, close beside Liskillaculloo. The latter is a large low earthwork, pear-shaped in plan, about 250 feet east and west, and 200 feet across, and only a few feet high. Ratharella is an earthen fort, and Caherbannagh[3] is a much-gapped, featureless ring-wall on a high spur; a sheepfold has been built out of the ruin; both lie in Kilnamona. The two largest forts are only of slight interest, being as usual low and featureless. That in Kilkee West is 200 feet across, while Kylemore fort in Killeen, near Lough Atedaun, opposite Corofin, is 300 feet across east and west, and but little less north and south. In it is a killeen graveyard for children. There are many traces of cairns usually nearly removed. One gives its name to Knockacarnaun. One on a low crag near Shallee Castle in Ballyneillan is 74 feet across, and has a polygonal chamber about 5 feet every way. It was explored in 1874-6; it yielded a skull and the bones of two bodies.[4]

KILCURRISH (O.S. 25). - An interesting group lies close to the curious church of *Cill Croise*, or Kilcurrish, in Kilnamona and Dysert. A cairn of large blocks stands on a spur about 300 feet above the sea on the edge of Caherbannagh. It is 57 feet across, and at present only 8 feet high, being hollowed out in the middle by treasure-seekers, but no cist is visible.

Down the eastward slope is a *cathair*, a ring of filling 7 to 9 feet high, with portions of the outer face of well-fitted, large blocks, with a batter of 1 in 4; the interior face is well preserved. The garth has been tilled, and is 102 feet across north and south, and 111 feet east and west.

Farther to the east in Dysert Parish is a huge natural block which some ignorant visitor has taught the local people to call 'the Cromlech'; the mistake, however, led to my discovery of two real dolmens near it[5]; one has collapsed, and is embedded in the roots of a venerable hawthorn 130 feet from the fort. The sides are 7 feet 3 inches north, 6 feet 10 inches south; the

---

[1] Report xvi, Dep. Keeper Rec. Ireland, p. 196. The place is Craig Corcrain in the Annals of the Four Masters, 1589. In all other documents of Elizabethan times it is Cahercorcaun; probably both names existed as Tullycommaun and Cahercommaun, Cluainsavaun, Dunsavaun, and Clochansavaun.

[2] They and an earthen fort to the west named Ratharella are in line. Only the east segment of Cahervickaun remains.

[3] Morogh, Earl of Thomond, granted Cahirbeanagh in Inchiquin to Michael O'Dea, 14th December, 1660. The latter assigned it to Samuel Burton (of Buncraggy), July 18th, 1685. (Patent Rolls, William and Mary, No. 5, Pars 4, *facie*).

[4] *Journal* xiii, p. 160, and xiv, p. 12, *Proc. R. I. Acad.* xxvi (c). Plate xxv for plan and section, p. 467 for description.

[5] Plan of the lower dolmen, *Proc. R. I. Acad.*, vol. xxvi (c), plate xxv, and p. 467.

cover is 6 feet 3 inches, by 5 feet. North from the last, in the bottom of a valley among thickets of tall hazel, is another unmarked dolmen. It is 9 feet 10 inches by 4 feet over all, with two very rude blocks to each side and one to each end; it is not tapering, but rectangular. The cover has been tilted off, but rests on the side; it is 6 feet 8 inches long, and 5 feet wide like the last, and did not slope. We explored the open fields back towards Magowna Castle, but found no antiquities.

TIRMICBRAIN (O.S. 17). - A remarkable little rock fort in Rath Parish. It is greatly defaced, standing on a knob of limestone[1] on a steep, high ridge covered with brushwood and overlooking the lake and marshy valley of Tirmicbrain on the edge of Rath Parish. Local tradition connects the name with Bran the famous hound of Finn Mac Cumhail,[2] which, pursuing a magic stag, sprang from the top of Keentlea (Ceann Sliabh) or Inchiquin Hill into the lake, where it and its quarry disappeared for ever. The fort faces the richly wooded hill, the tall ivied castle, and the picturesque old terraced garden and villa of the Burtons. Reached with difficulty through thorny brakes, little is found. Two rings of large blocks rudely built, the walls rarely 6 feet high, crown the knoll, clinging irregularly to its edges. The upper ring is a little over 40 feet across; the annexe is over 50 feet, but is almost impossible to measure on account of thorn bushes.

The forts of Kilnaboy have, for the most part, been fully described; but a few extra notes on them and certain other antiquities seem desirable. The misleading statement in the Ordnance Survey Letters of Co. Clare[3] that 'there are several cahers in this parish, but the most remarkable is Cahermore,' ignores all the really remarkable examples in which Kilnaboy parish is so very rich.

SLIEVENAGLASHA (O.S. 10). - The lofty ridge at the high cliffs, almost overhanging the beautifully situated fort of Cahermore,[4] in Lackareagh, at the mouth of Glenquin (*Gleanncaoin* in 1311), is crowned by a remarkable early cemetery. It is best reached past the Russells' house, up by the fort, along the echoing little glen below the cliffs, till we reach a vast talus of fallen blocks forming a rude ladder to the lofty summit. Cahermore, I may add, is a striking illustration of how little the fort-builders troubled themselves to secure an absolutely commanding site. Such a one was attainable on the ridge beside the little glen, yet the fort was built beside a high crag platform commanding its outer enclosures and the rampart of the central ring. Seeing it, Cahernawealaun and Caherlisaniska, in Co. Clare (even without considering the overhung forts in other parts of Ireland, and several

[1] It is marked, but not as an antiquity, on the new map at the 'R' of 'Riverstown.'
[2] The district appears in Irish literature as a haunt of Finn. 'The Dialogue of Ossian.' (*Trans. Ossianic Soc.*, vol. iv, p. 51) tells of his 'two hounds at the Lake of Inchiquin, two hounds at Formaoil' or Formoyle in the neighbouring parish of Inagh. The scene of the *Feis tighe Chonain* is laid on the summit of Inchiquin Hill, and the same summit figures as a battle-field between Finn and the Tuatha Dé in the local legend of the Glas cow.
[3] Vol. i, p. 67.
[4] *Supra*, vol. xxvi, p. 367 [21], plan. *Ancient Forts of Ireland*, Plate VII. It is called Cahermore in Glenkeane in 1655, in the Book of Distribution and Survey, p. 519.

promontory forts in Mayo, Kerry, and elsewhere), we cannot attach such weight as other antiquaries have done to the mere theory that a fort is not residential if its ambit is overlooked by neighbouring high ground. This view fails to recognize how rarely our so-called forts are 'castles,' how usually 'courts' round a residence, whose builders hardly thought of attack or of siege, or mural assault as more than a mere possibility. The masonry of this noble fort is similar in parts to Langough, near Newmarket,[1] in eastern Co. Clare, the stones being in certain cases rudely hammer-dressed to take the angle of the next block when necessary.

Three small carns stand on the cliff-bastion, which towers behind the fort and rock platform. They are much defaced, 12 feet to 16 feet across, and rarely 4 feet high. The middle one has a looped cattle shelter (for which it was dilapidated); much of the material was used to build the loose-stone wall on the dangerous edge of the precipice.

Far more interesting is the group of eight carns on the highest summit, 700 feet above the sea. The weird, bleached grey heaps[2] on the brown moorland overlook the curved grey rock terraces of Mullachmoyle and Glenquin, and all central Clare to the hills of Slieve Bernagh, across Co. Limerick to the Galtees. Southward we overlook glittering lakes and dark woods to Inchiquin Hill and Callan; westward we see out past the edge of the old world, for, when the sun gets low, a white blaze glows behind the low hills - the sunset on the waters of the Atlantic.

(1) The north-east carn is 18 feet across and 4 feet high; it is kerbed by a ring of slabs, set on edge, and usually 4 feet long and 2 feet to 3 feet high. There is a central cist, long since opened and partly filled; its cell is still opened for 5 feet inwards. (2) To the south is a levelled carn; part of its kerbing remains, but the stones are spread too widely for measurement. (3) At 50 feet farther southward is a third one kerbed, and 5 feet high, much dilapidated by rabbit-hunters. (4) At 140 feet to the south is a heap with remains of the kerb, and two slabs of the cist, which was 6 feet long. Another mass of stones of doubtful nature lies in a hollow to the north-west. (5) At 80 feet to the south of the last carn is the chief monument of the group, and perhaps on that account the oldest, being on the actual summit. It stands looking across the valley (where the bare brown patches are reputed to be the beds of the wonderful Glasgeivnagh cow and her calf), to the great cathair of Mohernagartan,[3] the fort and cave of the divine smith, Lon mac Liomhtha. Farther up the plateau are seen the largest carn on the hill, and the fine neighbouring dolmen at Cappaghkennedy, while far to the south-west the ruined cottage and shining slabs of the wrecked dolmens of

---

[1] *Proc. R. I. Acad.*, vol. xxvii, Plate X.

[2] The cairns in early times were sometimes the scenes of magic rites. The Annals of the Four Masters, under A.D. 555, cite a poem attributed to St. Columba, which alludes to 'the hosts which proceed round the cairns.' Also Annals in *Silva Gadelica*, vol. ii, p. 424, 'round the *brugh* let him walk right-handed.' I have heard of no relic of such observance in Western Ireland, though some attached to dolmens.

[3] See *Journal*, xxvi, p. 364 [18]. It is also called Cahermore, a very common name in north-west Clare.

Slievenaglasha[1] catch the eye. Everywhere lie the rain-fretted level pavements of the crag, showing (as the inhabitants believe) the actual tracks of the wonderful cow and Lon's sons. So, at Kinallia such markings represent in popular idea the footprints of the soldiers and hoofmarks of the horses of Guaire Aidne's guard pursuing the fugitive banquet, swept from the king's table by the Easter miracle of St. Colman MacDuach.

The identification of strange stones with cows is early in Ireland, *e.g.*, in a twelfth-century manuscript, 'the cows of Aife are stones which are on the sides of mountains, and are like white cows from afar.'[2] Tracks and lines of earthworks are frequently attributed to supernatural animals; the Rian Bo of Ardpatrick, Co. Limerick, and that near Ardmore, Co. Waterford, were made by the horns of St. Patrick's cow, while the Dane's Cast, the Worm Ditch, and the Duncladh in Ulster are believed to have been made by dragons, or by the Black Pig.[3] It is not impossible that the Cladh Ruadh trench from Kerry Head to Athea may have once been connected with another pig, as the strange boar, *Banbh Sinna*, son of Maelenaig, was slain at Temar Luachra, near its eastern termination.[4] The *leaba* patches are very apparent from the carn. I have given their curious legend elsewhere in these pages, and in *Folk Lore*, as it was preserved in 1839, and found practically unaltered in the recesses of these hills by Dr. Macnamara.[5] He and I were told by John Finn, in 1896 (I took it down at the time), a version mainly identical with O'Donovan's. 'At Slievenaglusha are the Glas Cow's beds; no grass ever grows on them; she used to feed near the herdman's house (at the dolmen),[6] and over Cahill's mountain, where she could get plenty of grass, on to Teeskagh.' His legend ended: 'And she went away, and how do I know where? and there were no tidings.' As another Tullycommaun version ended, 'She was taken by an Ulsterman,' one suspects that she was the cow hidden with the native of that province in the cave of *Leaba na haon-bo*, in Ballynahown, near Oughtdarra and Crumlin, farther west; but the natives say the 'Hean bo' was not the 'Glas.'[7]

---

[1] The dolmen was destroyed about 1880 by an idiot, who set the fuel stored in it on fire.

[2] *Revue Celtique*, 1892, p. 378.

[3] *Journal*, vol. xl, p. 126; Battle of Magh Tura, p. 65. See also 'Rian Bo' (Rev. Patrick Power), *Journal*, xxviii, p. 1, and xxxv, p. 110. For Mr. De Vismes Kane's 'The Ulster Earthworks,' see *Proc. R. I. Acad.*, vol. xxvii, p. 322; also Canon Lett in *Ulster Journal of Archæology* (new), vol. iii, pp. 23, 67 - all very full and valuable papers. Also *Ancient Forts of Ireland*, section 149. In the *Táin Bó Cuailnge* (ed. Faraday), p. 141, the Dun Bull digs a long double ditch.

[4] *Revue Celtique*, vol. ii, p. 93.

[5] *Journal*, xxv (1895), p. 227. *Folk Lore*, vol. xxii (1911), pp. 88, 89, also vol. xxiv.

[6] *Journal* xxvi, p. 365 [18].

[7] *Journal*, vol. xxxv, p. 346 [119]. Glasgeivnagh legends, see, for MacKineely and Balor at Tory Island, Donegal, *Ulster Journal of Archæology*, vol. i, p. 115, and *Bentley's Miscellany*, Nov. 1837; for Elin Gow at Cluainte in Kerry, J. Curtin's *Hero Tales*, p. 1; for the Clare Stories, *Folk Lore*, vol. xxii, 1911, xxiv, 1913; also *Journal*, xxv, p. 227. For the 'Gloss Gavlen' in Achill, see *West Irish Folk Tales*, W. Larminie, p. 1. She would pasture at Cruahawn of Connacht, and drink at Loch Ayachir-a-

The chief carn is 42 feet in diameter, 7 feet to 8 feet high, and fairly perfect; it has no kerbing, and the cist (if it exists) is concealed. The heap was an important trigonometrical station on the new survey, and a shelter was built on top visible far across the plains. (6) At 30 feet to the south is a large but greatly levelled carn, also 42 feet in diameter, unkerbed, and hardly 3 feet high; pens and cattle shelters have been built out of the stones close beside it. (7) On the edge of the platform to the extreme south, 135 feet from the last, is a defaced little carn 18 feet across. (8) The last of the monuments lies across a shallow depression, and is about 255 feet westward from the last, and 288 feet south-westward from the chief carn. It is 30 feet across, and 4 feet to 5 feet high, nearly perfect, save that it has been opened at one point, and the central cist exposed by treasure-seekers. This, unfortunately, is almost universal in Co. Clare, and took place everywhere too far in the past to recover any intelligible account of what was found. At the beginning of the last century it was recollected that pottery and crumbled bones, but no implements or gold, had usually been found. I carefully searched every open cist, but never found a particle of clay vessels or metal; only sometimes bones reduced to the smallest flakes. I know of no closed dolmen, save, perhaps, one, and four cairns apparently intact, which it is best not to specify at present. It is noticeable that the three southern carns of Slievenaglasha are unkerbed; if (as I believe) one of these is the oldest, then the more advanced form (such as we find at Poulawack and elsewhere), may be the later; however, kerbing is found round the mounds of important dolmens, such as Clooneen and Iskancullin.

GLENCOLUMBCILLE (O.S. 10). - The venerable church[1] dedicated to the great Columba, the patron of Ireland and of Iona, gives the name to the valley. I heard no tradition of the saint's sojourn here as I did at Crumlin. The church (as little known) I may describe, for it has been wrongly attributed to the fifteenth century,[2] because an inserted doorway is of that period. It is of the late eleventh or early twelfth century; the west end and much of the north wall are destroyed, and part of the south side rebuilt in modern times, from the jamb of an early window eastward. The east light has a chamber and recess, and a well-built splay; it is 16 inches wide, but the head is gone. There are projecting handle-stones in the east gable. The building measures 41 feet 9 inches outside by 21 feet 6 inches; it is 16 feet 6 inches wide inside, the walls being 2 feet 3 inches to 2 feet 6 inches thick. The upper half of a conical quern of sandstone, 13 inches across and 7 inches high, lies at the north-west angle of the ruin.

The ridge on which the church stands lies between the glens at the foot of Cappaghkennedy Hill, between Glenquin and the rich thickets of Glencolumbcille - golden, scarlet, and pink in the autumn, with ash, hazel, hawthorn, pegwood, and wild guelder rose - running up past Cappagh Castle to the lonely hermitage and well of St. Colman MacDuach, under the

---

guigala. The legend also occurs at Ballynascreen in Derry, and Glengavlen in Cavan. There was a mound of the Glas at Tara.

[1] *Proc. R. I. Acad.*, Ser. III, vol. vi.

[2] The Ordnance Survey Letters frequently describe essentially early churches as late when a Gothic door has been inserted.

huge Eagle Cliff of Kinallia. Glencolumbcille church commands lovely views
of these and the terraced hills, and down the 'pleasant valley' of Gleann
Caoin, with a broad, open view of the low land down the glen.

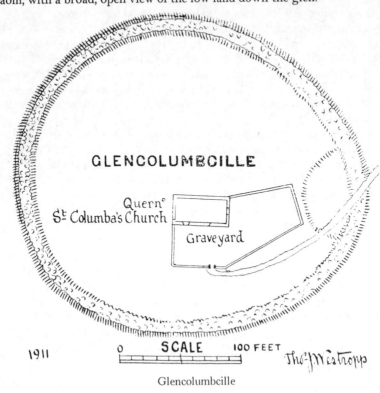

Glencolumbcille

I include this site, however, not for its religious interest or its beauty, but
because the church and burial-ground stand within a large low ringfort of
earth and stones 236 feet across the interior, north and south, 258 feet east
and west, and about 280 feet over all. It is largely of dry-stonework[1] to the
south, and is much removed; the mound round the north semi-circuit is 10
feet to 12 feet thick, and 6 feet high, faced with large stones in part, but now
featureless, for I found no trace of a gate. The area is terraced up on each
side of the ridge for about 4 feet over the field. The occurrence of churches
in forts is rare in the lower Shannon valley. Templenaraha oratory, with a
massive ring-wall, near Ruan, I have noticed. Tulla church, in eastern Clare,
had two circular ramparts about 150 feet and 480 feet across, stated in the
life of St. Mochulla, in 1142, to have been dug and stone-walled by the seven
converted soldiers of King Guaire, about A.D. 620.[2]

---

[1] Miss Stokes in *Three Months in the Forests of France*, p. 28, mentions her discovery
round the knoll on which once stood the monastery founded by St. Columbanus at
Annegrai, of a dry-stone wall, like Irish *cashels*, probably dating from the founder's
time, *circa* A.D. 580; a view is given. There was a cashel at St. Elois' Monastery of
Solignac, *ibid.*, p. xxxii.
[2] Vita S. Mochullei Episcopi, also *Journal*, xli, pp. 17, 18.

Moyarta and Kiltinnaun stood on low, flat-topped motes, with fosse and annexe; Killilagh and Rathborney, beside circular earthworks. In the neighbouring County of Limerick an imposing example occurs at Cloncagh church,[1] of which I give a plan. It is 750 feet to 770 feet across, and consists of two mounds with a fosse between, such as St. Enda of Aran raised about A.D. 480, round the monastery of his sister, Fanchea, at Rossory,[2] where a circular fosse and mound remain. Templebryan Church, Co. Cork, stands in a large ring 400 to 500 feet across, with a souterrain and pillar-stone inside the ambit. Abbey Grey, or Monasternalea, in Athleague, on the Suck, is girt by a large mound 600 feet inside, and 700 feet over all, with a fosse 25 feet wide. It is, therefore, quite as probable that the Glencolumbcille eathhwork[3] is ecclesiastical, as that some earlier chief gave his *dún* to God and the church in the days of St. Columba. To the north-east of this work, close to the road, is a plain cross with three steps, and a thin octagonal shaft, each face only three inches wide. Across the road, on the fence, is a large natural block of limestone 4 feet long by 3 feet high, with *six* little round holes, the third and sixth larger than the rest, the reputed marks of the saint's fingers.

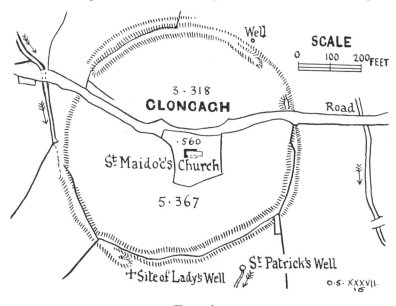

Cloncagh

MULLACH (O.S. 17). - I visited again the great cathair on Mullach ridge in Dabrien. I found that the hill (ridge) is locally named *Clochán wullach* and the fort *Caherwullach.* The large limestone boulder on the ridge is understood to be the 'Clochan.'

---

[1] *Proc. R. I. Acad.,* xxv (c), p. 413, xxvi (c), p. 60.
[2] Vita S. Fancheae.
[3] I found the supposed ecclesiastical earthwork at Kilmore, Co. Waterford, had no tradition or trace of a church or graveyard inside this strange but overrated earthwork. The name proves nothing, as the church (or wood) may have been elsewhere in the townland.

My first brief description in these pages[1] is from a letter of Dr. Macnamara; from notes on my subsequent three visits I may expand it here. It is
a fine oval ring-wall of good masonry, the batter in parts being curved and
in others in two slopes, 1 in 4 below for 6 feet up, and 1 in 3 above. The
outer face of good large blocks sometimes 3 feet long, the inner of small
stones. The rampart is often over 9 feet high and thick, the summit usually
6 feet 6 inches. Four inches lower is a narrow terrace from 27 inches to 36
inches wide (a part only 15 inches wide), being best preserved round the
northern half, and reaches to the south-east. It is usually 4 feet above the
garth. There are recesses perhaps for ladders, but the northern is only 10
inches deep, while 9 feet 6 inches long. The north-western is clearer, being
3 feet 3 inches wide. There is a well-defined rock cutting, a tank, or, more
probably, a souterrain, in the south-west segment. The fort measures 129
feet north and south, and 138 feet east and west outside, and the garth 112
feet and 120 feet inside respectively.

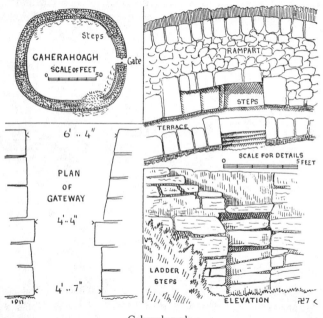

Caherahoagh

CAHERAHOAGH (O.S. 17). - Dr. George Macnamara got the bushes in the
overgrown garth of the fort cut away, disclosing once more the curious
ladder steps sketched by me[2] long before, but hidden for many years. I give
a plan and details of the curious ring-wall. The gateway is of cut stone
inserted about 1480; the steps near it are possibly as late, but have been
nearly destroyed since my first visit. The laneway to the fort is called
Bohereenacaheragh (*Boithrín na Cathrach*).

---

[1] Vol. xxvi, p. 367 [19].
[2] For the former description and views see *Journal*, vol. xxvi, pp. 366-7 [20] and
Ancient Forts of Ireland, fig. 13, No. 6.

CAHERBULLAUN. - It lies 58 feet to the south-west of Caherahoagh, and is now quite levelled; the walls are 8 feet thick, the garth 82 feet across. To the east of this townland is Ballard; the local name for the adjoining part of it is 'Bohaunnascraw,' while Ballyeighter is locally *Beol eighter*, and Lough Cullaun is known as Loch Monanagh. Aglish is Ballaglish.[1] Ashfield is called Garraunawhinshog.

CASHLAUNGAR (O.S. 10). - The townland of Tullycommaun is probably the Tuluauch-comyn held by (King Torlough) O'Brien in 1298 as given in the Pipe Rolls.[2] Through it in 1317 the army of Prince Dermot marched on his way to Corcomroe Abbey, 'along the fortress-begirt tracks' between Leana and Crughwill. Hugh O'Donnell's troops plundered it in their great raid into Thomond 1599. In again visiting the curious rock-fort I found two middens inside the wall at the south end of the platform, with bones of deer and oxen. The destruction of a bush revealed another fragment of wall not given on my first plan in 1896. I also found, utterly hidden in thick hazels on the platform spur below the rock tower on the north, a very massive walled enclosure or bawn, now nearly levelled. Mr. Richard Ussher made some experimental diggings in some of the caves in Glencurraun near the fort, and found very early traces of human habitation, such as he found at Edenvale. Unfortunately he was unable to carry on any works there. In Cahercommaun I also found a midden in the rock-cut drain; it yielded bones of oxen, deer, and swine, with shapeless iron implements greatly decayed. The fort name occurs in various records, as Kahirekamon in 1585[3] and Cahircomaine in 1655. The divisions of Tullycomon in the latter year were Glencrane, Leshene, Slewbegg, Lisheenageeragh, Dullisheen, Cahir-comaine, and Cahir-comane or Lyshinlyane.[4] The personal name Chumann or Coman has been long connected with the district of Burren and Corcomroe; its earliest recorded chief, Celechar, slain in 701,[5] was son of Coman.

CAHERFADDA (O.S. 16). - The cathair now bearing the townland name is most insignificant. It is a ring-wall of poor coarse crag slabs nearly levelled when some houses were built in it. The epithet, 'fada,' long, does not seem justified in any fort on these townlands. As may be seen (in the next section), the townland was 'Carrowfadda,' long quarter, in 1551 (*Ceathramadh*, not *Cathair*). The names, both in Irish and English forms, frequently interchange; but in this case the townland, not the fort, was 'long,' and the epithet probably passed to the fort. I may again point out that groups of nouns with the same terminal occur in place-names, e.g., Dun-savan, Clochan-savan, and Cluan-sumain, Cloghan-savaun, near Loop Head. The forts between Caherfadda and Lemenagh Castle are a levelled ring-wall near the avenue, a low fort of earth and stones over the little

---

[1] I have not, however, found the name Ballaglish in any document; the place is Eaglascarna in the Earl of Thomond's Estate Map, 1703.

[2] Pipe Roll No. 27, anno xxvii Edw. I.

[3] Fiants Elizabeth (Report D. K. R. App. No. xv).

[4] Book of Distribution and Survey (P.R.O.I., p. 520); the name, though found in common use in the townlands by Dr. Macnamara and myself, does not appear in the 1839 map.

[5] Or 704, according to the Annals of Ulster.

valley, and another low earth-ring on the summit of Knockloon Hill. Traces of two small ring-walls lie between Caherfadda and the dolmens of Parknabinnia.

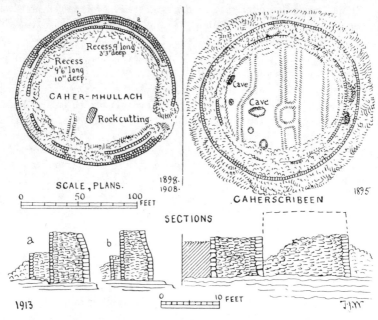

Cahermullagh and Caherscribeen

CAHERSCRIBEEN (O.S. 16). - I need only add to my former description of this rude but interesting and important fort[1] its plan and a record bearing on the early form of its name which hitherto I found in no document (though well known on the ground) till it was inserted on the new maps. The will of Murrogh O'Brien, 'The Tanist,' last recognized king and first Earl of Thomond and Baron of Inchiquin, is fortunately preserved in a contemporary copy at Dromoland, and dates 26th July, 1551.[2] In it occurs this passage – 'Item. Altri filio tertio Donato relinquo castellum, vulgo nuncupatur *Leamneh,* cum quinque quarteriis sibi vicinis quorum nomina sunt haec, scilicet. tres quart. terr. *Cnokloine* et *Carah-Scribnib* et quarteria in *Clundin* (Clooneen) et dimidiate quarteriae *Fahafane.'*[3] In the inquisition taken in 1626, after the death of Conor O'Brien in 1609, the three quarters of Lemeneagh are called *Carrowcastle, Carrowmoyle,* and *Carrowfadda.* The last two are evidently Cahermoyle-Roughan and Caherfadda, which also appear in the marriage settlement of the later Conor O'Brien and his formidable wife Maura Rhue, Mary, daughter of Therlogh Roe Mac Mahon

---

[1] *Journal,* xxvi, p. 368 [21]. The nearest equivalents to the long parallel traverses across the garth are, so far as I know, those in the ring-fort at Carrowmore, Co. Sligo. Such also occur in German forts.

[2] I have to thank Mr. C. MacDonnell, of Newhall, for the use of his copy of the will.

[3] It was called Cahirpolla, and adjoined Ballyganner; one document seems to place it next Lismoher.

of Clonderlaw,[1] October 19th, 1639. The gateway with his arms and an inscription in 1646 has only recently been pulled down and removed; it stood before Lemeneagh Castle, and was most injudiciously taken by the owner to his garden in eastern Clare.

SHESHY (O.S. 9). - This townland, lying to the north of Lemeneagh, has two ring-forts. Cahermore occupies a good position on a gently rising crag; it has fine rock masonry of the usual type, and is from 5 to over 6 feet high for much of its circuit. Caheraclarig, in a thicket of hazel bushes, near the Carran road, though far more dilapidated, has an unusual feature in the lower courses of its masonry. The bottom course is of large more or less rectangular crag blocks, but on these rests a course of thinner (header) slabs set on end like books on a shelf. I have only seen similar work in a *cathair* near Carrahan in eastern Clare, and even there all has been removed since 1892,[2] when I fortunately sketched it. There are somewhat similar courses in the upper part of the wall in Cahercommaun and Caherscrebeen, but they rather radiate like rude flat arches than stand upright.

Near these forts are two dolmens, one in the deep little glen of Deer-park or Poulquillika. Borlase published my description and plan of it in *Dolmens of Ireland*.[3] It stands on a low ridge, and consists of a chamber narrowing and lowering eastward, in all 18 feet long (in two compartments), and 7 feet to 5 feet wide. It has a fence of slabs around it. The covers are respectively 8 feet 2 inches by 5 feet 3 inches and 6 inches thick and 13 feet by 10 feet 3 inches to 9 feet and 9 inches thick. The remains of a small well-built house-ring appear on a small knoll to the west; the mere ring of large foundation blocks of a second cathair is seen on a boulder cliff between the Carran road and the old road to Castletown near their angle. There are also some defaced, roughly built, rectangular 'mohers.'

KILFENORA PARISH.

CLOONEEN (O.S. 9). The most beautiful of the dolmens in this part of the country is certainly Clooneen. Borlase's view,[4] though quite accurate, does not give any idea of its fine proportions; his plan is good. It lies in a dilapidated carn, and is a tapering cist of very regular slabs; its cell, 15 feet 3 inches long, 5 feet 6 inches to 3 feet 2 inches wide, and 5 feet 6 inches high. The cover is over 15 feet by 8 feet and 10 inches thick. A fence of slabs lay outside to the north, and a kerbing girds the mound. Such slab enclosures are no uncommon features in Co. Clare, as I have recorded their occurrence at a now levelled 'long dolmen' at Milltown, near Tulla, at Newgrove, Ardnataggle, and perhaps Killokennedy in eastern Clare, and at Iskancullin, Deerpark, and Clooneen. There is a small hole pierced in the south side-slab and the tops of the sides are hammer-dressed.

---

[1] Dromoland Papers. For her legends and history, see *Journal*, vol. xxvi, p. 363; vol. xxx, p. 408.

[2] Described in a paper on the remains in eastern Clare, *Proc. R. I. A.*, 1913.

[3] Vol. i, p. 70.

[4] *Dolmens of Ireland*, vol. I, p. 80. See also *Journal*, vol. xxxi, p. 291 [92].

ARDNAGOWELL (O.S. 16). - The most problematical of the early earthworks of Clare is certainly that on Knock Ardnagowell, a low green rise in the shale land, not far to the south of the road from Lemeneagh to Kilfenora,[1] in the townland of Ballyclancahill. It is a conspicuous object from the north and the south, consisting of two great parallel mounds over the saddle of the hill, but is not marked either on the old or the new maps. The mounds are 53 feet apart or 98 feet from top to top; they run north and south, looking in the distance like an old wide embanked road, on the summit of the ridge. They are respectively 185 feet and 198 feet long, the western being usually 40 feet thick, 5 feet 3 inches over the hillside, and 11 feet over the interspace; the eastern is 45 feet thick and of equal height.

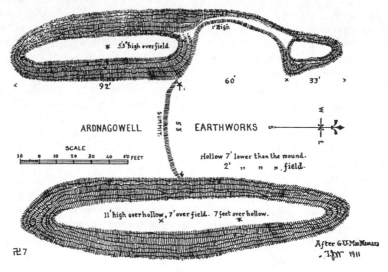

Ardnagowel Earthworks

The western runs for an even distance about 92 feet down each slope of the ridge and is dug into for 60 feet, leaving the outer edge only about 3 feet thick and a foot high. An old roadway runs to the south at 70 feet from the western mound, and a large boulder, 15 feet across, lies between it and the western mound. The ends die away into the slope, and nothing suggests that the works were joined by cross-mounds or loops. There is no tradition as to its nature. It is too wide for a road, too short for a mearing, too open for a fort, and being over a summit is of course unsuited for a reservoir, even if dew-ponds or artificial tanks were found in western Ireland. As we have seen, the ridge is slightly lowered between the mounds. I commend the problem of this strange work to other antiquaries.

KNOCKACARN (O.S. 16). - A conspicuous little tumulus stands on a ridge in Clooneen. It is 46 feet in diameter north-east to south-west, and 40 feet across, being oval. It is only 5 feet high; large blocks crop out of the sod, especially near the top.

---

[1] The plan is by Dr. G. U. Macnamara, who also measured the tumuli at Knockacarn and Ballyganner Hill for me. The townland is locally called Ballycloonacahill.

TULLAGHA (O.S. 16). - I limit this paper from Lemeneagh onward to the antiquities lying immediately south of the Kilfeneora road. Beyond these limits to the south there is but little to describe. Forts are few, and nearly all of the common type, about 100 feet across, of earth with rare traces of stone-facing and a fosse and low rings. The only ones worthy of any detailed notice about Milltown, Cahermurphy, and in the 'Irrus' peninsula from Loop Head to Dunbeg I have already described.[1]

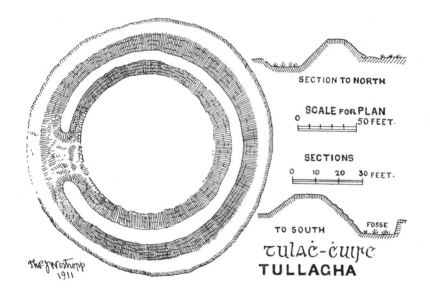

SECTION TO NORTH

SCALE FOR PLAN

0   50 FEET.

SECTIONS

0   10   20   30 FEET.

TO SOUTH   FOSSE

τυιλċ-ċυιγċ
TULLAGHA

Thos: J. Westropp
1911

Tullagha

Of dolmens, only those of Carncreagh and Callan and the problematical Ogham slab near the last needed and received notice. Two of the earthen forts lie near the road opposite the cross-road leading past Ballykinvarga, Noughaval, and Cahermacnaughten to Ballyvaughan; they are in Tullagh (locally Tullagha) townland, probably the ancient *Tulach Chuirc*. The one nearest the road is 220 feet over all, and is a mass of beautiful green sward, rising 13 feet over the fosse, which is 6 feet deep and 15 feet wide, with no outer ring. It is nearly filled up on the east and south, and is still wet in parts and filled with yellow iris. The rampart is 31 feet thick at the field-level to the south, and rises 6 feet over the garth; it is 41 feet thick at the base and 12 feet on top to the north. There are three gaps, two very shapeless and narrow, the third faces the east and was probably the ancient entrance. The garth is 117 feet across and nearly a true circle; it has been tilled, and is now much overgrown with docks. The rampart was once evidently faced by revetments of large regular sandstone blocks, but few traces remain, save along the inner foot of the mound.

---

[1] *Journal,* xli, p. 125, pp. 132-136; xxxviii, pp. 28, 114, 221, 344.

The earthen fort on the low rising ground of Knockalish lies about 400 yards away to the south-west. It is 150 feet across, but of little interest.

I have already described the more noteworthy forts of Kilfenora parish, Doon, Ballykinvarga, Ballyshanny, and Caherminaun. Doon was very probably the *Tech nEnnach*, the *dún* made by Ennach, son of Umor, on the river Dael, which rises from the ridge on which this great rock-cut fort sits imposingly, dominating the view from Roughan and the Tullycommaun ridges to far out to sea. Caherballagh is a featureless ring planted with hawthorns near Lough Ballagh. Cahersherkin is only a small defaced ringfort. The Down Survey, *circa* 1655, shows near it a large rectangular fort which is not given on the old or new Ordnance Maps, and I could not learn that any trace exists. Just within Kilnaboy parish lies Lissyogan, an oblong earthwork, 100 feet by 150 feet on Knockaunadrankady (Little Hill of the Fleas) in Moherbullog, while Cahergal in Maghera is a barely visible ring of filling on a pleasant hillock on the flank of Inchiquin Hill, overlooking the green valley towards Applevale. In the closing section of this paper I hope, so far as I am able, to conclude my survey of the ring-forts of north-west Co. Clare by notes on those undescribed round Lisdoonvarna, and the results of farther examination of the district thence to Ballyganner ridge and the Kilfeneora road, so as to meet the present survey.

6

CAHERMAKERRILA GROUP
KNOCKAUNS MOUNTAIN
BALLYGANNER GROUP

With the present paper I close the series[1] of twelve published in these pages during twenty-three years. The field work on which they are based was begun over thirty-six years ago, in May 1878. Though no trained antiquary is likely to deny the utility of such a work, there is sore need of apology for certain imperfections in its execution, patent even to a casual reader. When it was commenced I had no exemplar to follow; I had to learn what to do as the work proceeded. Matters at first little regarded proved important and called for insertion and further research. Forts and dolmens in that wilderness of crags and thickets are sometimes undistinguishable from rock ledges and boulders; often the most definite guide to a dolmen is a square patch of dark shadow in its open end. In some cases bushes of hawthorn, sloe and hazel[2] covered features, so that two flights of steps in Cahercuttine and two in Caherminaun, gateways in Roughane and the 'cairn-caher' and the terrace of Cashlaun Gar, were at first concealed from me. Thus supplemental matter had constantly to be added, destroying the consistency of the survey while increasing its value.

Theory, as a by-product to be constantly fused and recast, is of less moment. I have constantly altered my views, and hope no one may suppose that the theories in this conclusion even purport to be 'final.' Finality is impossible in our present ignorance; scientific excavation or critical

---

[1] Vol. xxi, p. 462; vol. xxii, p. 191; vol. xxiii, p. 281, p. 432; vol. xxvi, pp. 142 [1], 362 [17]; vol. xxvii, p. 116 [23]; vol. xxviii, p. 352 [35]; vol. xxix, p. 367 [47]; vol. xxxi, pp. 1 [62], 273 [76]; vol. xxxv, pp. 205 [94], 232 [116]; vol. xli, p. 343 [134]; vol. xliii, p. 232 [157].

[2] Like most matters relating to forts this finds a place in early Irish Literature. 'I saw a *liss* topped with trees' (MacConglinne, ed. Meyer, p. 68). 'Spiked thorn bushes grow on the site (*sic*, read 'side') of a half ruined *liss*, the weight of a heavy harvest bows them down, hazel nuts of the fairest crops drop from the great trees of the raths' (Guesting of Athirne, from Book of Leinster, *Eriu*, vol. vii, p. 3). The last well recalls the coral-like hedges of the forts in the autumn. 'An apple tree in every *liss*' (Battle of Magh Rath, p. 131, *circa* 1170-97), and other similar allusions.

examination to fix the dates of our literary sources has scarcely begun. Still progress is getting marked; the results of European research are no longer unstudied in Ireland, and such theories as attributed all our forts to the Firbolg or the Danes are left to a few belated followers of the older school. Nevertheless, there is still a prejudice that one who does not hold to his first theories is of no authority, and that one who does not adhere to the older school of 1840 is a lonely schismatic, even when he voices the views of the majority of European antiquaries, while the value of the study of dry fact appeals little to many whom country writers call 'great antiquarians.'

I keep for the actual conclusion my estimate of the broad results of these surveys of Co. Clare, so I need only note the lines of research. In 1892-93 two groups in eastern Co. Clare were described. From 1895 onward the papers deal with the Barony of Burren and the adjoining parishes of the Baronies of Corcomroe and Inchiquin. If we add the papers in 1908 and 1909 on the promontory forts of the Iorrus and the ring forts of Moyarta, and that in 1911 on Cahermurphy and the forts near Miltown-Malbay,[1] we get descriptions of the chief remains of this class in western Co. Clare. If we further add those in the *Proceedings of the Royal Irish Academy*[2] on the eastern forts, and those in the *North Munster Archaeological Society's Journal* on the forts near Kilkee,[3] and (as I do at the end of this paper) index and methodize it, the whole nearly attains to the dignity of a county survey - more I cannot claim to have done.

I never attempted to form a classification of the ring forts, but hope to do so tentatively at the end of the paper. Theories and classification in other countries do not fit Irish conditions. The English arrangement adopted by the 'scheme for recording ancient defensive earthworks and fortified enclosures' is absolutely unsuitable here. By its rules we should bring under one heading the widely divergent forts of Cahercommaun, Cahernakilly, Dundoillroe, and the Cashlaun Gar into Class A. We should have to classify Turlough Hill fort or Moghane differently from Cahercalla in Class B. So also the nomenclature of Great Britain and the Continent is unsuitable: 'late Celtic' with them means 'very early Celtic' here. The English assertion that while the great hill forts are prehistoric and tribal, the small ones are feudal, is contradicted here equally by our pre-Norman literature and by excavation. The English view separating promontory forts fenced all around from these only defended at the neck confuses instead of helping us; since so many of these walled headlands show fences, that we can hardly doubt that most were walled round before the edges and ends fell away.

Racial district types when sought for in Ireland are not discoverable; all the main types here are found in France, Germany, and Austria, and some also in Sweden, Switzerland, Holland, and farthest Russia, in Perm. The two oblong platforms at Bunratty and Culleen are probably Norman; the rest of the forts of Co. Clare represent no type that does not occur across Europe,

---

[1] Vol. xxxviii, pp. 28, 221, 344.
[2] Vol. xxvii, pp. 217, 371; vol. xxix, p. 186, and xxxii, p. 38; xxxix, p. 113; vol. xli, pp. 5, 17.
[3] Carrigaholt to Loop Head, vol. i, p. 219; vol. ii, pp. 103, 134, 225; Kilkee vol. iii, pp. 38, 153; for some of the Corcomroe forts, see also vol. i, p. 14.

from Perm to Kerry, and from the bronze age to late mediaeval times. Where the promontory forts of the Ural mountains and the Atlantic coasts are closely similar, and the great prehistoric 'Hausberge' of Central Europe resemble 'feudal mote castles,' we cannot be sufficiently cautious in laying down dates or tribal rules from external forms of earthworks. Excavation - our best means of dating - is hindered by the expense and by local jealousies, sometimes fostered by those who should know better, or by uninformed persons writing to newspapers.

At the commencement of this survey some (then recognised as 'authorities') said that 'such an attempt was useless, all had been worked out by O'Donovan and Dunraven.' The latter authorities, however, had each only described two types, while out of some 2,200 forts in Co. Clare, only five had been slightly described. So also when commencing a like work on the promontory forts I was told that 'nothing was left to be done,' when out of at least 106 only two had been adequately described and one inaccurately noted; of 104 no accurate plans had been made. There is a warning here to that complacent type of person who supposes all is done for any branch of Irish archaeology.

I may at least claim for these tentative notes, such as a pioneer can offer, that they are a record of what is being rapidly destroyed, and that they have led to wider studies of their field not a few who might never have surveyed it. What a noble field too it proved to be, what a museum of remarkable antiquities, and how full of beauty; 'the pride of the height, the clear heaven with its glorious show!' The forts lie amid the glimmering terraced crags, 'a barren and dry land' on the summits, but with underground rivers and silver-laced waterfalls in its glens. From some forts, like Caherdoonerish and Aghaglinny, we look across the sailess sea and seventy miles to either side from the huge domes of Nephin, in Co. Mayo, to Mount Brandon, and to the nearer mountains, the peaks of Bennabeola, in Connemara; the mote-like Kimalta; the Galtees and Slieve Mish. Nor is this all - rock-gardens of exquisite flowers, gorgeous cranesbills, creamy mountain avens, ferns and sedums adorn the nooks and shelves of the limestone. Magnificent sheets of colour carpet it, when the spring-giver 'makes it to bloom with flowers like sapphire,' and the loveliest of its flowers, blue gentian and violet, sheet the ground, and primrose and foam-white anemone the ledges. There the fissured grey crag, level as a pavement, sheltered in its clefts the hartstongue and maidenhair ferns. There the underground stream runs 'down to a sunless sea.' Amid all this varied loveliness the Corcomroe tribe and the Eoghanacht Ninussa and the forgotten races before them made their homes and monuments, often their only record. From its 'pages' these notes are taken, and it is still open to all who choose to revise or expand my copy from its wonderful original.

CAHERMAKERRILA GROUP (O.S. 9)

Had I been able to work my survey on consistent lines, this should have been included as part of the Cahermacnaughten group, which it adjoins; but by accident of means of access the two are practically cut off from each other, and I always found it more easy to reach the former forts from Corofin and the latter from Lisdoonvarna. From that spa-town we go eastward, crossing the river valley, and seeing on a bold bluff a lofty mound - a reputed 'fairy hill.'

LISSATEEAUN, *Lis an tsidheán*, the fairy fort, lies in a townland called Gowlaun, from the 'fork' (Gabhal) of the stream. It is a mote-like mound, shaped out of the natural bluff, but raised and rounded so as to form a high flat-topped platform sufficiently imposing as seen from the road bridge to the east. A shallow fosse runs round it on the side of the plateau in a semicircle. There are no other mounds or hut sites, nor is it easy to fix its actual height, as it runs into the natural slopes. The summit lies about 400 feet above the sea.

Its resemblance to a burial mound may have helped its reputation as a *sidh*, but it very probably was, if not in origin, at least in use, a true *lis* or residential fort, as its name implies. *Sidheán* in Co. Clare living usage, by the way, implies rather a passing gust or whirl of wind in which the fairies travel. It is a prophylactic usage to bow or take off your hat as the gust reaches you.[1] The fort is reputed to give its name to the Castle of Lisdoonvarna, 'the fortified fort of the gap.' The gap is the river gully, and the levelled ring wall at the head of the slope to the north is Caherbarna.

The mossy court walls sheeted with polypodium alone mark Lisdoonvarna Castle, long the residence of the Lysaghts (Gillisachta) and the Stacpooles. In the same townland, turning eastward, we pass the foundations of a *cathair* on a conspicuous green knoll. The road cuts through another levelled ring wall in Ballygastell. Nearly opposite to the south of the road are a *killeen* graveyard for children, and some old enclosures. Farther on in Ballyconnoe is a small house ring, its wall coarsely built, and now barely a yard high, on a knoll of crag. Near it, roads run northward towards Toomaghera (or 'Toovarra') chapel, and south-eastward (a bad, but ancient, road) along a green shale ridge, past a heap of fallen masonry, once Binroe Castle, to Cahermacnaughten. A rich marshy tract, as so often, runs from the foot of the ridge as far as the shale covers the limestone. The further reaches of the road run on to Noughval southward, and through Kilcorney valley eastward, past Caherconnell and the Cragballyconoal forts and dolmens, past Poulaphuca dolmen, down a steep descent into the Turlough valley, on to Corcomroe Abbey, being evidently one of the ancient thoroughfares of Corcomroe.

We have imperceptibly reached a considerable height above the sea, which is visible, both westward, beyond the high round castle of Doonegore, at the north end of the cliffs of Moher, and southward, in Liscannor Bay. Turning from the Toomaghera road into the craggy fields we enter the townland of Cahermakerrila. Beyond it lies the other large townland of Cahermaan.

---

[1] *Folk Lore* ('Survey of Clare'), vol. xxi, p. 198.

The names of these lands (so far as I am aware) first appear as *Cathair lapain* and *Cathair medhain* in the O'Brien rental, usually dated 1390.[1] No other record is known to me till two centuries later, when we find 'Kahirlappan' in the Fiants of 1583[2] then a deed of settlement of Turlough O'Brien of Dough (Dumhach) Castle at the close of Elizabeth's reign, in 1602, names 'Karrowmickerill *alias* Caherlappane.' The inquisition on the death of Donat, 'the Great Earl' of Thomond, has 'Cahervickarrelaw *and* Caher laffan.' Turlough O'Brien's inquisition, taken (after his death, August 1st, 1623) in 1627, recites the above settlement, by which he conveyed 'Cahermakerrilla and Ballyloppane' to his son Daniel O'Brien, who was born 1579, and was a most kind protector to some of the dispossessed English settlers in 1642. Finally, I need only mention the Down Surveys, 1655, with 'Karrowmeekereel *or* Carrowlupane.'[3]

There was probably a name group (such as occurs elsewhere) with the various prefixes; Bally (townland), Carrow (quarter), and Caher (fort), and the compounds *mac Irilla* or *lapane*. I may remind my readers that this place should be carefully distinguished from the great fort and townland in Carran parish.[4] The first is locally pronounced Cahermaakerry-laa, the other, Cahermacnole. These forts are called respectively Cahermakerrila and Cahermackirilla on the ordnance maps, but the Carran name is unwarranted by the best records and by local usage.

The Carran fort name is possibly miscopied in the Hardiman copy of the O'Brien Rental, where it is *Cathair meic iguil* (? iruil). It is possibly the Cahervikellie of the Fiants, 1583,[5] and appears as Cahermacknoull in the inquisition of Morogh O'Cashyn, 1623, and Cahermaconnela in the above cited inquisition, 1627. In 1754, in the will of Dr. Michael Moran (of the family living at Willbrook in later years) we find the same form: 'I leave my brother, Connor Moran, my part of the farm of Mohermollan and £6 to be paid him yearly during my interest in the farm of Cahirmacnoul and Knockaskeaghine,'[6] with reversion to the testator's sons, Patrick and Austin. Lastly, I need only cite Monck Mason's Survey, where (along with a list of clergy under the heading of 'natural curiosities') appears 'Cahermacconela.'[7] Revision is certainly badly needed in scores of names on the Ordnance Survey maps. Strange to say, in the opening centuries of our era, a Gaulish potter stamped his name, *Macirilla*, on his fragile wares,[8] which have survived so many wrecks of empires, and may survive others.

The anonymous form, 'Irial's son,' seems old, recalling such names as the local saints (Findclu) inghean Baoith, of Killinaboy, or (Sinnach) mac Dara, of Oughtdarra, also such names as Ardmhicchonail (named with Ardchonaill

---

[1] Hardiman Deeds, *Trans. R. I. Acad.*, vol. xv (sect. *c.*), pp. 38, 42.

[2] Fiants of Elizabeth (App. Report, Dep. Keeper Records, Ir., No. xv), Nos. 4263, 4274.

[3] Inquisitions, P.R.O.I. and Book of Distribution and Survey, Co. Clare.

[4] *Journal*, vol. xxviii, p. 363 [44].

[5] Fiants of Elizabeth, Nos. 4263, 4274.

[6] A fine fort described, *Journal*, vol. xxviii, p. 365 [46].

[7] 'Parochial Survey,' vol. iii, p. 287.

[8] *Revue Celtique*, vol. xiii, p. 317.

in the section of the Book of Rights, *circa* A.D. 1000, among the king of
Munster's nominal residences in Thomond in this district) and perhaps
Cahermacconnell and Caherconnell.[1]

Cahermakerrila was called after a local family, a branch of the
Corcamodruadh (O'Conor and O'Loughlin) tribe, called *Slicht Irriell,* from
some ancestor, who bore the name Irial, which occurs in the tribal descents
from the 14th century down. In 1396, Irial ua Lochlain, son of Rossa, Lord
of Corcumruadh, was killed by treachery, in revenge for Maelshechlainn ua
Lochlain, whom he had previously slain.[2] As the 'mac Irilla' form of the fort
name does not appear in 1390 it is possible that it originated from some son
of this chief about 1430 or later. Of course this does not prove that the
founder lived so late; forts are commonly called after their later occupants,
as in Co. Kerry.

The 'Sleyht Irryell' held lands in Gragans barony (Burren) in 1586, and
joined in the 'Composition of title' between Sir John Perrot and the Clare
gentry. In 1591, Irial son of Rossa (an interesting repetition of the ancestral
name two centuries earlier)[3] and others of the posterity of Mealaghlin
O'Loughlin, of Ballyvaughan and Benroe (Binroe) Castle, made an
agreement with Donat, the fourth Earl of Thomond, on the lines of one
made by their predecessors with the Earl's great grandfather, Conor, before
1540. They undertook not to mortgage or sell (even) a sod of land, or any
castle, without Donat's consent, and to submit to his decision, subject, in
certain cases, to the arbitration of Boetius Mac Clanchy, John, son of Tornea
O'Maelconary, and Owen O'Daly.[4] A copy of the deed remained with Mac
Clanchy (the chief brehon), and is found among the Mac Curtin MSS. in the
Royal Irish Academy.

The later history of the place tells us but little of moment. Piers Creagh,
of Limerick City and Adare, was transplanted by the Cromwellians to
Burren, about 1655. The family traditions are valueless; there is nothing to
show that the Creaghs were O'Neills;[5] they are called 'Russell, *alias* Creuagh,
of Adare,' in the late 13th and 14th centuries.[6] There is nothing whatever to
support the tale that the O'Quins exchanged these lands for Adare with the
Creaghs. Myth centres equally round the Quins and Creaghs of the latter
village. From the rich callows and oak woods of the Maigue the family was
brought to the bare uplands of Burren, and later we find them in the
goodlier heritage at the old chief castle of the Mac Namaras at Dangan
ivirgin near Tulla, where their representatives are still found. In 1664 Piers

---

[1] *Leabhar na gceart* (ed. O'Donovan), pp. 87, 91.
[2] Annals of Ulster.
[3] Fiants of Elizabeth, No. 4761.
[4] Frost, *Hist and Topog. of Co. Clare,* p. 20, also p. 303.
[5] Save the assertion on the 19th century inscription in Ennis Abbey founded on a
baseless Elizabethan conversation on the arms in Limerick Cathederal. MSS., Trinity
Colllege, Dublin, E3, 16. See *Journal,* vol. xxviii, p. 46. In usual genealogical logic
the carved panels dated 1460, *therefore* the modern inscription was about 1640, and
proved events in the 13th century.
[6] *Proc. R. I. Acad.,* vol. xxv (sect. *c.*), p. 376; vol. xxvi, p. 164. In the List of Mayors of
Limerick (though untrustworthy) in the 13th century we find, in 1216, J. Russell,
alias Creagh (M); 1263, John Russell *alias* Creaghe; 1312, John Creagh, of Adare.

was confirmed under the Act of Settlement in 'Cahermakerilla or Caherlappane,' and other lands; I know of no later mention of the older *alias*-name.

As to names of forts with personal compounds in Co. Clare much of interest could be written. Leaving out the mythic Fearbolg Irgus, whose name is connected with Caherdooneerish, at the beginning of our era we have Lismacain near Magh Adhair, named from Macan, slain in the raid of king Flann to the latter place in 877.[1] Cahercommaun is possibly called after Comán king of the Corcamodruadh, whose son died in 702, and Duntorpa from Torptha, another king of the tribe in 750. Grianan Lachtna, near Killaloe, is most probably called after the early chief Lachtna (whose 'camp' was on the slope of Cragliath above the Borhaime Ford[2] at the raid of king Felimidh of Cashel, about 840) rather than from the later king, uncle of king Brian. We have met many such names in Co. Clare, Cahermacclanchy, Caherhurley, Cahermurchadha, Cahershaughnessy, Cahermacnaughten, Cahermaccrusheen, Cahermacrea, Lismehan, Lissoffin (Lios Aedha fionn) and others.

THE FORTS. - In the field next to the road we first note a low mossy ring of filling, a house site, 27 feet inside. The foundations are 10 to 12 feet thick. It lies 30 feet from the south wall of the field. North from it on a flat low knoll are parallel rows of slabs, three about 4 feet square, lying north and south. I cannot suggest their purpose. About 70 feet eastward from the house ring is a second one, 386 feet westward from the great *cathair*. It has a wall of large oblong blocks, now rarely a yard high, 3 feet thick and 24 feet across inside. At the north-east part of its garth is a well built sunken and circular cell, of similar stones, and 6 feet inside, with a door to the west, the jambs 2 feet thick; thence runs a curved passage, 12 feet long and 3 to 4 feet wide, running under the outer wall at its north point. The souterrain was probably enclosed in a wooden or clay house with a stone fence or even basement.[3]

CAHERMAKERRILA is a ring wall of very fine regular masonry, the lower part of large blocks, the upper of regular thin slabs, laid as headers and closely fitted.[4] It is nearly circular, 96 feet across the garth, 115 feet over all. The frequent occurrence of small masonry in the upper part of the ring walls explains how it is that we so often find well preserved stone forts, with even tops, 5 to 6 feet high, the garth level with the summit, and no debris;

---

[1] Book of Ui Maine. Mr. R. Twigge gave me the extract. See *Proc. R. I. Acad.* vol. xxxii, p. 60. Macan was the first person slain at the *siege* of Magh Adhair.

[2] Book of Munster (MSS. R.I. Acad. 23 E. 26, p. 39.). See *Journal*, vol. xxiii p. 192. *Proc. R. I. Acad.* vol. xxix, p. 196.

[3] Such small house rings, like satellites, about the chief fort, are named in our Annals (eg., F.M.) 1014: 'The *dun* and the houses outside the *dun.*' As to souterrians, the Orvar odd saga (Baring Gould, *Deserts of France*, vol. i, p. 200) tells how such were found by the Norse, in Ireland, with women hiding in them, their entrances hiden by bushes. Some fine souterrains near Tuam are described by Dr. T. B. Costello (*Galway Arch. and Hist. Soc,* vol. ii, p. 109, and later).

[4] Some of it is nearly as fine as Cahermurphy (*Journal*, vol. xli, p. 129) or certain Kerry forts.

the small upper stones were easily removed for other purposes. The base courses here are 2 feet 8 inches to 3 feet thick, the 10 or 11 upper ones usually from 4 to 8 inches thick; the batter is very well laid, usually 1 in 7, but at the north-east part, where the wall is 11 feet high, it falls into the slight, characteristic S-curve owing to settlement. In the north-east section of the garth are two early hut enclosures, one circular the other slightly oval. The gateway faces the south-south-east and is 4 feet 8 inches (or if a loose slab be its jamb, 4 feet) wide. A long slab (too short to be a main lintel, but perhaps a relieving block) is 4 feet 7 inches long by 17 inches by 7 inches, and lies against the jamb.

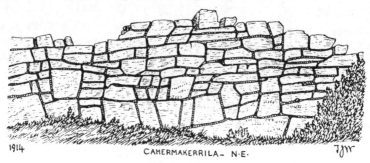

CAHERMAKERRILA- N·E·

Cahermakerrila, North-East.

An old oblong house abuts against the south-east section, two later ruined cabins to the south-west, and a little stone-roofed cell for goats or sheep to the east. On this side, wherever a facing block is removed, we can see that the inner filling is full of bleached and crumbled bones of animals; but whether these were built into the wall originally or slipped there in late times I cannot decide; I never saw bones elsewhere in the substance of a rampart. A featureless bawn lies near St. Colman's Well; this well is not in any fort.

HOUSE RING. - About a quarter of a mile to the east of the *cathair* is a little house ring, about 60 feet over all, and, as usual, reduced to about 3 feet high. The wall is rarely over 6 feet thick, of large blocks, with no filling. It may have been a bawn for protection against wolves, for 'the grey beast' was common in these wilds, and its name appears at Knockaunvicteera[1] (contrasted with Knockaunawaddera, or 'dog's ridge') near Lisdoonvarna, and at many other places, called 'Breffy' (Bregh magh).[2]

---

[1] A swampy plateau covered with heath, pinguicula and sundew. I speak with reserve, for there was a Macotire family, 'Maurice Macotere living at the end of the world in Ireland,' 1290 (*C.D.I.*, vol. i, p. 306), and the fort Cahermacateer in Co. Clare is called Cahermacteire in 1666, and Cahermacdirrigg in 1675. However, the contrasted name seems to decide the question for Knockaunvicteera.

[2] 'Breffy' is found at Lisdoonvarna, Miltown Malbay, Kilkee, and several places in Clonderlaw. Wolf remains are very rare in the Co. Clare caves, though bears are common.

CAHERMAAN. - *Cathair medhoin*, first named in 1390,[1] is identified on the new maps with an insignificant house ring, nameless in 1839. O'Donovan names it in that year as 'Cathair meadhoin – *i.e.*, the middle caher, a *large* fort in the townland of the same name.'[2] Evidently the real Cahermaan is the large cathair, 130 feet across, and nearly levelled, beside the laneway not far to the north-east of the house ring. All the facing is gone, and it is a mere low ring of grassy filling, rarely a couple of feet high. Its name evidently alludes to its position, midway between Cahermakerrila and Caher-macnaughten. Old people told me that the townland name was not attached to either of the forts in their time, so the Ordnance Survey too probably secured the identification by leading questions. The titular Cahermaan is barely 60 feet over all, 3 to 4 feet high, of rough slabs. The wall may be 7 feet thick, but the interior, like that of the previous little house ring, is full of rich soil and is cultivated.

1906 CAHERMAKERRILA AT WEST FACE

Cahermakerrila, at West Face.

WELL. - Before turning from these townlands, I may note that the Ordnance Survey Letters, quoted correctly by Mr. James Frost, do not state that the Well of St. Colman was in the fort; but some have taken 'Cahermakerrila' to mean the cathair and not (as it does) the townland.[3] Most of the wells I have seen in forts are merely flooded souterrains, as – *e.g.*, Glasha and Ballymacloon.[4] When Tulla church and its double-ringed enclosure were blockaded in 1086, the defenders were nearly reduced by thirst till the abbot, after a vision of St. Mochulla, found a spring under a boulder in the sacred edifice.[5] Mr. Orpen has noted a well in the mote of

---

[1] O'Brien's Rental.
[2] Ord. Survey Letters, Co. Clare, vol. i, p, 221, 222.
[3] See Frost, *loc. cit.*, p. 32.
[4] *Journal*, vol. xxxv, p. 355 [128]; *Proc. R. I. Acad.*, vol. xxvii, p. 377.
[5] Vita S. Mochullei, Analecta Bollaadiana, *cf. Journal*, vol. xli, p. 377, also *Silva Gadelica*, vol. ii, pp. 107, 110, and *Journal*, xi (1870), p. 95.

Castleknock, Co. Dublin. Streams occur beside several promontory forts, as Dun Fiachrach, Dunamo, Bonafahy, and Dunallia in Co. Mayo; Ballingarry, in Co. Kerry; Dunlecky and Dundahlin in Co. Clare, and many in Co. Cork - Dunkelly, Dunlough (Three Castle Head), Downeen, Dunsorske, Dunpoer, Ballytrasna, and Dooneenmacotter. One spring is known to me beside a ring fort in Co. Clare and not in a fosse - that in the abattis of Ballykinvarga.

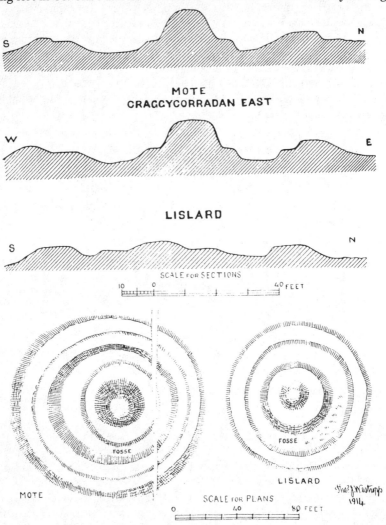

Craggycorradan and Lislard.

CAHERMACCRUSHEEN (O.S. 8). There is a fine oval cathair[1] near the fallen dolmen in *Cathair mhic croisin,* the townland bearing its name. It lies on an abrupt green knoll ending in a wall-like cliff, at the crown of the old road from Doolin northward. It looks up a glen along the straight line of inland

---

[1] *Journal,* vol. xxx, p. 355.

cliffs running from it to Ballinalacken, over which peel tower lies the pink heathery dome of Knockauns Mountain. A slight rise to the north shuts off from it the beautiful view seen from its neighbour, Cahermaclanchy. It was one of the finest forts in the district till, unfortunately, vandals used it for a quarry, though stone abounded everywhere around. Nearly every one of the useless field walls near it show its fine blocks, to the disgrace of the wanton destroyer, whoever he may have been.

The rampart is 9 feet thick, and is still 6 to 9 feet high, the garth being 6 feet above the field. The gate faces the east-south-east, it is 4 feet 9 inches wide, with coursed jambs and a pillar stone at its left inner corner. The garth is 117 feet east and west, and 144 feet north and south, or 135 feet and 162 feet over all. Only two courses of large, nearly square, blocks remain of the outer face. Inside are several irregular enclosures, a house site, a strange little slab cist, hardly 2 feet wide, and a long 'traverse' wall running north and south.

CRAGGICORRADAN (O.S. 8). The long marshy ridge (which falls abruptly beside Ballinalacken Castle and overlooks beyond it the bushy crags and rock-gardens of Oughtdarra[1] and the expanse of sea to Aran and to Moher cliffs) has two earthworks of a type very rare in Co. Clare, called the Mote and Lislard.[2] In eastern Clare 'mote' is always applied to a low earthwork, and in Oughtdarra to stone forts; here, alone, it applies to a high mound. I incline to the belief that the Mote (with perhaps Lislard) is not residential, though it has an outer ring and a fosse. The place was called *Cracc I corradain* in the '1390' rental.

THE MOTE - At the highest point of the road, at the steep end of the ridge, rises the mote. It has an outer ring 5 feet high to the south, but levelled to hardly a foot high to the north. This is cut through by a field fence to the east, but that segment is otherwise little injured and is in the same field as Lislard. The outer ring is about 84 feet across and is 12 to 18 feet thick. The fosse is 5 to 6 feet deep, and 9 feet wide below, and 15 feet at the field level. The central mound is slightly rounded, about 12 feet high, the same width on top, but 24 feet in diameter at the base; it has a 'berm' 3 feet high and 3 to 6 feet wide, round its foot; a similar ledge, 9 feet wide, running inside of the outer ring. It is sheeted with stunted heather and soapwort, and has furze bushes on the ring.

LISLARD. - About 420 feet from the mote, eastward, is another earthwork, called Lislard. The outer ring in parts is 5 feet high and 88 feet over all. The fosse is 9 to 12 feet wide, and rarely 3 feet deep, but wet and rushy to the south-east. The central mound is of two tiers, the base 48 feet in diameter, on its platform is a smaller mound 18 feet across, 6 feet on top and

---

[1] *Ibid.*, p. 342; also *Limerick Field Club*, vol. iii, p. 51. Oughtdarra is reputed to be named from the oratory of St. Sinnach Mac Dara, but the derivation is very doubtful. It is Wafferig in the Papal Taxation, 1302; Killagleach and Vetforoich form the Rectory of Glae, 1419 (*Cal. Papal Reg.*, vol. vii, p. 118); Owghtory (a separate parish from Killilagh) in 1584, and Ughdora in Petty's Map, 1655. None of these suggest the sound 'dara,' still less 'macdara.'

[2] *Journal*, vol. xxxv, p. 352 [125].

3 feet high, but defaced by treasure seekers. It may have been a residential fort in which a burial took place, while the mote was probably a sepulchral mound, not being flat-topped.

KNOCKAUNS MOUNTAIN (O.S. 4)

Eastward from Caherduff fort,[1] about a mile and a quarter away, lies a curious group of ring walls, seeming, with one exception, to be late and decadent. They lie on that ancient road from Ballinalacken to Faunaroosca, where it joins the steep zigzag laneway from St. Columkille's Church at Crumlin,[2] rising past the nearly levelled rectangular *cathair* on its rock ledge. To the east lies the shale dome of Knockauns. On its broad limestone base, rising 220 feet above them, and 976 feet above the sea, lie several forts. They command, like Caherduff, the whole Killonaghan Valley and the bluff Black Head, looking westward across the waves to the Connemara Peaks and Slyne Head.

The old roads are worth noting; the main one runs from Cahermac-crusheen past Oughtdarra. Beyond Knockauns Mountain, it runs northward, past Faunaroosca round castle and Ballyelly forts[3] over the mountain. It dips into the Caher Valley, near Formoyle, and runs up past Caheranardurrish, down through the Feenagh Valley, past the great forts of Caherfeenagh and Caherlismacsheedy[4] to Glenarraga, opposite the Ballyallaban forts. It then runs round the mountains past Lough Rask, Muckinish Castles, Bealaclugga Creek, and Corcomroe Abbey, up to the Carker Pass into Co. Galway. By it, apparently, the Siol Muiredaigh, in 1094, invaded the Corcamodruadh.[5] The latter, under Tadhg, son of Ruadri ua Chonchobhair, checked them at Fiodnagh (Feenagh) in a desperate but drawn battle, and they were glad to retire, both sides having lost heavily. Readers of the Cathreim Thoirdhealbhaigh will remember the appearance of the odious banshee Bronach to Prince Donchad and his army at Loch Rasga, and the fierce 'Battle of the Abbey' in 1317, as well as the ambuscade in which king Conchobhair Ruadh ua Briain fell in the wood of Siudaine near Muckinish in 1267.[6]

LISCOONERA. - A small ring wall stands on the edge of the bluff, very like Caherduff, save for its poor late-looking masonry and irregular plan. It has

---

[1] *Journal*, vol. xxxv, p. 351 [124]. My photograph of this interesting fort is published in Dr. A. Guébhard's very helpful monograph on European ring forts (*Congrés préhistorique*, iii, Antun), p. 1007.

[2] Local legend assigns the little oratory with its round-headed east and south lights to St. Columba, and the rock *Lecknaneeve* on which he landed after leaving Aran is shown on the shore below. His other church in a ring fort in Glencolumkille is described, *supra*, vol. xliii, p. 250.

[3] *Journal*, vol. xxxi, p.10 [69].

[4] *Journal*, vol. xxxi., pp. 275-6 [78-79].

[5] Annals of Tighernach, Ulster (1094), Chronicon Scotorum (1090), Four Masters and Loch Cé (1094). The Four Masters give under 1084 a raid of the Connacht men into Thomond, when 'they burned *duns* and churches and took away spoils.'

[6] Cathreim Thoirdhealbhaigh. See *Proc. R. I. Acad.*, vol. xxvii, pp. 292-3.

a very flat curve to the south-west, then an abrupt turn, nearly an angle, as at Caherdooneerish. Much was levelled when two cottages were built in its garth, but the northwest segment was kept for shelter. The wall had two faces and large coarse filling. The inner face is of small 'stretchers,' the outer of larger slabs. It is 7 to 8 feet high, bulged and irregular in its lines.

CAHERMOYLE. - A large fort, indifferently called Cahermoyle and Cahermore, lies about 300 yards from the last, about 770 feet above the sea. It is evidently the chief and oldest fort of the group, being of fine masonry and on the choicest site, overlooking a shallow grassy hollow, invaluable for keeping cattle under its occupants' eyes, but hidden from the rest of the plateau. The fort is circular: its wall, 7 to 8 feet thick, of large, regular courses, and still over 5 feet high, with a batter of 1 in 7. Only three courses remain to north and west, and there is little or no debris, so that evidently all the smaller stonework was removed for road making. It measures 122 feet over all and about 105 feet inside; there are no house sites.

CAIRNS. – A low heap of stones lies in Derreen West, just beyond the road, and 755 feet above the sea; west from it is another low grassy mound of earth and stones, also probably sepulchral.

Caherbeg, Masonry.

BAWN. - A late enclosure lies about 700 feet from the last and the same distance from Cahermoyle. It was probably a late cattle-pen, being poorly built of long blocks with field-stone filling. It has no describable plan, and is about 42 feet across at the widest point. The wall is in parts 5 feet high, and rarely over 4 feet thick; it resembles some of the 17th century enclosures near Leamaneagh Castle.

CAHERBEG. - The southern end of the grassy depression is guarded by a well-built little ring wall, about 300 yards from Cahermoyle on a slightly rising crag. It is correctly shown as a fort in the 1839 map, but not in the later survey. It is regularly oval, 70 feet across east and west, 86 feet north and south, and is built of large shapely blocks, with many upright joints, like the masonry of Chercloggaun; the inner face, as usual, is of far smaller stones, and but little remains. The wall is 6 to 7 feet thick, 9 feet high to the north, and 5 to 6 feet elsewhere, save where is in nearly levelled to the south. The gateway faces the latter point, but only its west pier remains. Several walls cross the garth.

Three more ring walls, now nearly levelled, lie eastward near the new road. One is in Derreen South (a long townland named from a long destroyed little oak wood),[1] another in Knockauns Mountain; both are low rings of mossy stones, the third is barely traceable. A more substantial one, but reduced to a heap, stands on a low crag, beside another grassy hollow suitable for cattle. Most of these little flimsy 'Mohers' and 'Cahers' are probably late bawns, degenerate representatives of the great ring walls of Ireland, Britain and the Continent. They are, however, far superior to the 'pounds' and 'bull parks.' Even these last are called 'Caher' and 'Moher.' 'It was my father built these Cahers' said a little boy proudly to me at Doolin.

The upland of Elva has no forts, and was doubtless once a vast 'booley'[2] where cattle were sent to feed in summer. The herds could easily be driven near the forts in cases of sudden alarm.

The new road runs across the boggy upland with deep gullies and runnels, rich in water-loving plants. At the crown of the ridge we overlook Munster for 70 miles to the blue peaks of Corcaguiny, out to Mount Brandon and back to the Galtees and the Silvermines. Hills in five out of the six Munster counties are visible, and Connemara is behind us. Thence the steep road runs past the ancient church and curious well, holy tree and pillar stone of Kilmoon, past Knockateeaun back to Lisdoonvarna.

CAHERDOONEERISH (O.S. 1). - The fort of Irgus,[3] a contemporary of Queen Medb, is on the summit of Black Head, about 650 feet above the sea. It is locally called Dunirias and Caherdooneerish.[4] I revisited this fine upland fort with Dr. Hugh G. Westropp in 1914, getting an unusually clear view to Mount Nephin and the Curlew Hills 60 to 70 miles northward. Some treasure-seeker had cleared out the gate, which I was able to plan. It is 2 feet 9 inches wide; its lintel, measuring 6 feet 2 inches by 2 feet by 9 inches lies before it; the piers are 6 feet deep, then the wall sets back to the north for 6 feet to what was either a ramp or flight of steps, as the terrace remains,

---

[1] What remained of the Cathair of Craggagh (a large ring fort between Liscoonera and Killonaghan church) was being carted away for road metal in May, 1914. It had, however, long ago been defaced, as a house adjoined it and is sharing its fate.
[2] It has not, however, got the numerous 'booley' names so notable on Mount Callan.
[3] *Journal,* vol. xxxi, p. 4 [63]. Black Head is the Mons Niger of certain early Portolan maps; 'm. negri' in the Upsal map, 1450; 'm. neig' in Agnesi's map, 1516; 'montes negros' in Voltius, 1593, and 'Niger mons' in the curious late map, 'Hybernia seu Irlant.' which combines Ptolemy, the Portolans and the late Elizabethan maps. It is Doinhooft in the *Zee Atlas* of Jacob Aertoz, 1668, but this is transferred to Hags Head in Jannson's Atlas, Amsterdam, 1661, and *Le Neptune François,* 1693, which rightly name Black Head Can Brayne or Can Borayne - *i.e.,* Ceann Boirne.
[4] Not Caherdoonfergus as on the maps. This was an obsession of O'Donovan, who was at the time seeking for traces of Fergus mac Roigh in Burren. Dr. MacNamara and I got the forms Dunirias, Dooneerish and Caherdooneerish before I noticed that the mythic Irgus was connected with Black Head or Ceann Boirne in the poem of Mac Liac.

being 5 feet high. Farther on is another slope beyond which the terrace is only 2 feet high: it is 3 feet 7 inches wide. The outer section of the wall is 6 feet higher (10 feet outside to the north, 13 feet high south from the gate); it is 6 feet 3 inches thick on top, with no batter, but bowed out in parts. The terrace can be traced all round. There are no hut sites in the garth or round the fort outside.

HOUSE RING. - Close beside the new road, and south from the long wall running down the western flank of the bluff, are two ruined cottages. Between them is a curious little oval house ring, shown on the 1839 map - not on the new one. It is of large blocks rising about 4 feet over the field, and is about 30 feet north and south, and 33 feet across; it is full of rich earth, and overgrown with brambles and hawthorns, covered with flowers: it was unusually full of birds on our visit.

CAHERDOONTEIGUSHA. - This fort[1] stands on a low knoll beside the new road and under the old road round Black Head. Just behind it rises an ivied rock terrace, and its walls are pierced and nearly hidden by the knotted ivy. A cottage has cut into the north-west flank, and the garth is cultivated. In face of all this, I had passed it by in 1885 and 1895 without recognising its character, despite the guidance of a map. What can be seen of the wall shows it to have been of large good masonry, with packing of round field stones. The inner face is everywhere gone; the wall was about 10 feet thick, and, though gapped here and there, is for the most part from 5 to over 6 feet high. The highest reach, next the road, is so ivy-capped that I could not measure it. The fort is oval, about 125 feet north-west and south-east, and 100 feet in the other axis, over all. The name, and even the fact of its being a cathair, seems forgotten. It has a fine view of the Aran Isles.

AGHAGLINNY (O.S. 2). - Ascending the old zigzag horse track behind Gleninagh peel tower and church, leading over the mountain to Feenagh, and now rarely used, we reach the summit to the west of the pass, in Aghaglinny South. There I was amazed to find a large earthen fort on the bare crags. One recalled the legend of the Firbolg serfs in Greece, toiling up the bare hills with their bags of earth. Who conceived the idea of such a fort, if fort, it were? The most gigantic *cathair* could have been raised more easily there from the loose slabs. I hardly venture to suggest that it was a temple;[2] the gods could repay such a work, but for human ends it was labour lost. A stone wall had been a better shelter and defence than it. Perhaps it was for some ceremonial purpose, like the mound of Magh Adhair or the great marsh-carn of Carnconnachtach, probably the inauguration place of the Corcamodruadh. If so, was it where the Eoghanacht chiefs were installed?

Leaving these unanswerable speculations, we turn to facts. The fort rests on the bald summit of the hill, 1,045 feet above sea. It overlooks nearly all Galway Bay, with its shores and the Aran Isles, the nearer of which look

---

[1] *Journal*, vol. xxxi, p. 7 [67].
[2] I have ventured to suggest this view for discussion, not for assertion, in these pages, vol. xl, p. 291. Turlough Hill fort and Ballydonohan, with, perhaps, Creevagh near Tullycommaun, may be also ceremonial or religious structures.

strangely near from our lofty standpoint. The 'fort' is a long oval platform of earth 6 to 10 feet high and exactly twice as long as wide, being 246 feet east and west, and 123 feet north and south. It is revetted with a facing of dry stone for the most part thrown down by the pressure of the earth.

The carn of Doughbranneen is seen lower down, but Caherdooneerish is hidden below the cliff. Descending into the wide valley towards Feenagh we reach in a lonely, utterly secluded spot, a fine ring wall, lying south-east from the summit. It is 240 feet inside and 260 feet over all, an unusual size in this district. The wall is of large blocks, well fitted, and usually from 2 feet 6 inches to 3 feet long and high: it is from 6 to 7 feet high and 10 feet thick, rarely less than 5 feet; the batter varies from 1 in 4½ to 1 in 7. The gateway faces the south (by compass), its passage is 7 feet wide, but the ope is defaced. There are traces of enclosures in the garth, but I could get no general view, as on my visit in 1906, the whole was filled with most luxuriant meadow-sweet in full flower, and often 4 feet high. The fine crescent fort of Lismacsheedy, already described in this series of articles,[1] lies at the end of this valley.

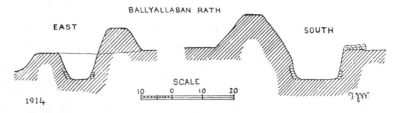

BALLYALLABAN RATH

EAST   SOUTH

SCALE
10   0   10   20

1914

Ballyallaban Rath.

BALLYALLABAN RATH (O.S. 5). - This fort, as being an earthwork, was only slightly noted by me in 1901.[2] It is one of the finest in the county, next to Bealboruma and Liscroneen; it stands beside the road in the bottom of Glenarraga, just below the great *Cathair*,[3] in a pleasant spot, well planted and well watered, girt on all sides, save the north, by the impressive terraced hills of grey and dove-coloured limestone. The outer ring was a drystone wall. The fort, with its stone-faced inner mound, once closely resembled one of the two ringed 'cahers' of the district; but when an enemy scaled the outer wall he was confronted by a deep fosse and swept by showers of stones from the high inner rampart. The outer defence was removed, probably when the road was made, and only the foundations, and here and there large blocks remain; it was 12 to, perhaps, 18 feet thick. Inside this is the fosse, fed by several springs, and 6 to 10 feet deep: it is 9 to 14 feet wide in the bottom. The inner ring is nearly perpendicular, so I presume that the revetment was removed in fairly recent days. It rises 8 to 9 feet over the garth, and 13 to 15 feet over the fosse, being 23 to 27 feet thick below and 6 feet on top, well preserved, and 430 feet in circumference. The garth is oval, 90 feet across north and south, by 111 feet east and west. It is planted with beech and sycamore, the ring being closely overgrown with hawthorn and hazel. The

[1] *Journal* vol. xxxi, p. 275 [79].

[2] *Journal*, vol. xxxi, p. 284 [84].

[3] *Journal*, vol. xxxi, p. 283 [85].

gateway, with a gangway, faces east; apparently the revetment continued so as to form built gate piers, and, I presume, a lintelled entrance at the gap,[1] probably reached by a trunk or plank across the ditch, like Doon fort. There is no local name save 'the Rath.'

Caherbullog.

CAHERBULLOG (O.S. 5). On revisiting the lower *cathair* in the valley I photographed and carefully sketched and measured its rampart, which, as I noted,[2] is in two sections. The inner section has as careful a face as the outer, and it is quite possible (here, as at Caherscrebeen) that the outer section was added to enlarge the garth. The northern section has been nearly destroyed since I first saw it in 1887. These walls of more than one section are regarded by French antiquaries as the 'murum duplex,' noted by Caesar, in Gaulish forts.[3] Two, and even three, sections occur in the French forts, as in Irish ones. The Co. Clare examples, besides Caherbullog, are Caheridoula, Poulgorm, Carran east cliff fort, the Cashlaun Gar (?), Caherscrebeen, Ballykinvarga (3), and the nearly demolished Cathair, beside Cahermore, in Ballyallaban. It occurs in three sections in Caherna-spungane, near Hollymount, in south Co. Mayo, where the two outer sections have only outer faces, as is generally the case.[4] In the Aran Isles it is found in Dun Aengusa (3), Dun Eochla, Dun Eoghanacht, Dubh-Chathair, Dun Conor (3), and I think Dun Moher (Dun Farvagh). In Co. Kerry it

---

[1] Of course the gate was always the weak spot in such forts. The early Irish allude to this - e.g., in Book of Leinster, p. 37 b 20: 'It is a peril to be upon the fort unfortified and the shout of the person in its door that has conqueréd it.'

[2] *Journal,* vol. xxxi, p. 15 [75].

[3] As for example, Casteon-Vasson (Alpes Maritimes). See *Comptes rendus de l'association française pour l'avancement des sciences,* xxxiii, session 1904 (Dr. A. Guébhard and M. Paul Goby); 'Enceintes préhistoriques, Castelars,' *Congrés préhist. de France,* 1905, p. 48; and 'Le Murum Duplex des Gaules,' Guébhard, *Soc. Préhist. de France,* Tome iii, p. 146.

[4] I owe this note to Mr. Hubert T. Knox.

occurs at least at Cahercarberybeg[1]; in Co. Limerick at Ballylin, to the south
of the old crag road from Old Abbey to Lismakeery. So far I have not seen it
farther south.

LISHEENEAGH. – 'The small rectangular fort of good masonry' mentioned
in these pages in 1901[2] has (as I have since observed) boldly rounded
corners, like Knockauns in Tullycommaun; there are no forts inside, and the
north side is much injured, as a modern house lies in ruins near it. The walls
are well laid slab work, and are 5 to 6 feet high to the south.

FINNAVARRA (O.S. 3). Dr. George U. Macnamara has sent me a photograph of a very curious and problematic structure, known as 'the Caves' at
Finnavarra. They lie in a heap of stones, perhaps an overthrown carn, in a
wood, and consist of three short straight passages, opening in the face of a
wall and roofed by an angular-headed arrangement of slabs 'pitched' against
each other, two and two. This is common in windows of round towers,
churches, and even late castles, but, I think, is unknown in souterrains.

I suspect this to be the ruin in Burren, described in 1780.[3] The note is so
curious as to bear repetition. 'From Burren[4] in the Co. of Clare, March 5th,
1780, on Thursday last, as Mr. Davoren was superintending some men who
were digging away the foundation of an old tower, near the Abbey of St.
Daragh,'[5] he discovered an opening. He cleared in seven hours a flight of 22
steps of granite[6] and found a square room of similar hewn stone, with 14
niches. In seven were skeletons,[7] set upright, in long oaken boxes; on the
south side was a slab, 'in the old Irish, or Bearla Firrna, which Dr. Dames
has thus translated: 'Cadh, the son of Aorth, the son of Osra, the son of
Cucullen Tiegernan, the son of Bracklahm; Lunduh, Greanaulin,
Farduragha, three brothers; Illan, Suilaulin, two sisters - all of the house of
Burren. From learned Phoenicia they drew their spark of life which was
extinguished, like the sun, in the Western ocean.'

With either touching guilelessness or wicked satire the writer adds: 'No
date has yet been discovered, nor any other monument of antiquity which
can enlighten this subject.' Surely this was much even for a follower of
Vallancey to believe! Even the five readings of the Mount Callan Ogham
may be charitably regarded as perverted ingenuity, but what can we say of
this other low water mark of Irish archaeology?[8]

---

[1] *Journal*, vol. xl, p. 124; xlii, p. 320
[2] Vol. xxxi, p. 14 [73].
[3] *Saunders' News Letter*, 11 March, 1790.
[4] 'Burren' is the village of Mortyclough near Finavarra
[5] This can only be Corcomroe, the only Burren *Abbey*.
[6] If anything was really found *conglomerate*, is possibly meant; as *granite* is often
confused with this rock.
[7] Note recurrence of seven hours, seven skeletons, virtually thrice seven steps, twice
seven niches. I presume the newspaper is answerable for such spellings as appear.
[8] Of course absurd and unfounded theories still find their way into newspapers.
Indeed, too often, the lowest form of Archaeology gets most publicity, fortunately
ephemeral.

What the 'Caves' may be, unless some one built a 'hermit's grot' or a 'gazebo' there, in the taste of the later 18th century, I cannot venture to suggest. I can only call attention to a curious enigma.

BALLYGANNER GROUP (O.S. 9).

So difficult is it to explore this tract, and so rich is it in lesser antiquities, that after examining its forts and dolmens (in 1895 and 1897), and revisiting it (in 1898, 1900, 1902 and 1907), I still found objects worth description.[1] I made another extensive exploration in 1911 for ancient roads and hut sites, and now give the results as a step towards completion. In that labyrinth of high walled fields and crags and bushes it were folly to claim completeness for these notes, but I believe I can have overlooked little of importance (after seven visits) in the area bounded by the roads, Ballyganner Hill, and a line through Caherkyletaan, Cahercuttine, the small house ring to the east of the last to Caheraneden, Mohercloghbristy, and the dolmen in Ballyganner South, and back to the dolmen on Ballyganner Hill and the enclosures and dolmen in Sheshy and Clooneen. In all I recorded some 55 forts and bauns - 6 of earth, 10 dolmens, 8 huts outside the forts, 4 souterrains, 4 rock-cut roads, 3 tumuli, some low earth mounds, and over 10 cairns, some 90 early remains in all, besides two castles and two churches.

I found nothing to add to the notes on the forts and dolmens save that Mr. O'Dea, of Ballyganner Castle, told me that the ring-wall enclosing the dolmen[2] is named Cahernabihoonach, the thieves fort (bitheamnach), and that he never heard the name Cahernaspeekee applied to the fort, so called on the maps. He says that the field called Parccauhernaspeekee (*Pairc cathrach na spice*) lies to the north-east beyond Caheraneden. Some of these fort names are very vague; in 1887 the name of Caheremon was transferred to the mortar-built ruin called Cashlaunawogga. In 1895 I was told by a herdsman that Ballykinvarga was 'called Cahernaspeekee, because of its spikes,' or abattis. As a rule I have rarely found any doubts about fort names in Co. Clare; usually the consensus of the old people is complete, and the doubt only introduced by a young, and therefore less authoritative, person. Dr. Macnamara and I found it equally hard to get genuine names inserted[3]

---

[1] *Journal*, vol. xxvii, p. 116 [23]; vol. xx, p. 287. *North Munster Archaeol. Soc.*, vol. i, pp. 14-29.

[2] *Journal*, vol. xxvii, pp. 119, 120 [26, 27]; vol. xxxi, p. 290 [92]. 'Ancient Forts of Ireland,' fig. 13, *North Munster Archaeol. Soc.*, vol. i, p. 23.

[3] I am glad to learn that Caheridoula (*Journal*, vol. xxvii, p. 119 [26]; vol. xli, p. 363 [154]) is about to be marked. The local officials acted with discretion in such cases, but names and objects were sometimes struck out in Dublin as not appearing on older maps. May I point out that the *cromlech* to the south-west of Cahercuttine, that at the Caher in Ballyganner South, were put on the map without antiquarian authority, and are unwarranted. The important west group at Parknabinnia was struck out in Dublin and only inserted on strong representation. In all this inconsistency the need for antiquarian referees is very marked.

and inaccurate names[1] altered on the maps, and sometimes the map names were got by leading questions,[2] a practice we carefully avoided. 'S. F.' (Sir Samuel Ferguson) in 1857 gives 'Caherflaherty'[3] as the name of Ballykinvarga cathair; this, in 1838, was the name 'Caherlahertagh,' given to a fort, beside which the new road from Kilfenora to Noughaval has since been made. Now, the latter name seems forgotten on the ground, and it is called 'Caherparkcaimeen.' In the Book of Distribution Ballykinvarga is called 'Caherloglin' in 1655; this last one suspects to be Caherlochlannach, the Irish equivalent of the late incorrect term 'Danish Fort;' but it may be *Cathair ui Lochlain* or O'Loughlin's fort' or 'Lochlan's fort.'

In the case of Ballyganner, I fancy that, as the craglands got deserted and became 'winterages' for cattle, and the people moved to the roadsides for convenience (especially after the great Famine), the names became useless, save to a few herdsmen, and gradually got confused, and at last forgotten. The younger herdsmen can rarely give any names, while a number known to the older men are almost impossible to locate, for those who remember them are usually too old to bring one spot. O'Donovan's sad lack of interest in all save the chief forts,[4] and his neglect of the Inquisitions of Elizabeth, James and Charles I and the great Surveys, left the surveyors free to put down names sometimes but vaguely located by their informants. Numerous names well attested in the documents (such as Cahercommaun, Caherscrebeen, Caherminaun, Cahercotteen, and Caheridoula) were found by us to be extant on the ground, and often widely known, though not on the maps.

BALLYGANNER HUTS.[5] In the field to the south of the large tumulus is a hut 19 feet long east and west, 24 feet north and south, with two cells, the western 6 feet by 5 feet, the eastern filled with the collapsed beehive roof. The west cell has walls 3 to 4 feet thick; the roof was formed of corbelled slabs, much tilted up to throw any wet out of the room; it has a small lintelled door 20 inches wide into a semi-circular room, 12 feet over all. The lintel is 5 feet 18 inches by 10 inches.

The largest tumulus is of earth and stones 51 feet across, 6 to 8 feet high, and perfect. The other lies 159 feet to the north-east, and is 37 feet across, only 5 feet 6 inches high, the top and centre dug out.

---

[1] One is generally told that they were 'approved by O'Donovan and O'Curry,' a method rather official than scientific, as we have no evidence to show that these scholars made any methodical researches *on the ground* to check the surveyor's notes. It recalls popular works of 1750-80 'approved by Mr. Smith.'

[2] I write this of my own knowledge of several cases, let one suffice - 'Maryfort,' near Tulla, where I have known the place from 1868, and a 'sapper' by this process got the name attached to a hitherto nameless fort. I had some trouble in getting this bogus name withdrawn.

[3] *Dublin University Magazine*, vol. xli, p. 505.

[4] In fact he does not describe a single fort of importance in north-west Clare in the Ordnance Survey Letters.

[5] By some accident a section containing notes on the tumuli and some huts at Ballyganner got ommited. I am anxious to embody all material for this important site, as I may probably rest assured of having passed by nothing of importance from Noughaval and Kyletaan to the road from Kilfenora to Corofin.

Another hut to the south-east of Caherwalsh is 33 feet across, a fan-shaped court. There is a hut 6 feet inside, with wall 3 feet thick at the south-east corner, touching which and outside it is a circular hut with walls of equal thickness and 6 feet inside. In the field to the south of this last is a house-ring 3 feet thick and 25 feet inside, shown as a small circle on the new maps.

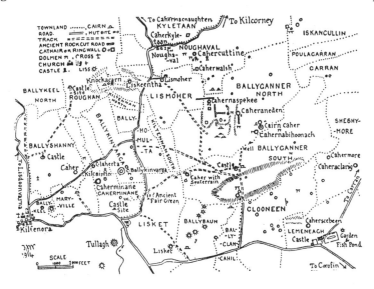

Map of the Ballyganner Group of Antiquities.

The ancient road near Cahernaspeekee may have been a cattle walk, leading to what appears to be a dry pond and continued beyond it. The only other ancient object I noticed on the last exploration of the townlands is a massive early wall of masonry like Caherwalsh at the O'Dea's garden, which was probably made in an early bawn.

CAHERCUTTINE. - The cairn between this fine fort and the dolmen opposite to its gate to the south[1] has been entirely removed and the blocks of the dolmen uprooted and overthrown since 1897. The dolmen to the south-west, marked 'Cromlech' on the new maps, is a slab enclosure of two compartments, each 3 feet wide, lying north and south, the whole 7 feet 8 inches square, of unknown use, and I think late, certainly not a 'Cromlech.' There seem to be remains of an actual dolmen in the same field to the west-north-west of Cahercuttine. A large slab stands east and west, and other stones lie near it forming a cist, 8 feet long and 6 feet wide at its west end.

LISMOHER. - This is not the imaginary fort shown on the 1839 map near and to the east of the Noughaval road from Caherminaun. It is correctly shown on the 1899 map as to the south of the lane to Noughaval House. Part of its northern facing has been removed to widen this lane, the rest is of large well laid blocks, and is fairly complete, but rarely more than 5 feet high. The garth is level with its top and thickly grassed. The ruined doorway faces the east; its lintel is 6 feet 3 inches by 2 feet by 1 foot.

---

[1] *Journal,* vol. xxvii, p. 117 [24].

KNOCKACARN. - Nearly due west from this on a low shale ridge, called Knockacarn, in line with Lismoher, is a row of sites. The first two, in Ballyhomulta, are an earthen liss called Liskeentha (*Lis caointhe*). I was told at Noughaval, in 1908, that its name was derived from 'fairy songs' which had even been heard 'not long before.' West from it, on top of the ridge (465 feet high), where the townland meets those of Rusheen and Kiltennan, are another liss, a smaller one in Kiltennan and the cairn which gives the ridge its name. If we extend the line, it meets in the next townland another alleged fort site, where the Castle of Roughan probably stood. The tradition of the last was rather vague as to its being a castle.[1] Beyond this, save Drimneen fort in Ballykeel and a larger ring mound in Knockavoarheen, no early remains or medieval ruins occur for over two miles, till we reach Cahermakerrila to the north-west.

The linear arrangement of forts, not uncommon in Ireland, is well marked at Noughaval; besides the five in line from Lismoher we see the great line west-north-west and east-south-east from Caherkyletaan (past Cahercottine, Caherwalsh, a ring fort, Cahernaspeekee, a slab enclosure and souterrain, the square bawn, the ring wall and castle) to the great dolmen on Ballyganner Hill. A third line at right angles to the last, passes (through a Cathair, the square bawn, Ballykinvarga, and a levelled fort) towards the great hill fort of Doon. The cause of this linear arrangement is unknown; some explain it as originating in a long ridge, but this is certainly not the case at Ballyganner. The two main lines evidently took as their goals the high standing dolmen and Doon fort, but no such prominent object fixed the line over Knockacarn.

CAHERNASPEEKEE. - This doubtfully named stone fort[2] has suffered horribly since 1895 by rabbit hunters and perhaps treasure seekers. The fine slabbed terrace is entirely defaced; the slabs were set upright along the face of the wall like a veneer. The gate has been cleared out by some treasure seekers and the jambs destroyed. The lintel lies across it and is intact, but is only 4 feet 6 inches long, so the ope was probably very narrow, hardly 3 feet wide;[3] the gate faced south. Only a portion of the rampart to the south-west is still 6 feet high, as most of the ring was on my first visit. The masonry is good, but open joined, and I think far later than the finely fitted work at Cahercuttine, Caheraneden, Caherminaun and Ballykinvarga. Between this fort and the bawn to the south is a long grassy depression artificially cleared, and shaped, perhaps, the *faitche* or green. The early laws[4]

---

[1] However, as there seems to have been one in the townland, I incline to accept the local statement.

[2] *Ibid.*, p. 119 [26]. It was suggested that this is a (very bad) corruption of *Cathair na easpuig* from some Bishop of Kilfenora, being near that cathedral. It is true that equally bad corruptions are not unknown – Lockwood for Lughid, Belvoir for Ballywire, Ballyvalley for Baile Ui Mhothla, and in the Co. Limerick, Mount Sion for Knockatsidhean! In this case, however, it is impossible to believe the phonetic *'n espuig* to have become *naspeekee*.

[3] I measured the passage as 4 feet in 1895.

[4] Book of Aicill, Brehon Laws, vol. iii, p. 253. See also Cormac's Glossary, *Three Ancient Glossaries* (ed. Whitley Stokes) under *Ramhat; Mesca Ulad* (ed. Hennessy), p. 43.

(Book of Aicill) provide for the upkeep of such 'greens.' To the west is a house site of large slabs set on edge; it is about 21 feet across, east and west, by 18 feet wide. The north wall is double, and in the north-east corner is a small souterrain under a large slab. The whole resembles the site in Knockauns fort near Tullycommaun. The baun is now quite defaced and overgrown.

There are three cairns or mounds of earth and stone slabs; two to the north of Cahernaspeekee, quite perfect; another to the south, with remains of a small slab cist; they vary from 5 feet to over 8 feet high. There are some regular oval green mounds, rarely 2 feet high, on the crag. One about 4 feet high has a set slab, evidently once a cist.[1] There is a fine well in the valley to the south of these, half way between the Castle Cathair and Cahernabihoonach. Due north from it are the fallen dolmen, the long rock-cut road from the latter to Caheraneden and the slab hut. The group of ruins farther eastward, besides Cahernabihoonach, includes the 'cairn caher' with its outer enclosure and perfect gateway[2] and a large bawn (near a curiously split and very conspicuous rock) which I think is almost certainly the 'Mohernacloughbristy' named along with Ballyganner in a deed of 1712.[3]

ROADS. - Besides the eastern one, probably from Caheraneden to the well, but not traced by me south from the fallen dolmen, there is another well-marked road, with at least two side, or cross, roads at right angles to it. They were formed, like the Creevagh avenue, near Glencurraun, by removing the water-fretted upper layer or layers of the crag. One runs nearly north and south from the direction of the great dolmen on the hill towards the cairns to the north of Cahernaspeekee and close to the east of the cairn near the bawn. When we get opposite to the pillared dolmen, a line but little to the north of Caheraneden, we see another road running to a little hut-ring close to the dolmen. I think there are traces of another road crossing this about half way between the main road and the hut parallel to the first. Yet another important road runs east and west (along the map line of the townland name, 'Ballyganner North') not far to the north of Caherna-speekee. I incline to attribute these works to the dolmen builders, who were accustomed to raise and transport large slabs, for the 'Caheraneden road' runs truly along a line through the great dolmen and the fallen dolmen (Caheraneden and the northern *cathair* on the ridge, being on its axis), while the first cross-road runs due east and west towards the pillared dolmen.

The site is so rich and remarkable that I hope some other antiquary may study it as a whole to some sound conclusion. Hard and painful as is the work done on fissured crags, hidden in grass and moss, I would urge others

---

[1] *Journal*, vol. xxxi, p. 287 [89].
[2] I retain the name 'cairn caher,' for distinction as representing the 'small ring wall surrounding a sort of cairn,' given in my first notes (xxvii, p. 119 [26]). The structure is described and the 'cairn' found to be a small house-ring (xxxi, p. 287 [89]). The house ring from the ammount of debris in which it was buried was probably a sort of tower of dry stone. See note on Dunnaglas Tower, Achill, in vol. xliv, p. 312.
[3] Dublin Registry of Deeds, vol. ix, p. 285.

to work it out. I give what I can, but a complete plan of a settlement occupied from the bronze age to the later 17th century with graves, residences, wells and roads should be worth obtaining, and it is possible that other roads and foundations may remain, especially to the east of the tract explored for this survey.

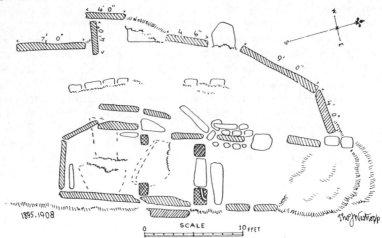

Pillared Dolmen near Caheraneden, Ballyganner North.

PILLARED DOLMEN. - I have been able to clear away the deep moss and debris and to plan this complicated monument in its entirety. The harp-shaped annexe to the north was entirely concealed in moss, bushes and debris till now.[1] There are two slab huts, possibly late, a short distance to the north of Cahernabihoonach.

I do not attempt to date the slab enclosures. The fences round such dolmens as that at Iskancullin are probably contemporary with the monument, so, possibly, are the circular slab rings, which are probably the basement of wooden and clay huts. On the other hand, the rectangular hut sites are probably far later, and the slab fences, such as we find at Leanna, still more recent. The same may be true of the cairns. In 1681, Thomas Dineley[2] notes of Burren that 'the particons are made of broad stones like slate turned up edgeways,' and in 1752 Dr. Pococke writes of Achill, Co. Mayo, that the people 'have a custom of raising heaps of stones, here called laktch (leachta), in other parts kerns (carns) to the memory of the dead.'[3] The custom has yet not died out in Aran and North Connacht.

The late huts of beehive shape, with corbelled roofs (found in Aran and some in Co. Kerry, on the Blasket Sound, so late that I saw one in the course of building near Dunquin in 1904), are also a serious warning against confident dating. As a rule, however, primitive work is of far larger

---

[1] See *Journal*, vol. xxvii, p. 119 [26]; vol. xxx, p. 402; vol. xxxi, pp. 288-290 [89-91]. *R.S.A.I. Handbook*, v, p. 56. *Proc. R. I. Acad.*, vol. iv, ser. iii, p. 542; vol. xxvi (c.), p. 461.

[2] *Journal*, vol. ix (1866-7), consec., p. 193.

[3] *Tour in Ireland* (ed. Rev. George Stokes), p. 94.

materials than its late descendants. Here I may warn against another error alleging old remains to be modern on insufficient authority. The 'oft told tale' of the British Association[1] is as a rule 'left half told.' The visitors in 1857 were informed that a supposed early hut had been built a year or so before, but the rest of the story is always garbled or suppressed by would-be jesters, for the hut was found marked as ancient in the maps of twenty years earlier, and the scoffer was proved a liar - as often happens. This shows how little any statement made by a native should be received, especially when made to a pic-nic party of strangers. Professor Macalister was told by an old man that certain huts in the Fahan Group were modern,[2] but the mendacious peasant was forced to confess the contrary by other natives present. I had very rarely had cause to doubt information, save on the tourist tracks,[3] or when tourists were by; it is always easy to test local belief by finding an informant not present on the first occasion. The 'educated classes' in Co. Clare, if not elsewhere, are rarely found to give any particulars of value or even of trustworthiness.

BALLYKINVARGA. - This very remarkable fort is getting widely known; it has recently been illustrated by Dr. Guébhard in the Report of the Prehistoric Congress, in France, 1906, and by Mr. Champneys in the valuable illustrations of his work on Irish Architecture. I have given in our *Journal,* 1913, a good general view by Dr. George U. Macnamara.[4] The bad practice of resketching has 'enriched' our pages with several false views, such as that of the crannog of Lough Bola and those of Ennis Abbey (especially the screen) in 1889 and the view of Cahercashlaun (so far as regards masonry) in 1899.[5]

Though apparently on a rather low site, there is a wide outlook; one can see from its wall the Telegraph and Snaty peaks in Slieve Bernagh in the far east of Clare, Inchiquin hill, Inchovea tower, Callan, Doon fort, Tully-commaun ridge, and the Noughaval forts and carns.

A coin of Alexander, King of Scotland, has recently been found in Ballykinvarga fort; it (like the hoard of coins of Edward II, found in the abattis, near the gateway) was probably plunder from the wars of the Bruces, in 1315, against whom Murchad O'Brien, King of Thomond, served.

---

[1] M. Haverty's *Handbook,* republished 1859.

[2] *Trans. R. I. Acad.,* xxxi (vii), p. 306.

[3] Any information can be obtained by leading questions, as I once exemplified by getting Greek myths for local legends to warn an English antiquary in search of true folk lore. Ask what the peasantry know and what names they use, never ask if a name or story exists.

[4] *Journal,* vol. xxvii, pp. 121-4 [29-30]. *Dublin Univ. Mag.,* vol. xli (1853), p. 505. Ordnance Survey Letters, vol. i, p. 287. Du Noyer's 'Sketches' (Library, R.S.A.I.), vol. vii. Dunraven, Notes on Irish Architecture, vol. i, p. 18. *Congrés préhistorique de France,* iii, p. 1017. Champney's *Irish Ecclesiastical Architecture* (1909), plate v, p. 8. *Ancient Forts of Ireland,* plate vii. I have to thank the Council of the Royal Irish Academy for leave to use the last named illustration.

[5] *Ennis,* vol. xix, pp. 46, 48; pointed arches made round, tracery altered, plan defective. Ballykinvarga, *Ibid.,* vol. xxvii, p. 125 [31]. Cahercashlaun, *Ibid.,* vol. xxix, p. 377 [57]. The same is true of some redrawn views in Borlase's *Dolmens of Ireland,* vol. i, pp. 87-94. Lough Bola, *Journal,* vol. xii, consec., p. 11.

A coin of King John has also been found recently in the gateway of Cahermacgorman fort, near Corofin; coins earlier than the reign of Elizabeth have rarely been found in Co. Clare.

I may add a late record of the place to my former notes.[1] Morough O'Brien, nephew of Boetius Clanchy of Knockfinn, in his will, Nov. 16th, 1630, mentions his properties of Ballykinvarga, Carrowkeele, Cahermeene, Ballykeile, and also Cahirmeenan (all fort sites). He leaves bequests to his cousins Gorman, Thomas, and Arthur, of Limerick, and Donogh O'Brien, and desires to be buried in Killilagh Church.

The only notes I need add are that two upright joints occur to the west of the gateway and one to the east.[2] The supposed dolmen to the south-east of the fort, beside the old hollow track from the gateway near the east wall of the field, consists of two small set slabs and two 'covers;' of the last, the southern measures 9 feet 3 inches by 7 feet 6 inches the others 7 feet 5 inches by 1 foot and 7 feet by 6 feet 6 inches. All is so pulled about that no plan is possible; the slabs probably belonged to a simple cist about 7 feet long.

In the next field to the south is the unmarked foundations of a ring wall, 87 feet over all, with an outer facing of large blocks; all the rest of the stonework has been removed.

CAHERLAHERTAGH.[3] - This remains as I saw it in 1895. I found in 1907 that it is locally called 'Caherparkcaimeen,' from a levelled fort used as a *killeen*, or child's burial ground, a short distance away. In this cemetery is a double cist of large thin slabs.[4] The southern compartment has two divisions, 7 and 8 feet long, and 3 feet 6 inches wide; the northern is of the same width and 7 feet 6 inches long. They are in a low enclosure, 14 feet 7 inches square, kerbed with large blocks. The cists have been cleared out, since 1895, when they were buried in debris and the partition hidden. The place, unlike many killeens, is believed to be consecrated ground, and was probably, from its name, Kilcaimeen, dedicated to the patron of Iniscealtra, a 7th century saint, half-brother to Guaire Aidhne, King of Hy Fiahrach Aidhne, the district round Gort.

CAHERMINAUN. - The late Dr. Joyce, in *Irish Names of Places*, is mistaken as to the townland being called from 'an old castle ruin,'[5] for the townland is called from a fine ring-wall of the name although even the new maps leave the fort nameless. The fort,[6] though much injured, is remarkable; the masonry is neither horizontal nor polygonal, but of long, sloping courses, running into wedges between the adjoining layers. I have rarely seen more than one such course in any other fort. The blocks show many signs of hammer work, such as we also find on other forts round the border of

---

[1] I have to thank Mr. J. R. B. Jennings (*Member*) for this extract.
[2] Such joints seem not to occur at regular intervals. In the outer ring of Cahercommane they are at intervals of 118 feet, 171 feet and 69 feet.
[3] *Journal*, vol. xxvii, p. 125 [32].
[4] Plan given, *Proc. R. I. Acad.*, vol. xxvi (c.), p. 469.
[5] *Irish Names of Places*, ser. ii (ed. 1893), p. 303.
[6] *Journal*, vol. xxvii, p. 125 [32].

Burren, Ballykinvarga, Roughan, and Glenquin, besides Cahermacrea and
Langough in eastern Co. Clare. Hammer work is alleged to exist in Dun
Aengusa, but I failed to see any trace of it. It is not a mark of late origin, for
numerous dolmens in Co. Clare have the top edges of their sides chipped to
an even line, and one at Gortlecka is even picked inside.[1]

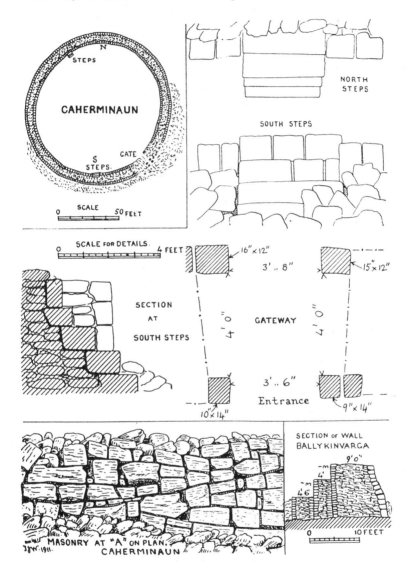

Caherminaun
N.B. – 'A' has become effaced on the plan; it was to the south-south-east.

---

[1] Creevagh, Caherblonick, Clooneen, Gortlecka, Baur, Cappaghkennedy, Rannagh,
Parknabinnia, Ballyganner Hill and other dolmens show this chipping.

The gateway is also unusual in having small pillars at each angle of its entrance; rarely do even two occur, and those are always at the outer side. The four measure - the outer, left 10 inches by 14 inches, right 9 inches by 14 inches; the lower ones nearly the same. They rise 3 to 4 feet above the debris, and are perhaps 6 feet high if cleared. The lintels have been thrown down, and are 4 feet 6 inches long by 30 inches by 18 inches, a broken one, 3 feet 8 inches long, also remains.[1]

The wall is 10 feet 6 inches thick at the gate, which is 3 feet 8 inches wide between the pillars. The wall is 4 feet to 5 feet high at the gate, but is lost in heaps of debris; it is 8 to over 10 feet high round the south and west segments; the inner facing is nearly entire, though (as usual) of far smaller stonework than the outer face; the filling is large and carefully packed; the batter is 1 in 6 and in parts as much as 1 in 3½ , a very unusual slope.

There are two flights of steps; the north-eastern was hidden in debris and coarse grass, and the southern nearly so in 1895. The latter now shows four steps over the debris, each is 10 inches wide, and is of two or three blocks in a recess 4 feet wide, and going straight up the wall. I incline to think this an older type than the 'sideways flight.' The other stair, instead of being in a recess, projects from the wall face; the steps are 5 to 6 inches wide and 8 to 13 inches high, 33 to 48 inches long; these flights most probably led to a terrace, but if so, this has left no trace. The rampart, when entire, may have been 14 or 15 feet high. The garth is 102 feet wide, the fort 123 feet overall, approximately circular. Only late pens remain inside.

BALLYKEEL. - Some forts occur - one on the edge of Ballykeel and Maryville, westward along the road from Caherlahertagh; another, the lowest courses of a well-built ring wall, is beside the road near the 'A' of Maryville on the map, it is of excellent masonry. There are two stone forts close to Kilfenora in Ballykeel South. The larger is on a knoll, well seen from the main road; it is much gapped, but of good masonry, with, I think, trace of an outer ring. These forts to the east of Kilfenora were examined for me with his usual kindness by Dr. Macnamara. That nearest to the Fair Green is shown on the map; though greatly overturned, it measures 102 feet across (it is strange how often this measurement occurs both in earth forts and ring-walls). The outer facing remains to the south and west in reaches of good masonry, one block is 4 feet long; its cathair is quite featureless. The rabbit hunters of the village have overthrown the forts near them, as is so usual.

The larger one on the east border of Ballykeel is the ruin of a fine structure, and is well seen from the road to Corofin. It consists of two concentric rings, and was a well built 'handsome' fort, but not very large. It is nearly all knocked down, and is in the same field as the last. There is a short reach of the facing of the inner ring about 8 feet long. The central fort is 47 paces across, the outer ring lies 10 to 12 yards outside it, and is 67 yards in diameter. It was built with blocks of unusual size - one 9 feet long, and apparently was a single stone wall, always a late feature.

---

[1] There was one nearly 7 feet long near it in 1895. It has perhaps been broken and part removed, or buried in the debris.

There is a standing stone in Ballykeel which, possibly, like the stone crosses, meared the *termon* of the old monastery and cathedral of Kilfenora. The forts from Doon and Kilfenora westward call for very little note, being featureless and the majority of earth, sometimes with remains of stone facing.

LISKET is an earthen fort 135 feet across: the 'platform' is 105 feet across and is flat-topped, but had a rampart rarely a foot high, giving the garth a slightly cupped appearance like one of the Coolreagh forts near Bodyke in the east of the county. The fosse is about 14 feet wide, the platform rising 5 feet above it. The fort, called 'Ballybaun fort' on the map, is nearly obliterated by tillage; it was about 30 yards across (north and south). A similar liss, 35 yards across (north and south), lies east of Ballybaun House where the 'R' of the parish name 'Kilfenora' is marked on the maps. The herdsman of Ballybaun knew of the other forts, but said that they were hardly noticeable. There is a curious single block of stone with a battlementled outline in the last described liss, 6 feet by 3 feet by 8 inches, like the side of a dolmen save for its irregular top.

CAHEREMON[1] is hardly traceable at a bend of the road north from Kilfenora. Petrie calls it 'a fine remain' if he be not confusing it with Ballykinvarga. Dutton in 1808 calls it Caheromond, and adds that its walls were covered with orpine. It is said to have had two rings, but I found bare trace of the ring of small filling of one. I seem to recollect the walls as standing in 1878 and 1887, but may be mistaken.

FANTA GLEBE contains a *cathair*, utilised as a feature in the Rectory garden, the former residence of the Protestant Deans of Kilfenora. It is a fairly complete ring of small stonework, 105 feet over all, and is thickly planted and quite featureless.

BALLYGANNER HILL (O.S. 9 and 16).

Though far from certain that I have exhausted this most important group that the apathetic archaeology of the last century left to my exploration, I must endeavour to close these notes. In 1896 I had to reserve the dolmens for Mr. W. Borlase with other limitations, which must be my plea for merciful criticism. Only the two fine dolmens of Ballyganner Hill and Clooneen had been accurately sketched and described at that time, while the unique Ballykinvarga fort was almost neglected and quite mis-described. I recently found that the west opening of the first named dolmen had been closed by a slab (like the sixth dolmen at Parknabinnia);[2] so violently and injudiciously had it been forced open that the great stone door had snapped at the ground level. These doors seem to imply that some of the dolmens

---

[1] Petrie, 'Military Architecture of Ireland'; Hely Dutton's *Statistical Survey*, Appendix, p. 12. 'Orpine, or live long, sedum telephium, covers the walls of an old fort, called Cahiromond, near Kilfeneora.'

[2] *Journal*, vol. xxxi, p. 291 [92].

were 'family vaults,' and could be opened to admit later burial.[1] The little
basins in the cover of this dolmen may imply observance of funerary
offerings in later generations. In Co. Clare science came too late to explore
them: probably every chamber has been violated by greedy, ignorant,
unobservant treasure seekers before the dawn of the last century. Tradition
alone told of finds of pottery. In our time one bronze age golden fibula of
the type of the 'Great Clare gold find' at Moghane (*circa* B.C. 500-700?) was
got at the dolmen of Knockalappa in eastern Co. Clare.

The nearly levelled cathair near the great dolmen stands on the most
commanding part of the ridge. It is of large blocks, one 6 feet 10 inches by
20 inches by 20 inches, the wall being 6 feet thick and rather coarsely built.
The more southern cathair, near the last, on the contrary is of fine large
masonry, regular blocks, set to a batter of 1 in 5 to 1 in 6. The wall is 7 feet
thick and over 5 feet high. The foundation of its gateway, recently
uncovered, shows that the passage faced south-east, and was 4 feet wide,
without posts. The foundation block of the north jamb is 6 feet 3 inches
long.

Beyond the steepest slope below to the south of the forts and to the west of
the laneway is a tumulus of earth and stones 56 feet across and 6 feet 6
inches high. It is intact save where some rabbiters made a hole into it on the
north side: no slabs were disclosed.

The *cathair*[2] to the west-north-west of the dolmen at the other foot of the
ridge is a fine example. Its ring is 120 feet across, but is somewhat
irregular. I have already described its details and the socalled 'cromlech'
before its gateway. It may be a grave, but again is unusual, if not unique.[3]

HUTS . - On the slope of the ridge, close to the west of the laneway, below
the great dolmen, is a hut site; it is circular, 29 feet across, of well laid
horizontal courses of blocks (like the house ring, with the souterrain, near
Cahercuttine); it is now barely 3 feet high. The Co. Clare huts are
practically of five types - two circular, two rectangular, the rest irregular.
(Type 1) A circle of slabs set on end like the ones south from
Cahernabihoonach and east from Moheraroon.[4] (2) A circular wall regularly
built with blocks in courses, like the one noted above; sometimes this
consists of several conjoined circular cells. In some cases it had a domed or
corbelled ('beehive') roof, in others, probably, a thatched or wooden one.
The most perfect are at Mohernaglasha, but foundations are not uncommon,
as at the Cashlaun Gar, Cahercommaun, Mohernagartan,[5] Ballykinvarga,

---

[1] The question of secondary burials does not seem to have been worked out for
Ireland. Here, above all other countries, caution is needed. If the four Maols, the
murderers of St. Cellach, were actually buried in the Clochogle dolmen near Ballina,
we have an example in the 7th century. A striking late case is in the Annals of Loch
Cé (ed. W. M. Hennessy) in 1581: 'Brien Caech O'Coinnegan** died, the place of
sepulture he selected for himself was *** at the mound of Baile an tobair.'
[2] *Journal* vol. xxxi, p. 289 [90, 91].
[3] See *Proc. R. I. Acad.*, vol. xxvi (c.), plate xxiv, 'slab enclosing No. 33, near western
Caher.'
[4] *Journal*, vol. xli., p 362 [152], and vol. xxxi, p. 289 [89].
[5] *Ancient Forts of Ireland*, fig. 13, No. 7.

and others. There is a curious domed hut having a lintelled east door and external offsets on Bishop's Island, once a promontory fort.[1] In eastern Co. Clare, where wooden huts probably superseded the stone ones, I have found the foundation of a two-celled hut at Carrahan near Spancel Hill. In Caherbullog are some very small circular cells (like those at Caherdorgan, Co. Kerry), some only 3 feet to 5 feet clear inside.[2] As we noted, the house site at Cahercuttine has a souterrain.

Of the third type are the rectangular enclosures, or huts, of slabs set on end near Caheraneden[3] and Cahernaspeekee and the one in Knockaun Fort;[4] the two last have souterrains. Of the fourth type it is hard to speak; it is probably late, approximates to the modern cottages. The fifth type is represented by the '9' shaped plan of the hut near Teeskagh and others, like those near Horse Island promontory fort.

DOLMENS - Borlase[5] makes an amazing mistake in speaking of the Co. Clare dolmens. 'Blocks of the size and symmetry of those used by the dolmen builders would nowadays be far to seek.' He cites certain 'intelligent farmers' as stating that 'it was a matter of astonishment how such slabs were raised.' In fact such slabs, of exactly the same size and regularity, abound, and at Parknabinnia, as we have noted, the blocks have been levered up and propped on small rounded boulders close to an important group of cists. I can only fancy that the 'Farmers' politely coincided with his expressed views, as every local person knows that such blocks could nearly always be raised near the sites of the dolmens in the north-west part of Clare.

Some apparent dolmens may have been slab huts (as long since suggested by George H. Kinahan,[6] but he carried his theory too far) however, I think the tapered cist, large or small, is always sepulchral. The 'long grave' type is not found in western or northern Co. Clare, and is rare in the eastern half. The finest example, at Milltown, near Tulla, was long since destroyed,[7] and we have only a brief description of it in the Ordnance Survey Letters. The dolmens seem nearly always to stand in the remains of a carn, or mound, rarely rising higher than the edge of the cover.[8] The fifth cist at Parknabinnia was, however, entirely buried in a carn, even after 1839.

---

[1] *Proc. R. I. Acad.*, ser. iii, vol. vi, p. 166. See also *North Munster Archaeol. Soc.*, vol. ii, p. 227; vol. iii, p. 38.

[2] *Journal*, vol. xxxi, p. 16 [75], for a sketch plan. Perhaps dog kennels like the *Croite na Catehragh* at Caherdorgan.

[3] *Journal*, vol. xxvi, p. 119 [26].

[4] *Ibid.*, vol. xxxv, p. 221 [107].

[5] *Dolmens of Ireland*, vol. i, p. 69.

[6] Kinahan calls them *Fosleacs*, but evidently included unmistakable dolmens (like Poulaphuca) with the slabs huts.

[7] *Proc. R. I. Acad.*, vol. xxiv. (c.) p. 113, from O.S. Letters, (MSS. R. I. Acad., 14 B 24), p. 255.

[8] The fairy mound, or *sidhe*, in early Ireland was supposed to open on the feast of *Samhain*. See *Echtra Nerai* (ed. D'Arbois de Jubainville). *Dolmens of Ireland*, p. 853. Nera's adventures on entering the fairy mound are worth detailed study. MSS., T.C.D., H. 2, 6, col. 658-662, Y.B.L. *Proc. R. I. Acad.*, 1879 (P.L.A.), p. 222.

Several dolmens were used for residence. Dr. George U. Macnamara remembers old women living in those of Cappaghkennedy, and Cottine, his father, the late Dr. Macnamara, attended one of these. Gortlecka dolmen also formed part of a cabin. One of those at Parknabinnia was used by a fugitive from justice, and I saw the straw of his bed in it. The one at Slievenaglasha was used as a calf shed and fuel store, to the burning of its contents it owed its destruction.

Legend regards them everywhere as the Beds of Diarmuid and Grainne, the famous fugitive lovers, and told how the hero spread seaweed on the covers so that when Finn bit his prophetic thumb, to learn whither his wife had absconded, he supposed them to be drowned.[1] A visit of a married couple to them cured sterility. In Hely Dutton's time (possibly on the same account) some sense of indecency attached, and a girl refused to guide him to those of Ballyganner in 1808, till she was assured that he was a stranger and ignorant of the local beliefs.[2] John Windele[3] in July 1855 notes of the Mount Callan Dolmen 'fruitfulness of progeny in that.' I learned of an indecent rite taking place about 1902 at a dolmen for the same purpose.

The confusion between dolmens and huts is not confined to Ireland, but occurs in the Pyrenees. Rev. Sabine Baring Gould notes[4] some that the French call 'cromlechs, circles of stone supposed to be prehistoric.' The local shepherds say 'that precisely similar stones are planted by themselves around temporary huts of branches and turf erected by them when they have to stay in the mountains.' These must be closely similar to the Burren circles of slabs. I myself have seen in the Corcaguiny peninsula, in Kerry, primitive looking beehive huts of recent date; one was being built so late as 1904 at Dunquin, and others were recently completed at Kilmalkedar. There also I saw 'long graves,' identical in design, but far less massive than the long dolmens (allées couvertes) rows of slabs set on edge, with slab covers, and buried in cairns. In Co. Limerick and Co. Clare it was courteous to bring a few stones to put on the modern cairn if you found one being made. I have also seen very primitive huts at Keel and elsewhere in Achill; while at Carna, on the north shore of Galway Bay, I have seen and photographed circular 'booley huts,' with dry stone walls roofed with long 'scraws' of sod thrown over the top like a tablecloth, and one 'dut out' in a sandhill, the roof resting on the surface with a low dry stone wall to the windward to prevent it being blown away. Nothing more primitive than these huts could well be imagined.[5]

---

[1] *Folk Lore*, vol. xxiii, p. 91.

[2] *Statistical Survey*, Co. Clare, p. 318. The idea of indecency is widespread, being found even in Holland and Belgium. See Borlase, *Dolmens of Ireland*, vol. ii, p. 555; vol. iii, p. 845; it probably rose from certain superstitious observances at the monuments.

[3] Topographical MSS. R.I.A., vol. i, p. 292.

[4] *Book of the Pyrenees*, p. 127.

[5] Primitive building traditions show in the fishing charm called *Cashlan pleiminhin*, or 'Cashlaun flaineen' locally. It is a stone circle, or rather miniature ring-wall, with its gateway towards the desired wind or direction from which the fish were expected. Despite the jealous secrecy of the people I secured a good photograph of this charm. See *Proc. R. I. Acad.*, vol. vi, ser. iii, p. 527, plate xxiii.

The great lesson to be learned in Irish archaeology (if not in that of other lands) is the risk of extreme, or exclusive, views; where all is so primitive, caution is most necessary, as the above facts show. Field surveys and excavations are the two master keys of the subject. I have attempted to supply the first for one district; I hope that the coming of the time and the man for the second may not be much longer delayed.

SHESHY (O.S. 9). - Before turning from the Burren uplands I must note two forts to the north of Lemeneagh.

CAHERMORE has been recently nearly entirely defaced. The outer face, in 1897, was nearly entire; now only a part to the west is 5 feet high, of fairly good slab masonry, the rest is a mere heap. The wall is 7 feet to 9 feet thick, and encloses a garth 81 feet across. There are no hut foundations, but some old looking pens and cattle enclosures adjoin the ring-wall.

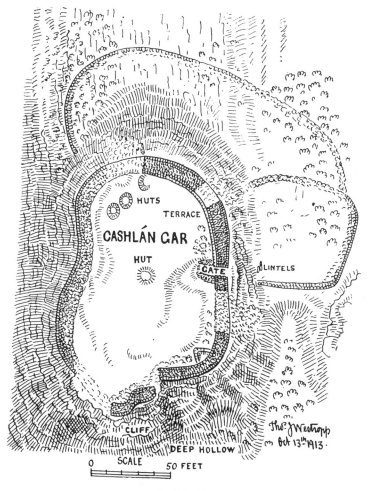

Cashlán Gar.

CAHERACLARIG. - This fort was a mere thicket on my former visit, it is now partly cleared. It is a ring-wall, the garth 90 feet across and grassy. The wall is 4 to 5 feet high in parts, but much gapped, and is only 6 feet thick. The gateway faces the east, and has a lintel 4 feet 6 inches by 15 inches by 8 inches. There is a hut enclosure to the south of the garth. The wall itself has two faces and but little filling of small stones. The layer of slabs set with their edges out, like books on a shelf, are to the north, in the outer face.[1] The cathair stands on a rock platform over a little glen.

CASHLAUN-GAR (O.S. 10). This remarkable fort[2] at the end of Glencurraun has been much cleared on its platform. The destruction of hazels, probably by goats, has brought to light a terrace, previously entirely concealed. It is 28 to 30 inches wide, and forms a separate section for perhaps 3 feet down but the base of the wall seems of one piece for 6 feet 8 inches from the ground. A reach of wall 15 feet long has fallen since my former visits; it is to the north of the east gate. More of the other walls is slipping down the slopes. I am now able to give a revised plan showing the outer enclosures, which are hard to measure, being covered with bushes. The huts are so covered with grass as to be now hardly distinguishable.

The wall of the outer enclosure (or bawn) to the north and east of the rock is, as a rule, 6 feet thick, of large blocks, usually 5 to 6 feet, one 8 feet 3 inches long and 2 to 3 feet high and thick. It is 61 feet from the inner fort to the north, running to what may be an older loop to the east, which turns back to the foot of the rock in line with the south jamb of the gateway, being there 63 feet out from the citadel wall. The main wall is 6 feet 2 inches thick, the terrace 2 feet 6 inches more; the whole in parts 10 feet, and at the gate 11 feet 6 inches thick and 8 feet high. It is 3 feet higher than the terrace and 12 feet 6 inches high outside.

TEMPLEMORE-KELLS (O.S. 17).

In my former visits in 1894 and 1898 I failed to recognise in the hedge of hawthorns, brambles and modern walls round the church anything notable or ancient. The new maps, showing a circular fence, led me to revisit it, and I am able to add a plan of another typical example of a church in a ring-wall, like Glencolumbcille.

The ruin[3] is situated in a pleasing position, among rich fields, near a lake, with a view of the flank and cliffs of the Glasgeivnagh Hill and Slieve-naglasha, and Mullach, with its great rock terraces and grey dome. The approach is by an old laneway to the north-east, and on that side the cashel is hardly traceable, being only marked by scattered bushes, small filling, and rebuilt modern walls. The ring measures 252 feet east and west, and 228 feet north and south over all; it is 8 to 10 feet thick, with filling of small field stones, and is 3 to 4 feet high. The foundation courses alone remain in parts

---

[1] I only know of this style of building elsewhere in a curious ring-wall at Carrahan in eastern Co. Clare. See *Proc. R. I. Acad.*, vol. xxxii, p. 73.

[2] *Journal*, vol. xxvi, p. 152 [10]; vol. xliii, p. 254 [175].

[3] *Proc. R. I. Acad.*, ser. iii, vol. vi, view and note, plate viii, and p. 139.

on the inside, but outside to the north and north-west, the outer face is well
preserved, in parts 5 feet high. It is of large blocks 3 to 4 feet high and
many 5 feet long, with good masonry above. Some large water-worn
boulders, in situ, are embedded in the wall,[1] and it is evident that before the
great drainage works the fort was washed by the lake; the garth being raised
some 4 feet higher than the field. To the south and east (as we noted) the
wall is entirely overthrown and a thick hedge of bramble and hawthorn
covers it, like the great, half demolished ring, in which the abbey of Canons'
Island in the Fergus stands.[2]

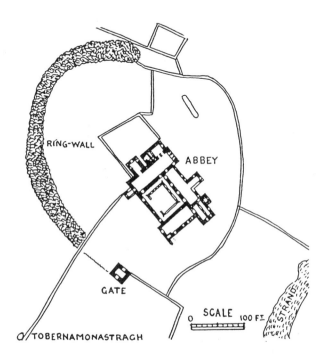

Canons' Island Abbey.

---

[1] This utilising of boulders when in a suitable position is characteristic of the
economy of labour in the early builders reaching its zenith in certain promontory
forts. Embedded boulders in ramparts are found outside of Ireland. Castal an Dui
fort, northern Perthshire, embodies a great boulder in its wall (*Proc. Soc. Antiq.,
Scotland*, vol. xi, ser. iv, 1912-13, p. 30), and other cases of embedded boulders.

[2] On my visit to this plain and interesting ruin in 1886 the curved heap of stones
was thickly overgrown with high bushes, so I cannot say whether any part of the
ring-wall remained intact. The southern and eastern parts have been long levelled,
perhaps for building the Abbey, before 1194. The Abbey gatehouse, however, seems
to be on its curve, and the outline may be traced, a later wall following the old line.
The ring measures about 320 feet inside, or 350 feet over all; it is about 310 feet
north-east and south-west, and encloses about 2½ acres (O.S. 60).

There are some old looking drains and embankments from the ring-wall, towards the lake, to the north-west and to the south-east, near the entrance, two holes in the field mark a souterrain. I am told that, when it was excavated long since by Col. Marcus Paterson, of Clifden, and Mr. Robert Burke Foster, of Rinroe, it was traced under the ring into the garth, but no antiquities were discovered. The field to the north-west is called 'Moher-animerish' (enclosed field of contention), and legend says that two brothers, O'Briens, fought and killed each other for its possession, in the perennial land hunger of Co. Clare. A somewhat similar legend attaches to the long earthwork of Killeen, south from Corofin.

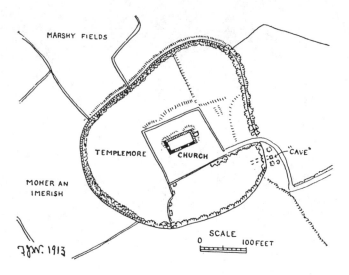

Templemore, Kells.

The cashel was evidently destroyed to build the modern graveyard wall, which lies from 70 to 110 feet inside it, and is roughly square. This habit of building mortared walls round graveyards has been fruitful in destruction for early remains besides destroying most of their charm. When we hear that the Rathblamaic round tower was levelled for this purpose, and see the carved blocks of the once beautiful romanesque church built into the new wall, there and at Tomfinlough, in this country, and recall the demolition of other Clare churches, Feakle, Kilnoe, Ogonnello, Moyferta, and many others, we can only regret that the power of vandalism was conferred by law on ignorant local bodies, without some restraint from some better educated source.

The church is locally named 'Templemoore,' 'Moor,' and 'Kells.' The plural form (Cealla) refers to it and St. Catherine's not far away; the latter is levelled, and its site forms an orchard in which graves and skeletons have been found. Curious to say, Aenghus O'Daly, the bitter satirist of the Tribes of Ireland, attacks, in 1617, the people of Cealla in Thomond for 'digging in the churchyard in the snow.'[1] This custom, by the way, was against the Ancient Law of Ireland, which is severe upon those 'digging in a graveyard and breaking bones.'

The building is of large and primitive masonry at its west end, perhaps of the 8th or 9th century. It has a lintelled door there, with inclined jambs, 26 to 24 inches wide, and still 4 feet high; the ground having being raised several feet by burials. The lintel is 6 feet 5 inches long and 2 feet thick. The church is elsewhere of poorer later masonry; it is 38 feet 8 inches by 23 feet 7 inches inside; the west end being 26 feet 8 inches across and the walls 2 feet 6 inches thick, the whole about 51 feet long. The north and east walls are only a few feet high. The south wall stands for 13 feet at the west, then a gap of the same length, then a reach of 18 feet long with a rude window slit for which the round head of an older window, cut in one block, has been utilised. There was a north-east buttress, now levelled. The vault of Michael Foster, Esq. (of Rinrow, who died on the 12th July, 1828, aged 42, erected by his brother, John Foster), abuts against what was once the east window.

LISMUINGA (O.S. 17). The fort, now called Lismuinga, is a small, well built ring-wall, about 100 feet across, the eastern half greatly overthrown. It stands on a little knoll in hazel thickets, and has a smaller fort, entirely levelled, about 400 feet to the west; a field wall passes through the last. Neither is a 'Liss.' To the south there is a trace of a curious rectangular fort, or bawn, between the 'Poulashantinna' and the road. It is oblong, and was of dry stone facing, with small filling, and entirely levelled, 120 feet across east and west, 96 feet north and south. The enclosure is divided into four by-cross walls. The owner says it is not haunted, but he has seen mysterious lights in the earth forts of Tully O'Dea near it, and he and others heard the Banshee cry before the death of his uncle.

The 'Poulashantinna' is one of those large funnel-shaped hollows down to an underground stream or to the sea. The name occurs at several places in North Mayo,[2] notably Downpatrick in Tirawley, and in the north Mullet. I do not know of its occurrence elsewhere, save at Lismuinga. Similar holes in Co. Clare, such as those near Ballycarr and Newmarket-on-Fergus, at Corbally near Quin, and Kilmorane to the south of Ennis, are reputed to be 'thunder holes,' and caused by a bolt. The name pronounced Pooláshantana, not 'Poulashantinna,' as on maps. Fish are caught in it.

---

[1] See paper by Dr. Macnamara, *Journal*, vol. xxx, p. 31.
[2] See *Journal*, vol. xlii, pp. 111, 204, 211.